Featuring 1,000 unpublished photographs, this is the first book about the 4,500 Norwegian volunteers in the Waffen SS. Written by Geir Brenden and Tommy Natedal - who have researched the Norwegian volunteers since the 1980s - the book is based on Geir and Tommy's large photo archive and covers the various fronts where most Norwegian volunteers fought, including the Caucasus, Leningrad and Karelia. Also covered in detail are the formations in which the Norwegian volunteers fought: *5. SS-Panzer-Division 'Wiking', SS-Freiwilligen-Legion Norwegen* and *1., 2.* and *3. Polizeikompanie, SS-Schikompanie 'Norwegen', 23. SS-Panzergrenadier-Regiment 'Norge', SS-Polizei-Schijäger-Bataillon 506 (mot.).*

I0869034

Geir Brenden was born in 1971. Educated and working in the security industry for more than 18 years, he began researching Norwegian volunteers in the Waffen SS when he was 16 years old. He has published the following books: *Norske frivillige på Østfronten, De som falt, Norske krigsfrivillige på tysk side* No. 1, 2 and 3 and *Norske offiserer I Waffen SS og Hitlers Norske Skijegere.* He has helped with researching information and pictures for 30 books on the subject. He also organises guided tours to the Eastern Front - where the Norwegians fought - and has led groups to Russia, Ukraine, Estonia, Latvia and Poland.

Tommy Natedal was born in 1966. He is an employee of Correctional Services with an educational background in defence. He has assisted a number of writers and historians with information and documentation about former veterans. He has also released the book *Norske offiserer I Waffen SS og Hitlers Norske Skijegere.*

NORWEGIAN VOLUNTEERS OF THE *WAFFEN SS*

Die norwegischen Freiwilligen in der Waffen-SS

Geir Brenden & Tommy Natedal

Translated from Norwegian into German and English by Thilo Reinhard

Helion & Company

Helion & Company Limited
Unit 8 Amherst Business Centre
Budbrooke Road
Warwick
CV34 5WE
England
Tel. 01926 499619
Email: info@helion.co.uk
Website: www.helion.co.uk
X (formerly Twitter): @Helionbooks
Facebook: @HelionBooks
Visit our blog at https://helionbooks.wordpress.com/

Published by Helion & Company 2016. This paperback edition 2025
Designed and typeset by Mach 3 Solutions (www.mach3solutions.co.uk)
Cover designed by Paul Hewitt, Battlefield Design (www.battlefield-design.co.uk)

Front cover: Soldiers from *11. Company 'Norge'* at Oranienbaum, January 1944. In the middle with binoculars is company commander *SS-Obersturmführer* Karl-Heinz Reinecke. He was killed on 2 February 1944 at Dubrovka. Rear cover: Enlistment Poster for *Legion Norwegen*.

ISBN 978-1-804518-44-1

British Library Cataloguing-in-Publication Data.
A catalogue record for this book is available from the British Library.

For details of other military history titles published by Helion & Company Limited, contact the above address, or visit our website: http://www.helion.co.uk

We always welcome receiving book proposals from prospective authors.

Contents

Vorwort

Während der achtziger Jahre begannen wir beide Bilder und Informationen über norwegische Freiwillige zu sammeln, die auf deutscher Seite gekämpft hatten, und kamen im Jahr 1994 durch den ehemaligen Frontkämpfer Knut Baardseth in Verbindung miteinander. Seit dieser Zeit arbeiten wir zusammen und teilen alles, was uns an Bildern und Daten in die Hände kommt. Zusammen mit Knut Flovik Thoresen haben wir ein Buch über norwegische Offiziere in der Waffen-SS herausgeben (*Norske offiserer i Waffen-SS*) und arbeiten zurzeit an der Herausgabe mehrerer Bücher.

Die Fotografien in diesem Buch stammen aus unseren privaten Archiven. Zusätzlich hat Helge Tunge uns eine Reihe seiner Archivbilder zur Verfügung gestellt. Die Bilder aus unseren eigenen Archiven wurden uns freundlicherweise von ehemaligen Frontkämpfern, mit denen wir in Verbindung kamen, zugestellt. Zudem haben wir auch einige Bilder im Nationalarchiv der Vereinigten Staaten, NARA (National Archives and Records Administration), gefunden.

Wir wollen allen Frontkämpfern, die uns Bilder zur Verfügung gestellt haben, herzlichst danken. Helge Tunge für die Bereitstellung von Bildern und deren Bearbeitung für dieses Buch. Vegard Sørlie für das Ausleihen von Werbeplakaten und Bildern. Arne Håkon Thomassen, Torgeir Lindtvedt Dalen und Linn Helene Gjervik für ihre Hilfe mit dem Text. Ein Dank geht auch an Morten Malmø für all seinen Beistand und Rat bei der Verwirklichung dieses Projekts.

Sollte es Leser geben, die imstande sind die Namen unbekannter Personen zu identifizieren, bitten wir sie sich in Verbindung mit dem Verlag zu setzen. Geir dankt Elizaveta Brenden für all ihre Hilfe und Unterstützung. Tommy dankt Lene Natedal für ihre Geduld und ihren Beistand.

Gjøvik/Jevnaker, 15. Juli 2014
Geir Brenden und Tommy Natedal

Preface

In the 1980s, we both started collecting pictures and information about Norwegian volunteers who had fought on the German side during the Second World War. Thanks to front line fighter Knut Baardseth, we came into contact with each other in 1994, and have collaborated and shared all photographs and information we have come across ever since. Together with Knut Flovik Thoresen, we have published a book about Norwegian officers in the *Waffen-SS* (*Norske offiserer i Waffen-SS*) and are currently collaborating on several book projects.

The images in this book are taken from our private archives, in addition to a number of pictures from the archive of Helge Tunge. Our own archive images were contributed by Norwegian volunteers we were able to contact, and who have kindly provided us with photographs and information about them. Additional images were furnished by the National Archives and Records Administration (NARA) in the US.

With this book, we hope to bring this large and unique collection of photographs to the attention of the public. Essentially, it provides a comprehensive picture of the lives of these front line fighters. We condone neither their actions nor their reasons for enlisting on the German side. Although they chose to fight for the wrong cause and were found guilty of collaborating with the Germans during the post-war trials, we feel that this material is of great historic interest today, nearly 75 years after the outbreak of the war.

We would like to thank all the Norwegian volunteers who have provided us with images. Thanks also to Helge Tunge for lending us photographs and processing the images for this book; Vegard Sørlie for contributing with propaganda posters; and Arne Håkon Thomassen, Torgeir Lindtvedt Dalen and Linn Helene Gjervik for help with the text. We would also like to thank Morten Malmø for all his help and advice throughout the project.

If any readers are able to identify the names of unknown persons depicted in this book, we encourage them to contact the publisher. Thanks from Geir to Elizaveta Brenden for her help and support, and from Tommy to Lene Natedal for her patience and assistance.

Gjøvik/Jevnaker, 15 July 2014
Geir Brenden and Tommy Natedal

Einleitung: SS und Waffen-SS

Die SS wurde 1925 als bewaffnete Streitkraft und Leibwache Adolf Hitlers ins Leben gerufen. Vier Jahre später übernahm Hitlers enger Vertrauter, Heinrich Himmler, die Leitung der Abteilung. Außer der Bereitstellung von polizeilichem Schutz für Hitler und die Leitung der NSDAP, erließ Himmler den Befehl, andere Parteien zu überwachen und alle internen "Unruhestifter" in der NSDAP unschädlich zu machen.

Als SA-Führer Ernst Röhm 1934 liquidiert wurde, hatte die SS eine zentrale Rolle gespielt. Die SA verlor ihren Einfluss, während die SS Macht und Status in der NS-Hierarchie gewann. Die SS war von nun an die Eliteeinheit der Partei. Mitglieder wurden sorgfältig ausgewählt, und strenge Disziplin war ein Teil des Alltags. Darüber hinaus wurde die SS schließlich der radikalste Vertreter der nationalsozialistischen Rassenideologie.

Nach einer gründlichen Umstrukturierung wurde die SS in drei Hauptgruppen unterteilt:

1: **Die Allgemeine SS** bestand aus den verschiedenen Parteiabteilungen, die auch in den besetzten Ländern repräsentiert waren, einschließlich der 1942 gegründeten Germanischen SS Norwegen.

2: **Die Waffen-SS** bestand aus Infanterie, Artillerie und Panzertruppen, was sich im Jahre 1940 auf ca. 100 000 Mann belief. Im Dezember 1944 war die Zahl der Waffen-SS-Mitglieder auf fast eine Million gestiegen, etwa die Hälfte von ihnen als Freiwillige.

3: **Der Sicherheitsdienst (SD)** war das politische Kontrollorgan der SS, dem auch die Gestapo unterstellt war.

Letztendlich übernahm die SS auch die Konzentrationslager in Deutschland und anderen besetzten Ländern, eifrig von Himmlers rechter Hand, Reinhard Heydrich, verwaltet. Um für die Sicherheit zu sorgen, wurden SS-Totenkopf-Divisionen aufgestellt. Die SS verübte auch Massenmorde an der Ostfront, nachdem Deutschland die Sowjetunion und Polen angegriffen hatte. Die sogenannten Einsatzgruppen, die aus Freiwilligen der verschiedenen SS-Einheiten, der Polizei und des Sicherheitsdienstes bestanden, ermordeten 1,5 Millionen Zivilisten, darunter eine Million Juden.

Die Waffen-SS war somit der militärische Arm der SS. Der Kern der zukünftigen Waffen-SS entstand zunächst in Berlin im Jahre 1933 durch die Einrichtung einer eigenen Stabswache, gefolgt von der SS-Verfügungstruppe. Im Zweiten Weltkrieg wurde die Waffen-SS weitgehend als Eliteeinheit eingesetzt, und Reichsführer-SS Heinrich Himmler verblieb oberster Befehlshaber während des gesamten Krieges.

Die erste Formation der späteren Waffen-SS war die Leibstandarte-SS Adolf Hitler, eine speziell ausgewählte Einheit, die als Hitlers persönliche Leibwache fungierte. Im Anschluss an die "Nacht der langen Messer" wechselten viele SA-Mitglieder über zur SS, aus der schließlich die SS-Verfügungstruppe hervorging, die wiederum in die SS-Divisionen "Das Reich" und "Totenkopf" unterteilt war.

Die Waffen-SS war als eine aus deutsch-germanischen Rekruten bestehende Armee geplant. Zu Beginn des Krieges war dies mehr oder weniger der Fall, aber nach mehreren Kriegsjahren wurden sowohl deutsche als auch ausländische Soldaten rekrutiert. Daher wurde die Division "Wiking" unter der Führung von Felix Steiner aufgestellt. Die Truppe bestand aus 55 000 Niederländern, 43 000 Belgiern, 20 000 Franzosen, 6000 Dänen, 5000 Norwegern, 200 Schweden und 800 Schweizern. Darüber hinaus meldeten sich auch viele Freiwillige aus Estland und Lettland. Zunächst wurden nur "Arier" in der SS zugelassen, aber schließlich gab Himmler sein Einverständnis, auch anderen, wie z.B. Bewerbern aus dem Balkan, den Beitritt zu gewähren. Muslimische Einheiten wurden auch aufgestellt, wie z.B. die 13. SS-Waffen-Gebirgs-Abteilung der SS "Handschar", die 23. Waffen-Gebirgs-Abteilung der SS "Kama" und die 21. Waffen-Gebirgs-Division der SS "Skanderbeg". Ironischerweise hatte diese sogenannte "rein germanische" Armee zuletzt den größten Anteil an Rekruten aus Ländern außerhalb Deutschlands in der gesamten deutschen Kriegsmaschine.

Die Waffen-SS als politisches Phänomen

Der britische Historiker Antony Beevor hat die Endschlacht um Berlin im Jahr 1945 als "den letzten Scheiterhaufen des europäischen Rechtsextremismus" beschrieben. Bei der Verteidigung Berlins gegen die Rote Armee kämpften Einheiten der Waffen-SS gemeinsam mit französischen, norwegischen, dänischen, schwedischen und anderen ausländischen Freiwilligen. Daher ist es längst überfällig, den Mythos der Waffen-SS als militärisches Phänomen aufzuheben. Die Waffen-SS war und blieb ein Teil der Weltanschauung Hitlers, Himmlers und der SS, und war damit ein auf langfristiger Planung basiertes politisch-ideologisches Phänomen. Die multinationale Waffen-SS muss

Introduction: SS and *Waffen-SS*

The SS was established in 1925 as an armed force and personal bodyguard for Adolf Hitler. SS stands for the German word *Schutzstaffel* (protection squadron). Four years later, Hitler's trusted right-hand man Heinrich Himmler became head of the division. In addition to providing police protection for Hitler and the leadership of the Nazi Party, Himmler charged the SS with monitoring other parties and stopping all 'troublemakers' within the Nazi Party.

When the chief commander of the SA (*Sturmabteilung* – storm battalion), Ernst Röhm, was liquidated in 1934 during the so-called Night of the Long Knives, the SS played a central role in the event. The SA lost its influence, while the SS gained power and status in the Nazi hierarchy. The SS would from here on become the party's elite group. Members were chosen carefully, and strict discipline was part of everyday life. Moreover, the SS would eventually become the most radical exponent of racial ideology in the Nazi state.

After a thorough reorganisation, the SS was divided into three main groups:

1: ***Allgemeine SS*** consisted of the various party branches that also existed in occupied countries, including the Germanic *SS Norway*, founded in 1942.

2: ***Waffen-SS*** consisted of infantry, artillery and armoured forces. In 1940, this amounted to approximately 100,000 men. By December 1944, nearly one million men had joined the *Waffen-SS*, approximately half of them as volunteers.

3: ***Sicherheitsdienst (SD)*** was the political monitoring organ of the SS, and also oversaw the Gestapo.

The SS eventually took charge of the concentration camps in Germany and other occupied countries, keenly administered by Himmler's own right-hand man, Reinhard Heydrich. *SS-Totenkopf* divisions were formed to provide security. The SS also carried out mass killings on the Eastern Front after Germany's attacks on the Soviet Union and Poland. The so-called *Einsatzgruppen* – factions made up of volunteers from various SS units, the German police and the SD – murdered 1.5 million civilians, including a million Jews.

The *Waffen-SS* was the military branch of the SS, its core initially forged in Berlin in 1933 through the establishment of a special *Stabswache* (HQ guard), followed by the *SS-Verfügungstruppe*. During the Second World War, the *Waffen-SS* was largely employed as an elite force, and Heinrich Himmler, as *Reichsführer-SS*, remained its commander-in-chief throughout the war.

The first formation of what would later become the *Waffen-SS* was the *Leibstandarte SS Adolf Hitler*, a unit specially selected to act as Hitler's bodyguard. After the Night of the Long Knives, many SA members joined the SS, eventually leading to the emergence of the *SS-Verfügungstruppe*, which in turn was divided into two SS divisions: *'Das Reich'* and *'Totenkopf'*.

The *Waffen-SS* was to be an army of 'Germanic' recruits. At the beginning of the war, this was more or less the case, but after several years of war, German as well as foreign soldiers were enlisted. At this point, *Division 'Wiking'* was activated under the leadership of Felix Steiner. The troops included 55,000 Dutchmen, 43,000 Belgians, 20,000 Frenchmen, 6,000 Danes, 5,000 Norwegians, 200 Swedes and 800 Swiss. Many volunteers also joined from Estonia and Latvia. Initially, only 'Aryans' were admitted into the SS, but eventually Himmler gave the green light for others to join, such as people from the Balkan states. Muslim units were established as well, such as the *13. Waffen-Gebirgs-Division* of the *SS 'Handschar'*, the *23. Waffen-Gebirgs-Division* of the *SS 'Kama'* and the *21. Waffen-Gebirgs-Division* of the *SS 'Skanderbeg'*. Ironically, this so-called 'purely Germanic' army eventually made up the largest number of recruits from countries outside of Germany in the entire German war machine.

The *Waffen-SS* as a political phenomenon

The British historian Antony Beevor has described the final battle for Berlin in 1945 as 'the last funeral pyre of European right-wing extremism'. As Berlin defended itself against the Red Army, *Waffen-SS* units fought together with French, Norwegian, Danish, Swedish and other foreign volunteers. It is therefore long overdue to abolish the myth of the *Waffen-SS* as a military phenomenon. The *Waffen-SS* was and remained part of the world of Hitler, Himmler and the SS: a political-ideological phenomenon rooted in long-term planning. The multinational *Waffen-SS* must be seen against the background of other European fascist movements and the polarisation between communism and fascism in the interwar period.

vor dem Hintergrund der europäischen faschistischen Bewegungen und der Polarisierung von Kommunismus und Faschismus in der Zwischenkriegszeit gesehen werden.

Vom skandinavischen Blickwinkel aus ist das III. (Germanische) SS-Panzerkorps besonders interessant. Vor allem Himmlers Vision einer multinationalen "Waffenbrüderschaft" in der Waffen-SS sollte hier, im Anschluss an Hitlers und Himmlers langfristigen Plan für ein "Tausendjähriges Großgermanisches Reich", zu einer "rassisch überlegenen pangermanischen Armee" führen.

In der Weltanschauung Hitlers und Himmlers waren es nicht die traditionelle Nationalstaaten, sondern die menschlichen Rassenmerkmale, die allen Beziehungen zwischen den Völkern zu Grunde lagen. Die pangermanischen Bestrebungen der SS hatten zwei Hauptziele: erstens die Schaffung eines großgermanischen Reichs, das den Großteil Nord- und Westeuropas umfassen würde; und zweitens die Erweiterung des "Lebensraums" im Osten durch Krieg, Völkermord und Kolonisation. Der Traum von einem großgermanischen Reich und einem "Vernichtungskrieg" gegen die Slawen und Juden waren zwei Seiten derselben Medaille. Die Waffen-SS spielte eine wichtige Rolle bei beiden Aufgaben durch die Rekrutierung und Ausbildung nicht-deutscher aber germanischer Funktionäre, und die militärische Sicherung der besetzten Ostgebiete.

Die Aufnahmekriterien der ideologisch profilierten, paramilitärischen SS-Verfügungstruppe waren äußerst hart, sowohl in Bezug auf "rassische Voraussetzungen", als auch auf die ideologische Treuepflicht dem nationalsozialistischen Ideal gegenüber. Die SS-Verfügungstruppe bildete den Kern der 38 Divisionen der Waffen-SS. Bei Kriegsausbruch im Jahr 1939 fusionierte die SS-Verfügungstruppe mit Teilen des KZ-Personals der SS-Totenkopfstandarten und Abteilungen der Reserve-Polizei. Zu Beginn des Krieges bestand die Waffen-SS aus 50 000 politisch indoktrinierten Soldaten und treuen Anhängern des Nationalsozialismus. Himmlers Bemühungen für eine umfassende Personalpolitik innerhalb der SS führten zu einer Reihe von wichtigen Berührungspunkten zwischen den verschiedenen Zweigen der SS, einschließlich der Waffen-SS.

Ein wichtiger Faktor war die gezielte Personalrotation zwischen den Feldeinheiten der Waffen-SS, den Einsatzgruppen, und dem Personal der Konzentrations- und Vernichtungslager. Während des ganzen Krieges wurde diese Strategie aufrechterhalten, und führte zu immer tieferer Menschenverachtung und einer zunehmend destruktiven Mentalität. Ein typisches Beispiel ist der berüchtigte Dr. Josef Mengele, der 1940 bis 1941 Bataillonsarzt beim SS-Pionier-Bataillon 5 "Wiking" war und am Unternehmen Barbarossa teilgenommen hatte, wofür er mit dem Eisernen Kreuz 1. Klasse ausgezeichnet wurde. Später wurde er nach Auschwitz befördert und diente dort bis zum Kriegsende. Dass die Waffen-SS nicht, wie SS-Generäle Hausser und Steiner nach dem Krieg behaupteten, "Soldaten wie alle anderen" waren, liegt auf der Hand.

Der übliche militärische Ehrenkodex galt im Krieg gegen die Sowjetunion nicht. Alle Offiziere müssten sich von ihrer überholten Denkweise befreien, verlangte Hitler in einer Rede vor deutschen Generälen. Der deutsch-sowjetische Kriegsschauplatz zeugte von einer neuen und unerwarteten Brutalität in der Kriegsführung beider Seiten. Angesichts der Massenmorde an Kriegsgefangenen übertraf die Ostfront alle anderen Kriegsschauplätze Europas und Asiens an Rohheit und Barbarei. Die Ostfront hatte einen besonders verderblichen Einfluss, und nicht nur Hitlers Truppen, sondern auch Stalins Rote Armee und die äußerst brutalen Kriegshandlungen, Vergeltungsmaßnahmen und Massendeportationen der Partisanenbewegung trotzten bewusst allen völkerrechtlichen Regeln. Der Feldzug gegen die Sowjetunion führte die Kriminalisierung des Krieges auf beiden Seiten mit sich. Hitlers Befehl an sämtliche Einheiten der Wehrmacht und Waffen-SS, die sofortige Hinrichtung aller gefangenen russischen Kommissare und Politruks zu veranlassen, ist das bekannteste Beispiel. Neuere Forschung hat gezeigt, dass nicht nur die Waffen-SS, sondern auch die deutsche Wehrmacht häufig gefangengenommene russische Kommissare auf Hitlers Befehl hinrichtete.

Gleichzeitig muss man aus Gründen der Nuancierung beachten, dass es in der Waffen-SS Soldaten und Einheiten gab, die nie direkt am Krieg oder an Massenverbrechen beteiligt waren. In vielen Fällen war die Haltung der Truppe vermutlich ein Spiegelbild der Persönlichkeit und des Charakters der Offiziere, die die verschiedenen Feldeinheiten der Waffen-SS befehligten. Inwieweit waren die befehlshabenden Offiziere von ihrer Ideologie geprägt? Das Urteil erlaubt viel Spielraum und Variation, und es ist heute äußerst schwierig, das Verhalten der Truppen an oder hinter der Front zu rekonstruieren. Das harte ideologische Profil der Waffen-SS und ihre belastende Personalpolitik, insbesondere im Offizierskorps, wo Idealisten und Massenmörder in einen Topf geworfen wurden, hatten zur Folge, dass allzu viele Waffen-SS-Einheiten im Zweiten Weltkrieg häufig eine blutige Spur hinterließen. Der Gesamteindruck der Waffen-SS ist weder Idealisten oder Massenmörder.

From a Scandinavian perspective, the *III. (Germanic) SS Panzer Corps* is a particularly interesting case. Above all, Himmler's vision of a multinational brotherhood in arms (*Waffenbrüderschaft*) within the *Waffen-SS* was to spawn a 'racially superior pan-Germanic army', in combination with Hitler and Himmler's long-term plans for a 'Thousand-Year Greater Germanic Empire'.

Hitler and Himmler's worldview considered racial characteristics, rather than the traditional nation-state, to be the basis of all relations between different peoples. The pan-Germanic ambitions of the SS had two main goals: firstly, the creation of a Greater Germanic Empire that would include the bulk of Northern and Western Europe; and secondly, the territorial expansion of 'living space' – *Lebensraum* – to the East by means of war, genocide and colonisation. The dream of a Greater Germanic Empire and a 'war of extermination' against the Slavs and the Jews were two sides of the same coin. The *Waffen-SS* played an important role in both tasks by recruiting and training non-native German - albeit Germanic - officials, and securing the occupied eastern territories by military means.

The requirements to join the *SS-Verfügungstruppe*, a paramilitary group with a distinct ideological profile, were stringent, both in terms of racial standards and ideological commitment to the Nazi ideal. The *SS-Verfügungstruppe* was the basis for the 38 divisions of the *Waffen-SS*. When war broke out in 1939, the *SS-Verfügungstruppe* merged with parts of the concentration camp staff from *SS-Totenkopf* divisions and units from the reserve police force. At the beginning of the war, the *Waffen-SS* consisted of 50,000 politically indoctrinated soldiers and Nazi zealots. Himmler's efforts to implement a comprehensive staff policy within the SS led to a number of important points of contact between the various branches of the SS, including the *Waffen-SS*.

An important factor was the deliberate rotation of personnel between field units of the *Waffen-SS*, special task forces and concentration and extermination camp staff. This strategy was employed throughout the war, resulting in an ever-deeper contempt for other human beings and an increasingly destructive mentality. A typical example is the infamous Dr Josef Mengele, who from 1940–41 was enlisted as a battalion physician in the *SS Pioneer Battalion 5 'Wiking'* and had received the Iron Cross 1st Class for his participation in Operation Barbarossa. Later he was ordered to Auschwitz, where he served for the remainder of the war. It is plainly evident that the *Waffen-SS* did not, as SS generals Hausser and Steiner claimed after the war, consist of 'soldiers like everyone else'.

The regular military code of honour did not apply in the war against the Soviet Union. 'All officers,' Hitler announced in a speech to German generals, 'have to rid themselves of an outdated mode of thought.' The German-Soviet theatre of operations witnessed a new and unexpected kind of brutality on both sides. When it came to the mass murder of POWs and civilians, the Eastern Front surpassed all other European and Asian war arenas in terms of callousness and savagery. The Eastern Front had a particularly corruptive influence, whereby not only Hitler's troops, but also Stalin's Red Army and the partisan movement's extremely brutal warfare, retaliatory actions and mass deportations deliberately defied international law. The campaign against the Soviet Union brought with it the criminalisation of war on both sides. Hitler's directive to all the units of the *Wehrmacht* and *Waffen-SS*, ordering the immediate execution of all captured Russian officials and commissars, is the most famous example. Recent research has shown that not only the *Waffen-SS*, but also the regular German *Wehrmacht*, frequently and summarily executed captured Russian commissars in accordance with Hitler's orders.

For the sake of nuance, it must be noted that the *Waffen-SS* included soldiers and units that never came into direct contact with war or other mass crimes. In many cases, the troops' conduct is likely to have been a reflection of the personality and character of the officers commanding the various *Waffen-SS* field units. To what degree were these officers influenced by their ideology? Judgement allows for considerable room and variation, and the troops' behaviour at or behind the front is extremely difficult to reconstruct today. The austere ideological profile of the *Waffen-SS* and the strain on its personnel policy - in particular among the officer corps, where idealists and mass murderers were lumped together - far too often left a trail of blood in the wake of many *Waffen-SS* units during the Second World War. The overall impression of the *Waffen-SS* is as neither idealists or mass murderers.

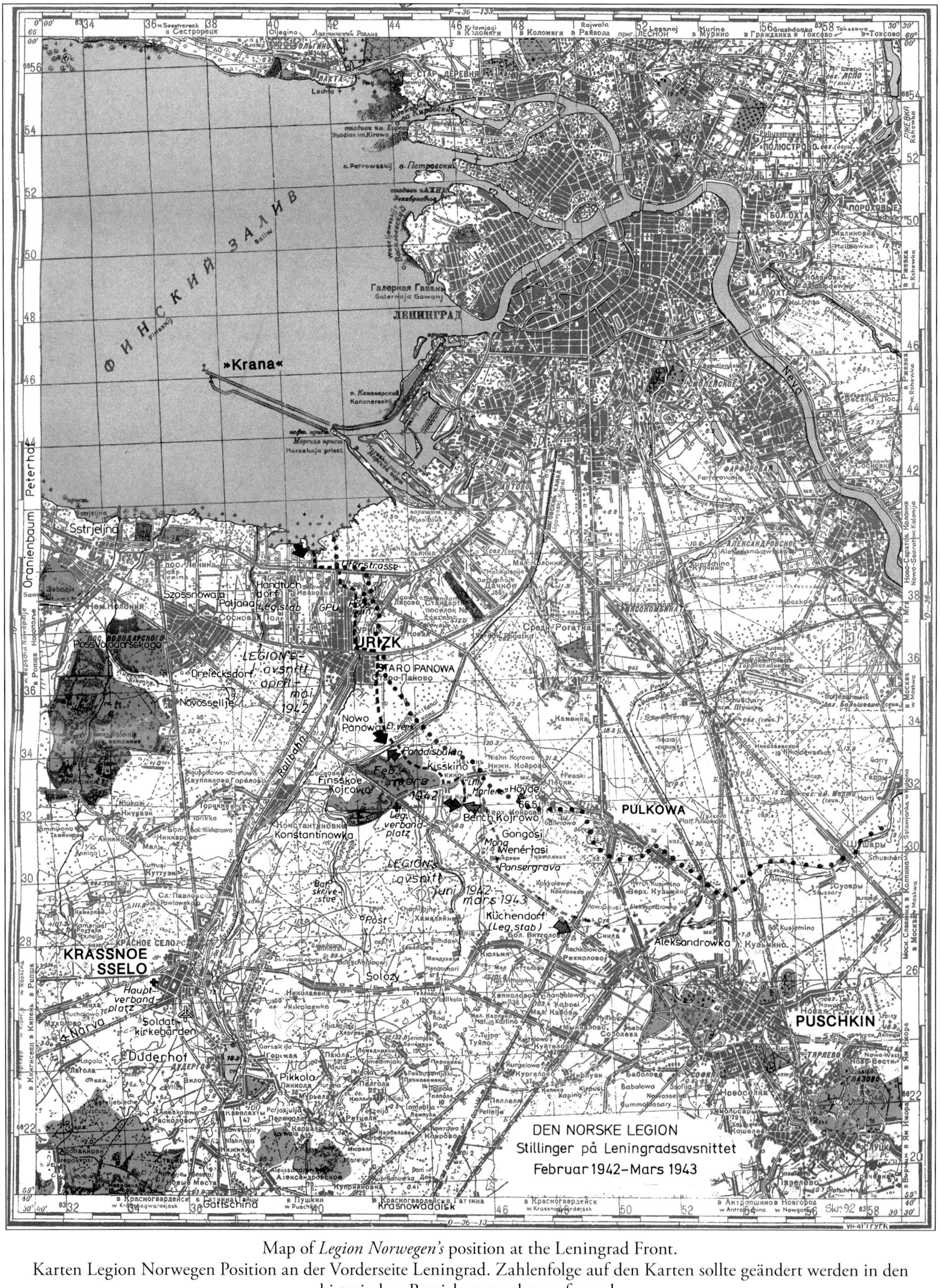

Map of *Legion Norwegen's* position at the Leningrad Front.
Karten Legion Norwegen Position an der Vorderseite Leningrad. Zahlenfolge auf den Karten sollte geändert werden in den historischen Bereich zu machen aufgrund.

Map of the combat zone of the *6 SS Division Nord*.
Karte des Bereich 6 SS Division North.

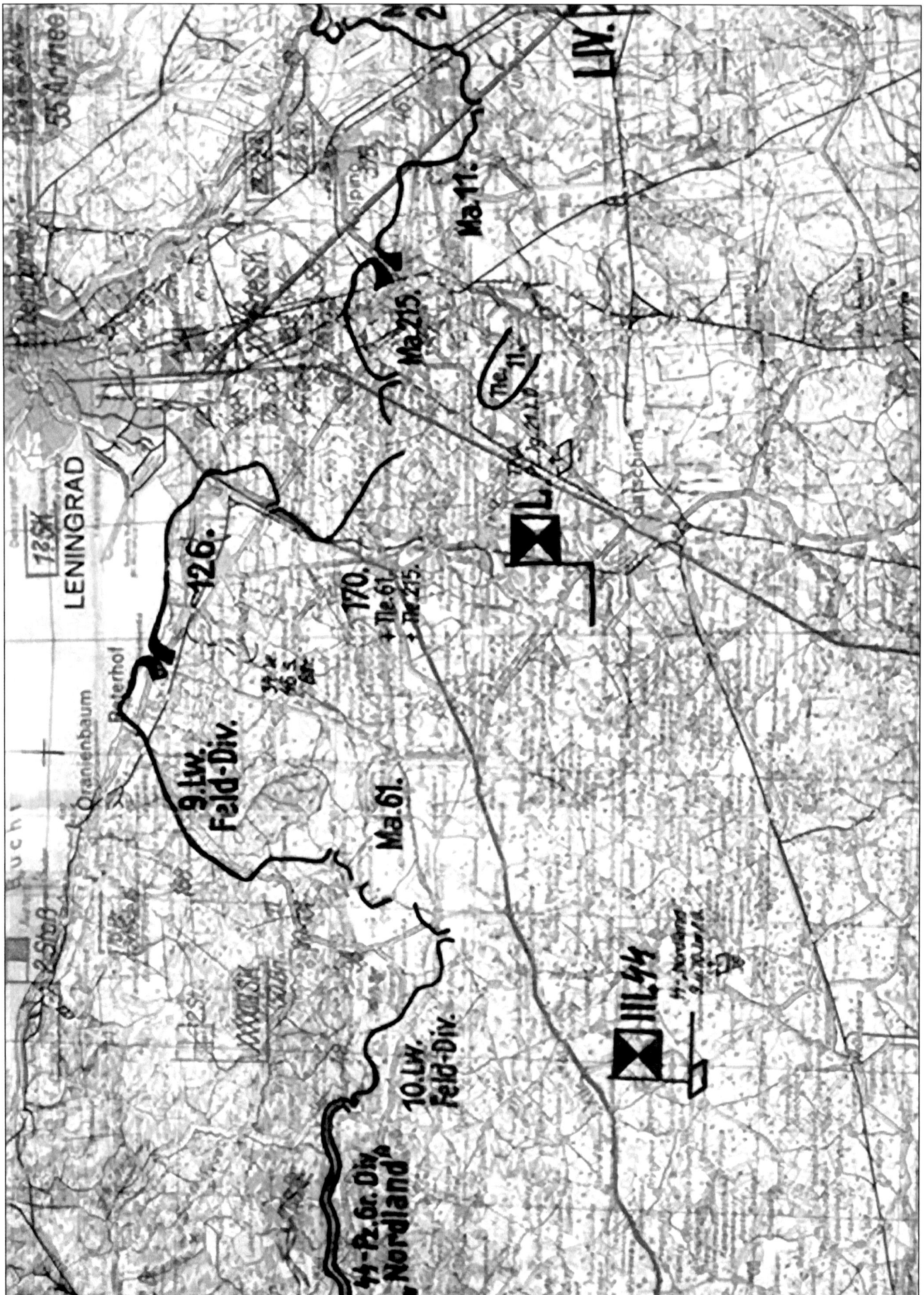

Map of Oranienbaum Front.
Seite xi Karte von Oranien Front.

Map of Narva Front.
Karten Narva Front.

1

5. SS-Panzer-Division “Wiking”

Im Dezember 1940 wurde die 5. SS-Panzer-Division “Wiking” unter Kommando von SS-Brigadeführer Felix Martin Julius Steiner offiziell aufgestellt. Die Anwerbung hatte schon im Sommer 1940 in Dänemark, Holland und Belgien begonnen. Die ersten norwegischen Freiwilligen meldeten sich am 13. Januar 1941, nachdem der norwegische NS-Führer Vidkun Quisling am Tag zuvor durch einen Radioaufruf öffentlich angekündigt hatte, dass Norweger sich freiwillig zur Waffen-SS beim Regiment “Nordland” melden könnten. Der wichtigste Grund, sich als Freiwilliger zu melden, sei der Aufbau eines zukünftigen norwegischen Heers, sowie der Beitrag zum Sieg Deutschlands im gegenwärtigen Krieg. Dadurch würde man die Stellung Norwegens im zukünftigen Europa mit Deutschland als führender Nation untermauern.

Im Frühjahr und Sommer 1941 reisten die ersten norwegischen Freiwilligen in sechs Gruppen nach Sennheim und Graz, und wurden in die 5. SS-Division “Wiking” eingegliedert. Die norwegischen Freiwilligen wurden nicht als gesammelte Einheit innerhalb des Regiments “Nordland” eingesetzt, sondern über die ganze Division verteilt. Die meisten Freiwilligen kamen zum Regiment “Nordland”, aber viele kamen auch zum I./SS-Infanterie-Regiment “Germania”, dem SS-Artillerie-Regiment 5, und der SS-Flak-Abteilung 5. Die Angeworbenen, die mit den Gruppen 1–4 reisten, absolvierten ihre Ausbildung und nahmen am Unternehmen Barbarossa – dem deutschen Angriff auf die Sowjetunion – teil. Ungefähr 300 Norweger beteiligten sich an dem Feldzug.

Die 5. SS-Division “Wiking” wurde am 29. Juni 1941 an der Ostfront eingesetzt, nur eine Woche nach dem Beginn des Unternehmens Barbarossa. Die ersten Gefechte mit russischen Einheiten fanden am 1. Juli statt, und einer der ersten Verluste der Division war der Regimentskommandeur des SS-Inf.Rgts. “Westland”, SS-Standartenführer Hilmar Wäckerle. Bei einigen Kompanien des Regiments löste sein Tod Pogrome gegen die jüdische Bevölkerung und willkürlich gefangengenommene russische Soldaten aus.

Im Juli 1941 wurden die ersten norwegischen Verluste an Toten und Verwundeten gemeldet. Im September, nach den schweren Kämpfen um Dnjepropetrowsk, hielt der Vorstoß bis November 1941 an. Vor der Stadt Rostow wurde die Division abermals in schwere Kämpfe verwickelt, und bezog am Mius-Fluss die Winterstellung. Hier verschanzte sich die Division bis der Vormarsch auf Rostow im Sommer 1942 begann. Die Stadt Rostow wurde im Juli 1942 erobert, und die Division nach Süden in den Kaukasus kommandiert. Hier nahm die Division im Oktober 1942 an schweren Kämpfen bei Mosdok teil, und wurde daraufhin in nordöstlicher Richtung in die Kalmückensteppe beordert, wo es im Januar 1943 zu schweren Gefechten kam. Im Frühjahr 1943 wurde die Division nach Issjum-Ssredny verlegt. Im April 1943 trat das Regiment “Nordland” aus der Division aus, und wurde zum Truppenübungsplatz Grafenwöhr verlegt. Daraufhin wurde das Regiment aufgelöst, und die Mannschaft zum neuaufgestellten SS-Pz.Gren.Rgt. “Norge” versetzt. Die meisten Norweger der Division “Wiking” kamen zu dem neuen Regiment, oder wurden aus der Waffen-SS entlassen. Ab Sommer 1943 waren daher nur noch etwa ein Dutzend Norweger in der 5. SS-Division “Wiking”.

Im Juli 1943 kämpfte die Division bei Isjum in der nordöstlichen Ukraine, und im November bei Korsun. Im Januar 1944 wurde die Einheit zusammen mit mehreren Divisionen der Wehrmacht bei Tscherkassy umringt, und brach am 17. Februar aus der Einkesselung aus, wobei später mehrere Norweger als tot oder vermisst gemeldet wurden. Im April 1944 wurde die Division neu aufgestellt und bei Kowel eingesetzt, bevor sie Ende des Jahres in eine Verteidigungsstellung bei Modlin in Polen verlegt wurde. Im Januar 1945 wurde die Division, nun dem IV. SS-Pz. Korps unterstellt, nach Komárom in Ungarn kommandiert, und nahm am Unternehmen “Konrad I” teil, um die Besatzung der Stadt Budapest, die von russischen Truppen eingekesselt war, zu entlasten. Als “Konrad I” scheiterte, begann man eine neue Offensive vom Norden aus, um Budapest über das Pilis-Gebirge zu erreichen. Aber auch dieser Vorstoß scheiterte, und man versuchte die Südlösung, “Konrad III”, die Ende Januar 1945 auch fehlschlug. Dann ging es gegen Westen nach Österreich, wo die Division am 9. Mai 1945 kapitulierte und in amerikanische Gefangenschaft geriet. Nur eine Handvoll Norweger waren noch in der Division, und keiner der ursprünglichen Freiwilligen aus dem Jahr 1941. Der letzte Norweger, SS-Unterscharführer Paul Sæther, der seit Juni 1941 mit dabei gewesen war, fiel im März 1945 als Unterscharführer in der SS-Flak-Abt. 5.

1

5. SS-Panzer-Division 'Wiking'

In December 1940, *Division 'Wiking'* was officially activated under the leadership of SS-*Brigadeführer* Felix Martin Julius Steiner; recruitment had begun in the summer of 1940 in Denmark, the Netherlands and Belgium. The first Norwegian volunteers enlisted on 13 January 1941. In a radio appeal on the previous day, NS-leader Vidkun Quisling had announced that Norwegian nationals could volunteer for the *Waffen-SS Regiment 'Nordland'*. The main incentive for signing up was to secure the establishment of a prospective Norwegian army as well as Germany's victory in the ongoing war, strengthening Norway's position in a future Europe under German leadership.

In the spring and summer of 1941, Norwegian volunteers travelled in six batches to Sennheim and Graz before joining the *5. SS-Division 'Wiking'*. Rather than being installed as a single unit within *Regiment 'Nordland'*, the men were distributed throughout the division. Most of the volunteers ended up in *Regiment 'Nordland'*, but many Norwegians were recruited into the *I/SS-Infanterie-Regiment 'Germania'*, the *SS-Artillerie-Regiment 5* and the *SS-Flak-Abteilung 5*. Those who enlisted and left Norway together with groups 1–4, completed their training and participated in Operation Barbarossa, the German attack on the Soviet Union. Consequently, some 300 Norwegians took part in the campaign.

On 29 June 1941, the *5. SS-Division 'Wiking'* was installed on the Eastern Front, one week after the beginning of Operation Barbarossa. The division's first encounter with Russian forces took place on 1 July, and one of the first men to fall was the commander of *SS-Infanterie-Regiment 'Westland'*, *SS-Standartenführer* Hilmar Wäckerle. His death provoked some companies in the regiment to respond with pogroms against the Jewish population and randomly chosen Russian POWs.

The first Norwegians were wounded or killed in action in early July 1941. In September, heavy fighting broke out at Dnepropetrovsk, and the advance continued until November 1941, when the division experienced heavy fighting west of Rostov and retreated to positions at Mius River. Here, the division dug in for the winter and held its position until the summer of 1942, when it began to advance on Rostov. The city of Rostov was captured in July 1942, and the division was ordered to move south towards the Caucasus. Here it was involved in heavy fighting at Mosdok in October 1942, before being ordered to move north-east towards the Kalmyk Steppe in late 1942. Heavy battles were fought here during the winter of 1943, before the division was ordered west. In April 1943, *Regiment 'Nordland'* was pulled out of the division and transferred to Grafenwöhr training camp, where the regiment was disbanded and the men assigned to the newly activated *SS-Panzer-Grenadier-Regiment 23 'Norge'*. Most of the Norwegians in *Division 'Wiking'* were either transferred to the new regiment or demobilised. As of summer 1943, only a dozen or so Norwegians were left in *Division 'Wiking'*.

In July 1943, the division fought at Izium in the north-eastern part of the Ukraine, and in November at Korsun. In January 1944, the division and several *Wehrmacht* units were surrounded at Cherkassy, and although the division managed to break away on 17 February, several Norwegians were reported killed and missing. In April 1944, the division was once again mobilised and deployed at Kovel, before being assigned to a defensive position at Modlin in Poland in late 1944. In January 1945, the *Division 'Wiking'*, now attached to the *IV. SS Panzer Corps*, was relocated to Komárom in Hungary and participated in Operation 'Konrad I' in the relief effort for Budapest, which was surrounded by Russian forces. When 'Konrad I' had to be aborted, an attempt was made to reach Budapest from the north via the Pilis Mountains, but that also failed. Finally, a third solution from the south – 'Konrad III' – was attempted, but had to be called off as well in late January 1945. From here, the division continued westward with a delaying action in Austria, where it was disbanded on May 9 near Fürstenfelde and the men taken as prisoners of war by the Americans. At that point, only a handful of Norwegians were left in the division, and none of the veterans of June 1941. The last Norwegian to be killed in action – Paul Sæther, who had enlisted in June 1941 – fell in March 1945 as *SS-Unterscharführer* in *SS-Flak-Abteilung 5*.

Abreise aus Norwegen | Departure from Norway

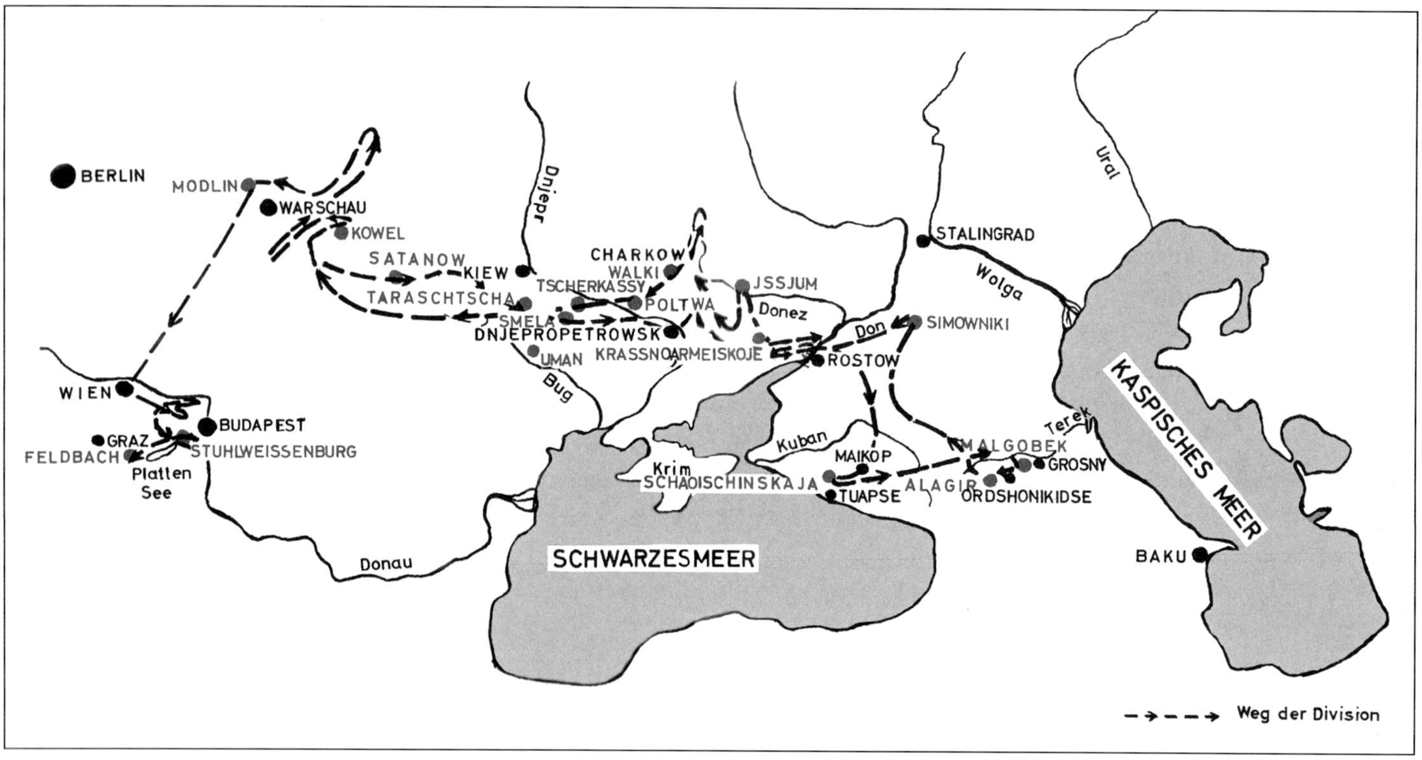

In early 1941, the first volunteers travelled in two groups to undergo training in Graz. One group travelled by air from Fornebu near Oslo, another by boat and train. Several groups that also travelled by sea and rail followed later, but this time to Sennheim for the first part of their training.

Die ersten Norweger, die sich Anfang 1941 als Freiwillige gemeldet hatten, reisten in zwei Gruppen zur Ausbildung in Graz. Eine Gruppe mit Flugzeug von Fornebu bei Oslo, eine andere mit Zug und Schiff. Weitere Gruppen reisten später auch mit Zug und Schiff, aber in diesem Fall nach Sennheim zur vormilitärischen Ausbildung.

The Hippodrome at Vinderen, Oslo, 30 January 1941. The first Norwegian volunteers of *Regiment 'Nordland'* are lined up to listen to speeches by *Reichsführer* Himmler, Vidkun Quisling and *Reichskommissar* Terboven.

Das Hippodrom in Vinderen, Oslo, 30. Januar 1941. Die ersten norwegischen Freiwilligen des Regiments "Nordland" sind aufgestellt und warten auf die Reden von Reichsführer Himmler, Vidkun Quisling und Reichskommissar Terboven.

A group of *Hirden* who have volunteered for *Regiment 'Nordland'*. Front row from the left: Ove Mele, unknown, Arne Mathisen and Rolf Halmrast. Second row from the right: Bjørn Myhre.

Eine Gruppe von *Hirden* die sich freiwillig zum Regiment "Nordland" gemeldet haben. Erste Reihe von links: Ove Mele, ein Unbekannter, Arne Mathisen und Rolf Halmrast. Zweite Reihe von rechts: Bjørn Myhre.

The *Hirdhuset* (Hird House) in Skien, 5 February 41. Regiment leader Per Dahlen, standing underneath the SS-insignia, addresses volunteers who have signed up for *Regiment 'Nordland'*. Sitting second from left in a checkered shirt is Sigurd Stridsklev, fourth is Gunnar Vetlesen, sixth Bjørn Heisholdt and seventh Alf Seeberg wearing a Hird uniform.

Das Hirdhaus in Skien, 05.02.41. Hirdregimentsführer Per Dahlen steht unter den SS-Runen und hält eine Rede an Freiwillige die sich zum Regiment "Nordland" gemeldet haben. Sitzend Nr. 2. von links in kariertem Hemd Sigurd Stridsklev, Nr. 6. Bjørn Heisholdt, Nr. 7. Alf Seeberg in Hird-Uniform.

The first group travelling by airplane from Fornebu airport near Oslo. First from the left is Bjørn W. Johannesen; the rest are unknown Germans.

Die erste Gruppe, die mit dem Fleugzeug vom Flughafen Oslo Fornebu abreist. Nr. 1 von links Bjørn Walberg Johannesen, die anderen sind unbekannte Deutsche.

Volunteers billeted at Rosenhoff School in Oslo.

Freiwillige werden in der Rosenhoff Schule in Oslo untergebracht.

Third or fourth group. Standing: first from right, the German tour leader; second, Olav Hangeland, the Norwegian tour leader. Front row from the left: Wiggo Dahlstrøm, Per Hasselknippe and Martin Skjefstad. Second row from the left: Adolf Bye, Nils Norvik Quisling and Osvald Olsen. Third row from left: Roy Rud.

Dritte oder vierte Gruppe. Stehend von rechts: Nr. 1 der deutsche Reiseleiter, Nr. 2 Olav Hangeland, der norwegische Reiseleiter. Erste Reihe von links: Wiggo Dahlstrøm, Per Hasselknippe und Martin Skjefstad. Zweite Reihe von links: Adolf Bye, Nils Norvik Quisling und Osvald Olsen. Dritte Reihe von links: Roy Rud.

The volunteers marching to the train.

Die Freiwilligen marschieren zum Zug.

Oslo train station, ready for the trip to Sennheim.

Oslo Hauptbahnhof, klar zur Abreise nach Sennheim.

At Moi railway station while travelling to undergo training in Germany.

Moi Bahnhof während der Fahrt zur Ausbildung nach Deutschland.

Moi railway station again while travelling to undergo training in Germany.

Moi Bahnhof während der Fahrt zur Ausbildung nach Deutschland.

Group 2 crossing over into Germany. Far right: Rolf Solum (KIA/killed in action July 1941), followed by Kåre Brynestad wearing a white hat. At the very left of the picture, sitting and wearing a Hird hat, is Hans Petter Hoff. Tore Moss is in a white jacket and Odd Berle Christiansen with a hat in the middle of the picture, standing just below the chimney holding a wire. On the left, flanked by two Germans and wearing a sixpence hat, is Bernhard Flå.

Gruppe 2 während der Überfahrt nach Deutschland. Ganz rechts: Rolf Solum (gefallen im Juli 1941) und Kåre Brynestad mit weißer Mütze. Ganz links, sitzend mit Hird-Mütze Hans Petter Hoff. Tore Moss mit weißer Jacke, Odd Berle Christiansen in der Mitte unter dem Schornstein. Bernhard Flå mit Sixpence zwischen zwei Deutschen.

Ausbildung in Graz und Klagenfurt | Training in Graz and Klagenfurt

4. Company barracks, dining hall and officers' mess in Graz, 21 May 1941.

Kaserne der 4. Kompanie, Speisesaal und Offizierskasino in Graz, 21.05.41.

Inspection before marching in Graz.

Besichtigung vor dem Ausmarsch in Graz.

The dining hall in Graz. Third from the right side of the table is Jan Schneider.

Speisesaal in Graz. Nr. 3 an der rechten Tischseite: Jan Schneider.

At the barracks in Graz. First from the left side of the table is Arne Tvedt. On the right side of the table are Arne Hassel (first) and Henry Brock-Moe.

Kaserne in Graz. Nr. 1 an der linken Tischseite: Arne Tvedt. Rechte Tischseite: Nr. 1. Arne Hassel und Henrik Brock-Moe.

In one of the barrack windows in Graz. Bottom left, Guttorm Falk; top left, Yngvar Kofoed; bottom right, Fritjof Hansen.

An einem Kasernenfenster in Graz. Unten links Guttorm Falk, oben links Yngvar Kofoed, unten rechts Fritjof Hansen.

Bottom from the left: Per Sinding, Bernhard Johannessen and Henrik Brock-Moe. Top from the left: Tore Moss and Sigurd Aas.

Unten von links: Per Sinding, Bernhard Johannessen und Henrik Brock-Moe. Oben von links: Tore Moss und Sigurd Aas.

The entrance to the barracks in Graz.

Eingang zur Kaserne in Graz.

A group of Norwegian recruits in Graz. Front row from the left: two unknowns, Rolf Halmrast and Olav Borgir. Back row from the left: Tore Moss, unknown and Knut Steenstrup.

Eine Gruppe norwegischer Freiwilliger in Graz. Erste Reihe von links: zwei Unbekannte, Rolf Halmrast und Olav Borgir. Hinten von links: Tore Moss, ein Unbekannter und Knut Steenstrup.

From the left: Sverre Nilsen, Tore Moss, two unknowns, Knut Steenstrup and Hans Holtan.

Von links: Sverre Nilsen, Tore Moss, zwei Unbekannte, Knut Steenstrup und Hans Holtan.

Labour service in Klagenfurt.

Arbeitsdienst in Klagenfurt.

Sports in Graz. Physical exercise was a major part of the curriculum.

Sport in Graz. Körperliches Training war ein wichtiger Teil der Ausbildung.

Another image of physical exercise in Graz.

Sport in Graz. Hartes körperliches Training war ein Teil der Ausbildung.

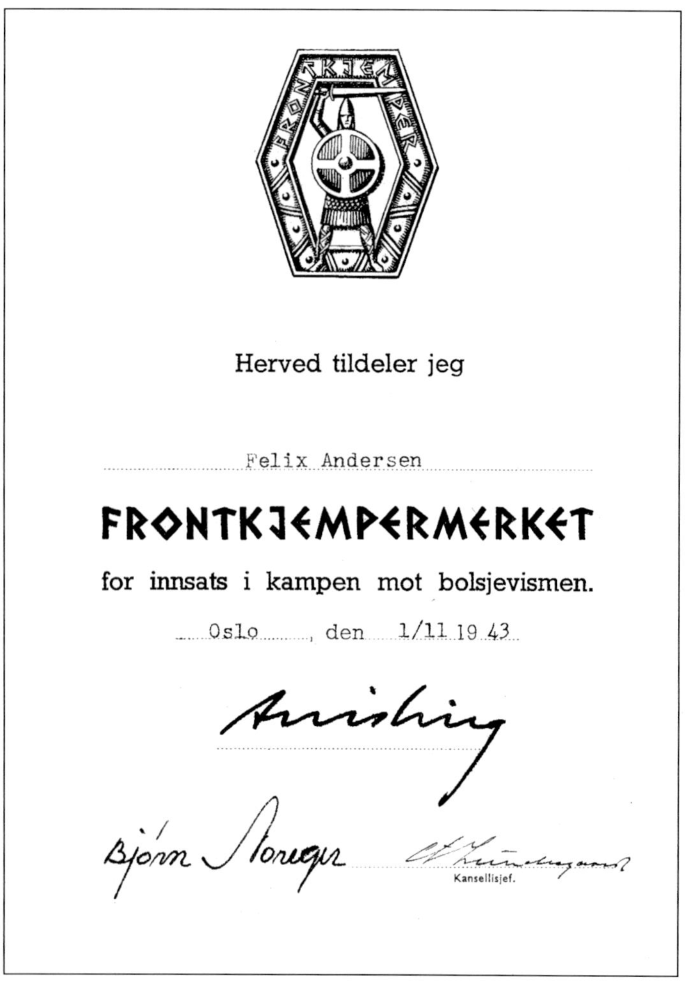

Herved tildeler jeg

Felix Andersen

FRONTKJEMPERMERKET

for innsats i kampen mot bolsjevismen.

Oslo, den 1/11 19 43

Kansellisjef.

For a while, *SS-Hauptsturmführer* Felix Andersen was the highest-ranking Norwegian officer of *Division 'Wiking'* in Graz. He briefly served as orderly officer in *Regiment 'Nordland'*, was awarded the Iron Cross 2nd Class and promoted to *SS-Sturmbannführer*. After returning to Norway, he became fire chief of Aker municipality.

Eine Zeit lang war SS-Hauptsturmführer Felix Andersen der ranghöchste norwegische Offizier der Division "Wiking" in Graz. Er diente kurz als Ordonnanzoffizier im Regiment "Nordland", erhielt das Eiserne Kreuz 2. Klasse und wurde zum SS-Sturmbannführer befördert. Nach seiner Entlassung wurde er Brandmeister der Gemeinde Aker.

The dining hall in Graz.

Der Speisesaal in Graz.

The barracks in Graz.

Die Kaserne im Graz.

NS leader Vidkun Quisling visits the camp in Graz.

NS-Führer Vidkun Quisling besucht das Lager in Graz.

Ready for departure to the front. From the left: Emil Bruun-Evers (KIA 6 May 1944), Ottar Lie Motland, five unknowns, Holger Tau (executed 1945), unknown and Jens Martin Slettebø.

Klar zum Abmarsch an die Ostfront. Von links: Emil Bruun-Evers (gefallen am 06.05.44), Ottar Lie Motland, fünf Unbekannte, Holger Tau (hingerichtet 1945), ein Unbekannter und Jens Martin Slettebø.

Ausbildung in Sennheim | Training in Sennheim

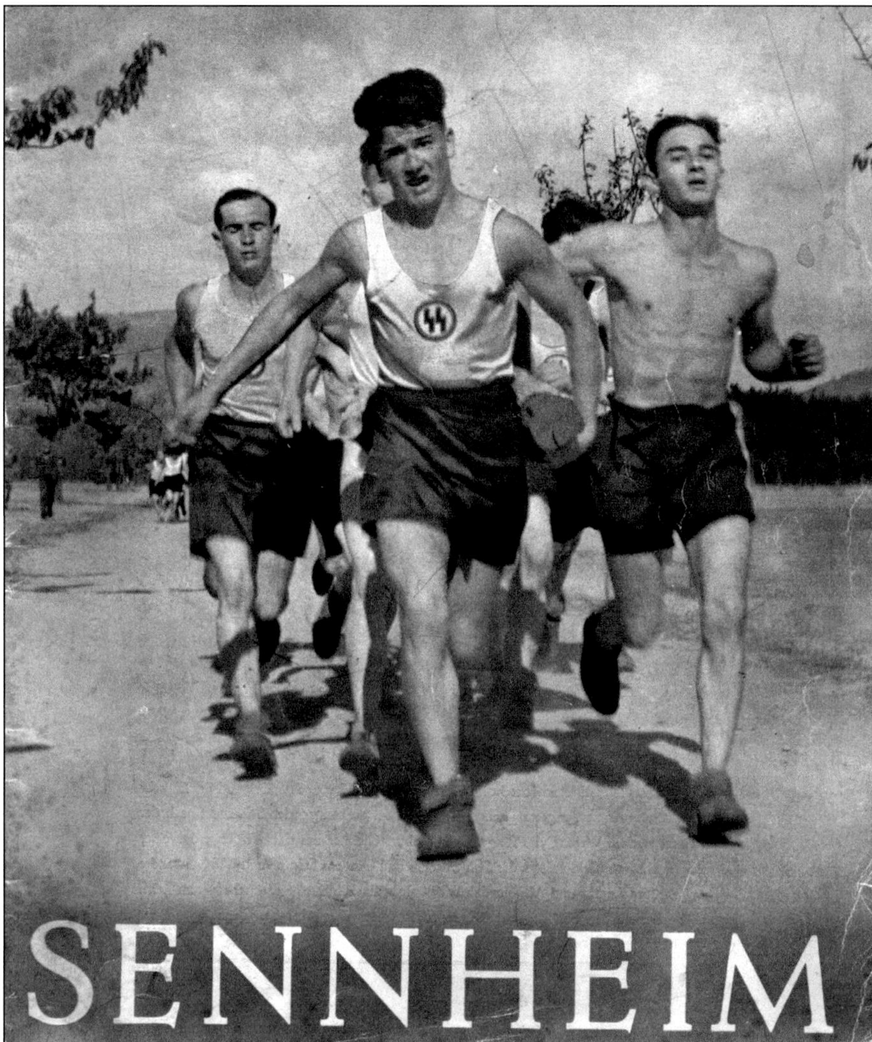

SS training camp Sennheim.

SS-Ausbildungslager Sennheim.

Jens Slettebø in Sennheim.

Jens Slettebø in Sennheim.

The barracks in Sennheim.

Die Kaserne in Sennheim.

The barracks in Sennheim.

Die Kaserne in Sennheim.

Jens Slettebø in Sennheim.

Jens Slettebø in Sennheim.

The main building in Sennheim.

Das Hauptgebäude in Sennheim.

The canteen in Sennheim.

Die Kantine in Sennheim.

Another view ofd the canteen in Sennheim.

Die Kantine in Sennheim.

Preparing for guard duty in Sennheim.

Aufstellung zum Wachdienst in Sennheim.

Obstacle course in Sennheim.

Hindernisstrecke in Sennheim.

From the left: Ragnar Homb, who later joined *Regiment 'Nordland'*; Osvald Olsen, who joined the *SS-Standarte 'Kurt Eggers'* as a war correspondent for the remainder of the war; Nils Quisling Nordvik, who was killed in 1942; Per Hasselknippe, who never made it to the front. Odd Røstad joined *Regiment 'Nordland'* and Ivar Hagen was a veteran of the Winter War in Finland and the Battle for Norway; the latter was enlisted in *Regiment 'Nordland'* for 28 months.

Von links: Ragnar Homb, der später zum Regiment "Nordland" kam; Osvald Olsen, der als Kriegsberichter zur SS-Standarte Kurt Eggers versetzt wurde und am Krieg bis zum Schluss im Jahre 1945 teilnahm; Nils Quisling Nordvik (gefallen 1942); Per Hasselknippe, der nach seiner Ausbildung als Rekrut aus gesundheitsmäßigen Gründen aus der Waffen-SS entlassen wurde. Odd Røstad trat dem Regiment "Nordland" bei, und Ivar Hagen war ein Veteran des finnischen Winterkrieges 1939/40 und des Kampfes gegen die deutschen Truppen in Norwegen. Er kämpfte an der Ostfront und war insgesamt 28 Monate beim Regiment "Nordland".

From the left: Jens Slettebø and Ottar Lie Motland in Sennheim.

Von links: Jens Slettebø und Motland in Sennheim.

SS-Regiment "Germania" an der Front | *SS-Regiment 'Germania'* at the front

The headquarters of *Regiment 'Germania'* somewhere on the Eastern Front.

Hauptgefechtsstand des Regiments "Germania" an der Ostfront.

Ottar Birkeland (in Sennheim or Graz).

Ottar Birkeland (in Sennheim oder Graz).

Odd Berle Christiansen was seriously wounded while serving in *'Germania'*. He was shot in the hip and became 70 percent disabled.

Odd Berle Christiansen wurde während seiner Zeit in der "Germania" schwer verwundet. Er erlitt einen Hüftschuss und wurde zu 70 Prozent invalid erklärt.

A break during the advance on the Ukraine.

Ein Pause beim Vormarsch in die Ukraine.

Preparing food while advancing through the Ukraine.

Essenszubereitung beim Vormarsch durch die Ukraine.

From the left: Kåre Berge, a Dane, Arne Stangeland and Hugo Skansen.

Von links: Kåre Berge, ein Däne, Arne Stangeland und Hugo Skansen.

A quiet moment during the fighting at Kamenka.

Ein ruhiger Augenblick während der Kämpfe um Kamenka.

Alexander Lakso on the Ukrainian plains.

Aleksander Lakso in den ukrainischen Steppen.

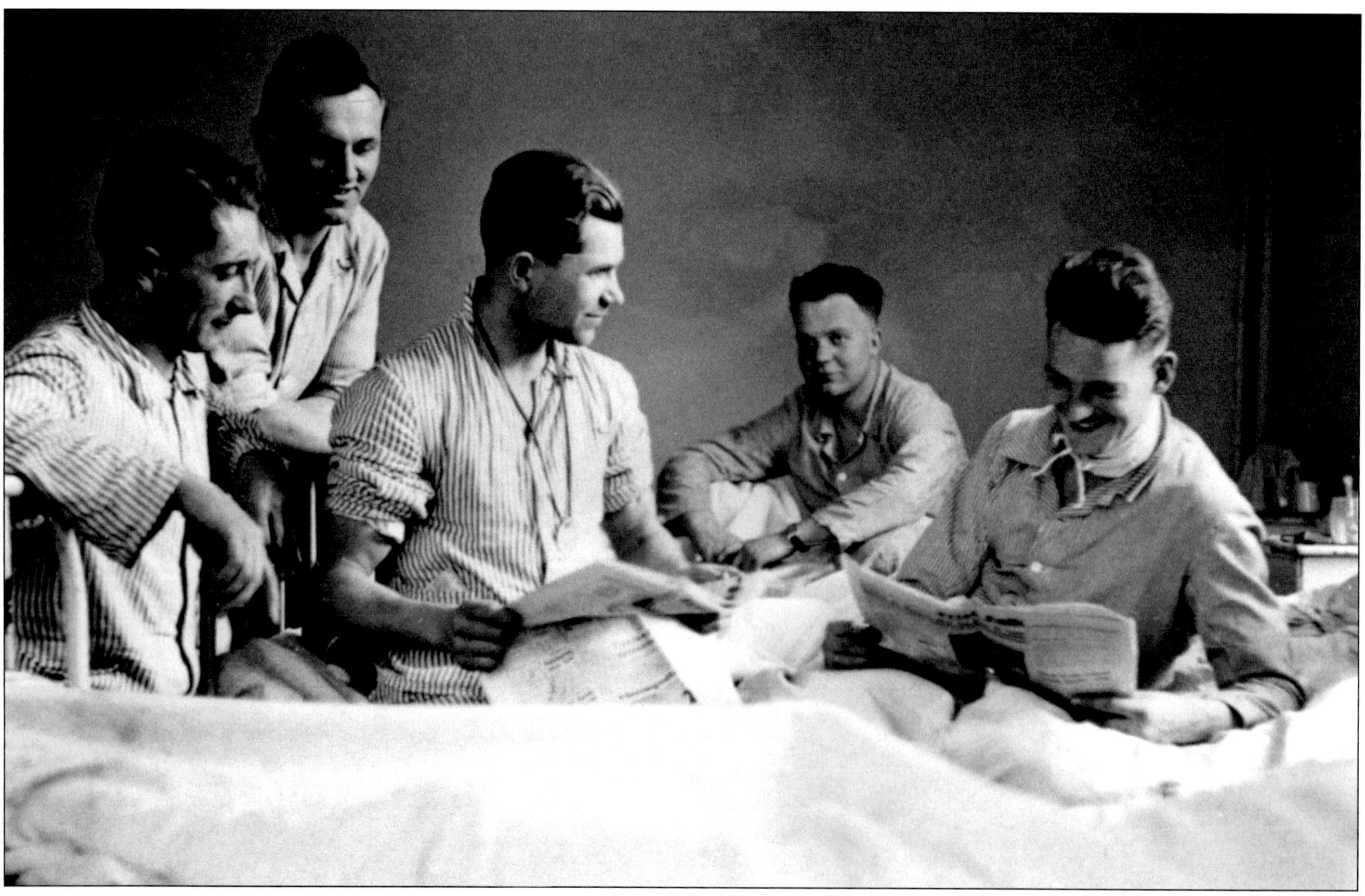

Two wounded Norwegian volunteers. From the left: Bjarne Peder Karlsen and Erling Rennesund.

Zwei verwundete norwegische Freiwillige. Von links: Bjarne Peder Karlsen und Erling Rennesund.

Regiment 'Germania' is relieved by the Italians. Back row: first from right, Axel Jøndal; fifth from right, his brother Oddvar Jøndal.

Das Regiment "Germania" wird von Italienern abgelöst. Hintere Reihe von rechts: Nr. 1 Axel Jøndal, Nr. 5 sein Bruder Oddvar Jøndal.

From the left: *SS-Sturmmann* Nicolai Rach-Kiil, *SS-Sturmmann* Aleksander Lakso and *SS-Sturmmann* Richard Sem-Jacobsen. All three survived the war.

Von links: SS-Sturmmann Nicolai Rasch-Kiil, SS-Sturmmann Aleksander Lakso und SS-Sturmmann Richard Sem-Jacobsen. Alle drei haben den Krieg überlebt.

A group from *Regiment 'Germania'* advancing through the Ukraine.

Eine Gruppe des Regiments "Germania" beim Vormarsch durch die Ukraine.

Oddvar Jøndal after receiving the Iron Cross 2nd Class. After *'Germania'* he served as a courier at *SS-Hauptamt* in Berlin.

Oddvar Jøndal nach der Verleihung des Eisernen Kreuzes 2. Klasse. Später diente er als Kurier am SS-Hauptamt in Berlin.

This picture bears the following text: From our position, winter 1941–42, taken in the spring. We're sitting on our bunker, the entrance is between our legs. Jan Taarneby is sitting to the right. The other two were later killed in action.

Der Text dieses Bildes: Von unserer Stellung Winter 1941–42, aufgenommen im Frühling. Wir sitzen auf unserem Bunker, der Eingang ist zwischen unseren Beinen. Jan Taarneby rechts, die zwei anderen sind später gefallen.

SS-Unterscharführer Søren Modolf Sørensen fought in *Regiment 'Germania'*. After returning to Norway, he joined the German Security Police (SD) and took his own life on 21 April 1945.

SS-Unterscharführer Søren Modolf Sørensen kämpfte beim Regiment "Germania". Nach der Entlassung war er beim Deutschen Sicherheitsdienst (SD) und nahm sich am 21.04.45 das Leben.

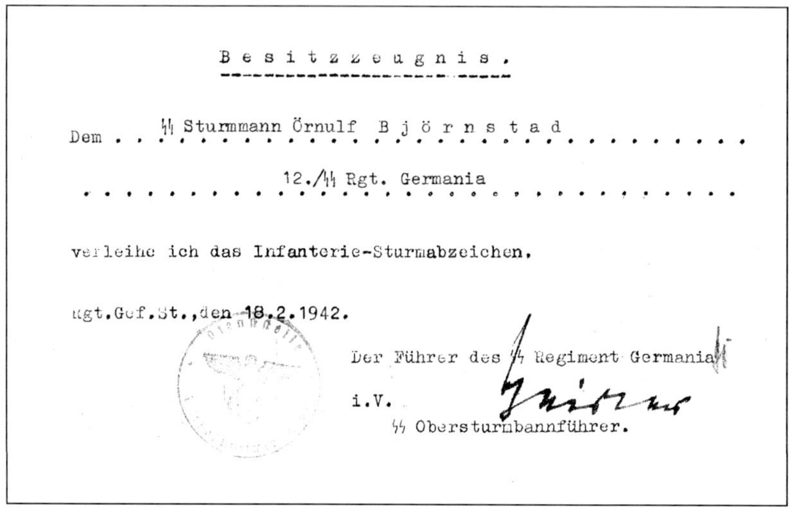

B e s i t z z e u g n i s .

Dem . . SS Sturmmann Örnulf B j ö r n s t a d . . . .

. . . . 12./SS Rgt. Germania . . . .

verleihe ich das Infanterie-Sturmabzeichen.

Rgt.Gef.St., den 18.2.1942.

Der Führer des SS Regiment Germania
i.V.
SS Obersturmbannführer.

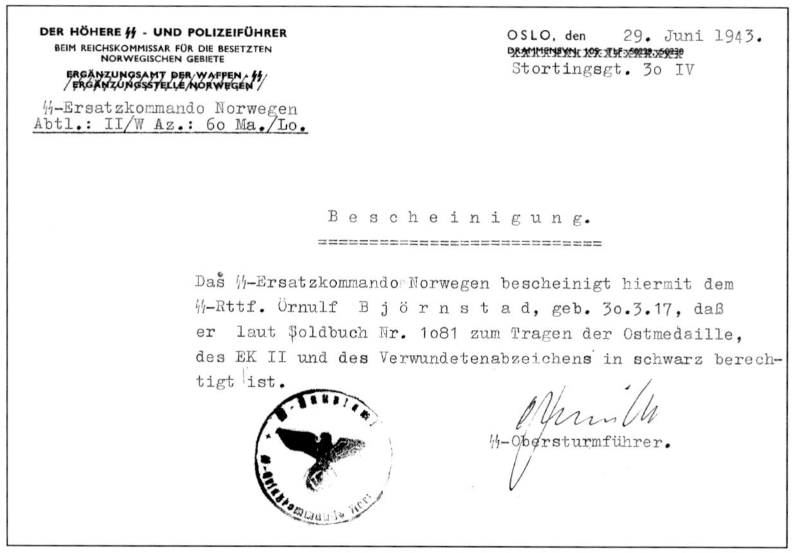

DER HÖHERE SS - UND POLIZEIFÜHRER
BEIM REICHSKOMMISSAR FÜR DIE BESETZTEN NORWEGISCHEN GEBIETE
ERGÄNZUNGSAMT DER WAFFEN-SS
ERGÄNZUNGSSTELLE NORWEGEN

SS-Ersatzkommando Norwegen
Abtl.: II/W Az.: 60 Ma./Lo.

OSLO, den 29. Juni 1943.
Stortingsgt. 30 IV

B e s c h e i n i g u n g.

Das SS-Ersatzkommando Norwegen bescheinigt hiermit dem SS-Rttf. Örnulf B j ö r n s t a d, geb. 30.3.17, daß er laut Soldbuch Nr. 1081 zum Tragen der Ostmedaille, des EK II und des Verwundetenabzeichens in schwarz berechtigt ist.

SS-Obersturmführer.

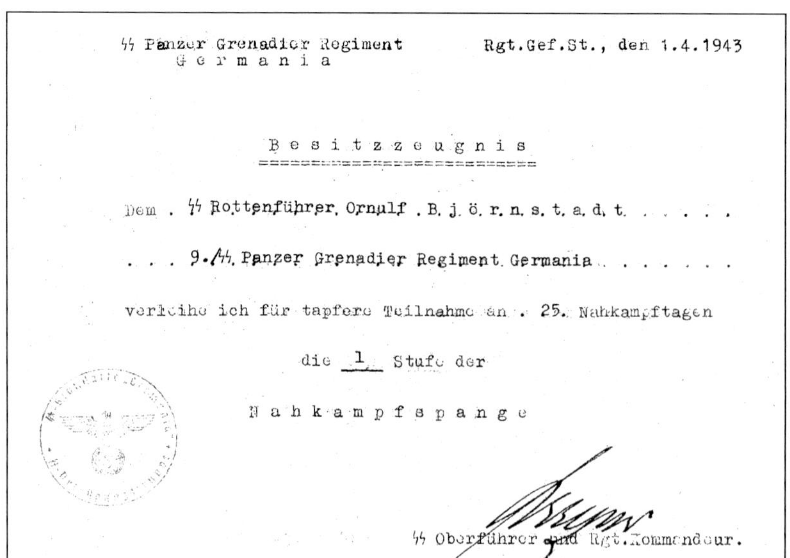

SS Panzer Grenadier Regiment
G e r m a n i a

Rgt.Gef.St., den 1.4.1943

B e s i t z z e u g n i s

Dem . SS Rottenführer Ornulf . B. j. ö. r. n. s. t. a. d. t. . . . . .

. . . 9./SS Panzer Grenadier Regiment Germania . . . .

verleihe ich für tapfere Teilnahme an . 25. Nahkampftagen

die 1 Stufe der

N a h k a m p f s p a n g e

SS Oberführer und Rgt.Kommandeur.

SS-Rottenführer Ørnulf Bjørnstad served in *Regiment 'Germania'* from 15 January 1941 to 15 June 1943. He was wounded twice, received the Iron Cross 2nd Class, an Infantry Assault Badge and a Close Combat Clasp in Bronze.

SS-Rottenführer Ørunlf Bjørnstad diente vom 15.01.41 bis zum 15.06.43 im Regiment "Germania". Er wurde zweimal verwundet und erhielt das Eiserne Kreuz 2. Klasse, ein Infanterie Sturmabzeichen und die Nahkampfspange in Bronze.

SS-Unterscharführer Alf Fjeld volunteered for *Division 'Wiking'* in April 1941. He was wounded several times and fought at Cherkassy and Kovel, among others. He received the Iron Cross 1st Class and the Close Combat Clasp in Bronze.

SS-Unterscharführer Alf Fjeld meldete sich als Freiwilliger im April 1941. Er wurde mehrmals verwundet und kämpfte bei Tscherkassy und Kowel, wo er das Eiserne Kreuz 1. Klasse und die Nahkampfspange in Bronze erhielt.

Norwegian members of *II./Germania*, summer 1941. Sitting in front from the right, Torbjørn Dambo; with paper, Magne Holter; sitting in the middle row on the right, Per Wickstrøm; standing far left, Nygaard.

Norweger in der II./Germania, Sommer 1941. Vorne sitzend von rechts: Torbjørn Dambo, Nr. 6 mit Papier Magne Holter, sitzend in der mittleren Reihe Per Wickstrøm, ganz links stehend Nygaard.

The grave of Per Møller. He was killed on 20 July 1941 when a piece of shrapnel struck his head.

Das Grab von Per Møller, der am 20.07.41 fiel als ein Granatsplitter seinen Kopf traf.

Krug, a *Volksdeutscher* (ethnic German) with the *6./Germania*, August 1941.

Der Volksdeutsche Krug von der 6./Germania, August 1941.

SS Untersturmführer Fredrik Jensen with a group from *7. Company* of *Regiment 'Germania'*.

SS-Untersturmführer Fredrik Jensen mit einer Gruppe der 7. Kompanie des Regiments "Germania".

SS-Untersturmführer Fredrik Jensen is awarded the Iron Cross 2nd Class. He later received the Iron Cross 1st Class and the German Cross in Gold. He was the most highly decorated Norwegian front line fighter.

SS-Untersturmführer Fredrik Jensen erhält das Eiserne Kreuz 2. Klasse. Später wurden ihm das Eiserne Kreuz 1. Klasse und das Deutsche Kreuz in Gold verliehen. Er war damit der am höchsten ausgezeichnete norwegische Frontkämpfer.

SS-Untersturmführer Fredrik Jensen is awarded the Iron Cross 2nd Class. He later received the Iron Cross 1st Class and the German Cross in Gold. He was the most highly decorated Norwegian front line fighter.

SS-Untersturmführer Fredrik Jensen erhält das Eiserne Kreuz 2. Klasse. Später wurden ihm das Eiserne Kreuz 1. Klasse und das Deutsche Kreuz in Gold verliehen. Er war damit der am höchsten ausgezeichnete norwegische Frontkämpfer.

SS-Regiment "Nordland" an der Ostfront | *SS-Regiment 'Nordland'* on the Eastern Front

Regiment 'Nordland' during the invasion of the Ukraine.

Das Regiment "Nordland" rückt in die Ukraine ein.

Charging an MG-34 before the attack.

Ein MG 34 wird vor dem Kampf geladen.

Regiment 'Nordland' occupies a town.

Das Regiment "Nordland" besetzt ein Dorf.

Anti-aircraft machine guns mounted on a vehicle.

Fliegerabwehr an einem Fahrzeug montiert.

Gunnar Haug during a break in the advance.

Gunnar Haug während einer Unterbrechung des Vormarsches.

Guard duty on the Mius Front, winter 1941–42.

Wachdienst an der Mius-Front, Winter 1941–42.

A group of volunteers in an MG position on the Mius Front.

Eine Gruppe Freiwilliger in einer MG-Stellung an der Mius-Front.

An MG position on the Mius Front.

Eine MG-Stellung an der Mius-Front.

Fritz Ihlen was one of the first and most renowned Norwegian war correspondents. Before joining the *Waffen-SS*, he had participated in the Winter War in Finland in 1939–40.

Fritz Ihlen war einer der ersten und bekanntesten norwegischen Kriegsberichter. Bevor er als Freiwilliger in die Reihen der Waffen-SS eintrat, hatte er an dem Winterkrieg in Finnland 1939–40 teilgenommen.

Smoke mortar position on the Mius Front, winter 1941–42.

Nebelwerferstellung an der Mius-Front, Winter 1941–42.

MG on an anti-aircraft mount, operated by *SS-Unterscharführer* Petter Pedersen. Before becoming a volunteer, he had attended the Norwegian Officer Candidate School.

SS-Unterscharführer Petter Pedersen an dem als Fliegerabwehr montierten MG. Er war norwegischer Offizier.

Olaf Fermann as an enlisted man in *Regiment 'Nordland'*. Later he became commander of the Norwegian front fighter office and Vice President of the Norwegian Red Cross in 1942.

Olaf Fermann als SS-Schütze beim Regiment "Nordland". Später wurde er Leiter des Norwegischen Frontkämpferbüros, und ab 1942 Vizepräsident des norwegischen Roten Kreuzes.

View from an MG position of *Regiment 'Nordland'*.

Aussicht von einer MG-Stellung des Regiments "Nordland".

Crossing a river in an inflatable boat.

Flussüberquerung in einem Gummiboot.

2./Nordland. On the left is Gabriel Wartano from Baku, Russia, who was captured by the Germans in August 1942. To the right is *SS-Unterscharführer* Robert Stock from Tyrol.

2./Nordland. Von links: der Russe Gabriel Wartano aus Baku wurde im August 1942 gefangengenommen. Rechts: SS-Unterscharführer Robert Stock aus Tirol.

Two volunteers from *SS-Regiment 'Nordland'*. The person to the right is carrying a captured Russian PPSh machine gun.

Zwei Freiwillige des SS-Regiments "Nordland". Der Freiwillige rechts im Bild hält eine russische Maschinenpistole vom Typ PPSch.

Einar Østvold, a volunteer of *Regiment 'Nordland'*, at the Mius Front.

Einar Østvold vom Regiment "Nordland" an der Mius-Front.

Einar Østvold, left, and Arne Skjæveland at the Mius Front.

Von links: Einar Østvold und Arne Skjæveland an der Mius-Front.

A short rest period during the advance.

Eine kurze Ruhepause während des Vormarsches.

Regiment 'Nordland' used a *Kübelwagen* ('bucket seat car') to carry ammunition to the front lines.

Ein Kübelwagen des Regiments "Nordland" wurde als Munitionsträger zur Front benutzt.

Volunteers from *Regiment 'Nordland'* next to a downed Russian plane.

Freiwillige des Regiments "Nordland" an einem abgestürtzen russischen Flugzeug.

Fredrik Kaatorp was a veteran of the Winter War in Finland from 1939-40 and served as a driver for *Regiment 'Nordland'*.

Fredrik Kaatorp, ein Veteran des Winterkrieges in Finnland 1939–40, diente als Fahrer beim Regiment "Nordland".

Fredrik Kaatorp to the right of his truck.

Fredrik Kaatorp an der rechten Seite seines Lkws.

Four drivers with Regiment 'Nordland'. Second from the left is Fredrik Kaatorp.

Vier der Fahrer vom Regiment "Nordland". Nr. 2 von links: Fredrik Kaatorp.

SS-Sturmmann Oddvar Nes was killed on 22 November 1941 during the assault on Rostov. He was part of *7./SS-Inf. Rgt. 'Nordland'*.

SS-Sturmmann Oddvar Nes, der am 22.11.1941 bei dem Angriff auf Rostow fiel. Er war Angehöriger des 7./SS-Inf. Rgts. "Nordland".

Bjørn W. Johannessen, fourth from the left, is awarded an Infantry Assault Badge. He was a member of *5. Company* of *Regiment 'Nordland'*.

Nr. 4 von links, Bjørn W. Johannessen, bei der Verleihung des Sturmabzeichens. Er war Angehöriger der 5. Kompanie des Regiments "Nordland".

A group of volunteers from *Regiment 'Nordland'* at the Mius Front.

Eine Gruppe Freiwilliger des Regiments "Nordland" an der Mius-Front.

A *Regiment 'Nordland'* MG position.

MG-Stellung beim Regiment "Nordland".

NS-leader Vidkun Quisling visits the Norwegian volunteers of *Division 'Wiking'* with Felix Steiner.

NS-Führer Vidkun Quisling besucht die norwegischen Freiwilligen der Division "Wiking". Hier zusammen mit Felix Steiner.

From the left: Otto H. Gille, Finnish general Öhqvist and Felix Steiner during the general's visit to the so-called 'Finnish Battalion' of *Division 'Wiking'*.

Von links: Otto H. Gille, der finnische General Öhqvist und Felix Steiner während eines Besuchs des Generals beim finnischen Bataillon der Division "Wiking".

Finnish general Öhqvist with Felix Steiner and Otto H. Gille during the general's visit to the 'Finnish Battalion' of *Division 'Wiking'*.

Der finnische General Öhqvist mit Felix Steiner und Otto H. Gille während eines Besuchs des Generals beim finnischen Bataillon der Division "Wiking".

Finnish general Öhqvist again with Felix Steiner and Otto H. Gille during the former's visit to the 'Finnish Battalion' of *Division 'Wiking'*.

Der finnische General Öhqvist mit Felix Steiner und Otto H. Gille während eines Besuches des Generals beim finnischen Bataillon der Division "Wiking".

Two volunteers at the Mius Front in the freezing winter of 1941–42.

Zwei Freiwillige an der eiskalten Mius-Front im Winter 1941–42.

Two drivers of *Regiment 'Nordland'*.

Zwei Fahrer des Regiments "Nordland".

SS-Regiment "Westland" an der Front | *SS-Regiment 'Westland'* at the front

A group of volunteers from *Regiment 'Westland'* near Rostov.

Eine Gruppe Freiwilliger des Regiments "Westland" in der Nähe von Rostow.

A group of volunteers from *Regiment 'Westland'* in September 1942. At the back to the right is Norwegian volunteer Gunnar Høy.

Eine Gruppe Freiwilliger des Regiments "Westland" im September 1942. Hinten rechts der Norweger Gunnar Høy.

Regiment 'Westland' in Rostov.

Das Regiment "Westland" in Rostow.

The German squad leader Braad in Rostov.

Der deutsche Gruppenführer Braad in Rostow.

50° Celsius (120° F.) while advancing across the Ukrainian plains.

50 Grad Wärme beim Vormarsch durch die ukrainischen Steppen.

Wounded volunteers of *Regiment 'Westland'* in a field hospital on 1 October 1942. At the back to the right is Norwegian volunteer Gunnar Høy.

Verwundete Freiwillige des Regiments "Westland". Hinten rechts der Norweger Gunnar Høy. Feldlazarett, 01.10.1942.

Norwegian volunteer Inge Oliver Martin Bakken, third from left.

Nr. 3 von links der Norweger Inge Oliver Martin Bakken.

Cleaning an MG-42 with *Regiment 'Westland'*.

Reinigung eines MG 42 beim Regiment "Westland".

An unknown Dane, left, and Inge Bakken, who received the Iron Cross 1st Class after the Battle of Cherkassy.

Von links: ein unbekannter Däne und Inge Bakken, der nach der Schlacht um Tscherkassy das Eiserne Kreuz 1. Klasse erhielt.

Group 1 of *5. Company, Regiment 'Westland'*, in 1944.

1. Gruppe der 5. Kompanie, Regiment "Westland", 1944.

Inge Bakken instructing in the use of an MG-42 during the summer of 1944.

Inge Bakken demonstriert die Anwendung eines MG 42, Sommer 1944.

A *Regiment 'Westland'* MG position in the summer of 1944. Inge Bakken is in the background.

MG-Stellung des Regiments "Westland", Sommer 1944. Inge Bakken im Hintergrund.

Inge Bakken in Poland during the summer of 1944, manning one of the assault guns (*Sturmgeschütz*) of *Division 'Wiking'*.

Inge Bakken an einem Sturmgeschütz der Division "Wiking" in Polen, Sommer 1944.

Norwegians from *Division 'Wiking'* who fought at Cherkassy visit *Reichskommissar* Terboven at Skaugum, Norway.

Norwegische Tsckerkassykämpfer der Division "Wiking" zu Besuch bei Reichskommissar Terboven in Skaugum, Norwegen.

Inge Bakken on home leave in Lillestrøm during the summer of 1944.

Inge Bakken beim Heimaturlaub in Lillestrøm, Norwegen, Sommer 1944 .

Inge Bakken with his wife Aasa, a front-line nurse, during their leave of absence in Norway.

Inge Bakken mit seiner Frau, der DRK-Schwester Aasa, während des Heimaturlaubs in Norwegen.

Artillerie-Regiment 5 "Wiking" und Flak-Abteilung 5 "Wiking" an der Front | *Artillery Regiment 5 'Wiking'* and *Flak-Abteilung 5 'Wiking'* at the front

SS-Unterscharführer Thoralf Gjølberg during the attack on Russia.

SS-Unterscharführer Thoralf Gjølberg während des Angriffs auf die Sowjetunion.

Four artillerymen with *SS-Art.Rgt. 5* in the Ukraine.

Vier Angehörige des SS-Art.Rgts. 5 in der Ukraine.

An artillery position during the advance through the Ukraine.

Eine Artilleriestellung während des Vormarsches durch die Ukraine.

During a break. At the back on the left is Hans Holtan.

Eine Ruhepause. Hinten links Hans Holtan.

SS-Unterscharführer Thoralf Gjølberg somewhere in the Ukraine.

SS-Unterscharführer Thoralf Gjølberg in der Ukraine.

A group of artillerymen from *SS-Art.Rgt. 5* in front of their gun.

Eine Gruppe des SS-Art.Rgts. 5 vor ihrem Geschütz.

A group of artillerymen aiming their gun.

Eine Gruppe von Kanonieren beim Einschießen ihres Geschützes.

A group of artillerymen being awarded the Iron Cross 2nd Class in the Ukraine.

Eine Gruppe von Kanonieren wird in der Ukraine mit dem Eisernen Kreuz 2. Klasse ausgezeichnet.

On the left is the Norwegian volunteer Bjørn Conrad Heisholdt.

Links: der Norweger Bjørn Conrad Heisholdt.

To the right is the Norwegian volunteer Arvid Johannessen.

Rechts der Norweger Arvid Johannessen.

Ole Brunæs was a volunteer in the artillery before attending the Officer Academy in Bad Tölz and becoming the Norwegian liaison officer at *SS-Hauptamt*, *Germanische Leitstelle* (SS Head Office, Germanic Control Centre).

Ole Brunæs war bei dem SS-Art.Rgt 5 bevor er die SS-Junkerschule in Bad Tölz besuchte und als Verbindungsoffizier ans SS-Hauptamt, Germanische Leitstelle, kommandiert wurde.

Hans Holtan was a member of *SS-Flak-Abt. 5*. He enlisted on 31 January 1941 and was discharged in July 1942.

Hans Holtan war bei der SS-Flak.Abt. 5. Er hatte sich am 31.01.41 gemeldet, und wurde im Juli 1942 entlassen.

Oddvar Solberg was a member of *SS-Art.Rgt. 5* until his discharge on 10 June 1943.

Oddvar Solberg war Angehöriger des SS-Art.Rgts. 5 bis zu seiner Entlassung am 10.06.43.

Arthur Hjelt served in *'Wiking'*, was promoted to *SS-Unterscharführer* and received the Iron Cross 2nd Class. He was a member of *SS-Flak.Abt. 5*, 3rd battery.

Arthur Hjelt war bei der SS-Flak.Abt. 5, 3. Batterie, wurde zum SS-Unterscharführer befördert und mit dem Eisernenen Kreuz 2. Klasse ausgezeichnet.

SS-Unterscharführer Paul Sæther was killed in March 1945 near Veszprém, Hungary. For a long time he was a member of *'Wiking' Flak Abteilung* 5. He received the Iron Cross 1st Class after destroying three tanks with his anti-aircraft gun. He took part in the fighting at Cherkassy and Kovel.

SS-Unterscharführer Paul Sæther fiel im März 1945 in der Nähe von Veszprém, Ungarn. Er war Angehöriger der SS-Flak.Abt. 5 und wurde mit dem Eisernen Kreuz 1. Klasse ausgezeichnet nachdem er drei sowjetische Panzer mit seiner Fliegerabwehrkanone zerstört hatte. Er nahm unter anderem an den Kämpfen im Kessel von Tscherkassy und in Kowel teil.

Oluf Brenna at his gun in *SS-Art.Rgt. 5*, 5th battery.

Oluf Brenna an seinem Geschütz im SS-Art.Rgt. 5, 5. Batterie.

On leave are, from the left, unknown, Yngvar Kofoed and Guttorm Falk.

Auf Urlaub. Von links: ein Unbekannter, Yngvar Kofoed und Guttorm Falk.

The attack on Dnepropetrovsk.

Angriff auf Dnjepropetrowsk.

A group of artillerymen in front of their gun.

Eine Gruppe von Kanonieren vor ihrem Geschütz.

Another view of the artillerymen in front of their gun.

Eine Gruppe von Kanonieren vor ihrem Geschütz.

Second from the left is *SS-Unterscharführer* Thoralf Gjølberg.

Nr. 2 von links: SS-Unterscharführer Thoralf Gjølberg.

Motor vehicles of *SS-Art.Rgt. 5* at the Mius Front.

Fahrzeuge des SS-Art.Rgts. 5 an der Mius-Front.

A group of anti-aircraft fighters with their gun.

Eine Flakgruppe mit ihrem Flakgeschütz.

Anti-aircraft fighters with their gun near Uspenskaya.

Eine Flakgruppe mit ihrem Flakgeschütz bei Uspenskaya.

A group of anti-aircraft fighters with their gun somewhere on the Eastern Front.

Eine Flakgruppe mit ihrem Flakgeschütz an der Ostfront.

Anti-aircraft guns were mounted on trucks while moving to new positions.

Die Flak wurde während des Stellungswechsels auf dem Fahrzeug montiert.

On the Mius Front, early summer 1942.

An der Mius-Front, Frühjahr 1942.

An anti-aircraft gun mounted on a half-tracked vehicle.

Flakgeschütz, auf einem Kettenkrad montiert.

Field graves of *Division 'Wiking'* somewhere on the Eastern Front.

Feldgräber der Division "Wiking" an der Ostfront.

An MG position used by the artillery for close-quarter defence.

MG-Stellung des SS-Art.Rgts. 5 zur Nahverteidigung.

Another view of anti-aircraft guns mounted on trucks while moving to new positions.

Die Flak wurde während des Stellungswechsels auf dem Fahrzeug montiert.

Nordic crew, from the left, Jolki (Finland), Hans Lindèn (Sweden), unknown and Kåre Holstad (Norway).

Nordische Besatzung. Von links: Jolki (Finnland), Hans Lindèn (Schweden), ein Unbekannter und Kåre Holstad (Norwegen).

On the Mius Front, spring 1942.

An der Mius-Front, Frühjahr 1942.

Mius, spring 1942.

Mius, Frühjahr 1942.

To the right is the Norwegian volunteer Anker Sundby, who served as *SS-Rottenführer* in *Flak-Abteilung 5, 1. Company.*

Rechts der Norweger Anker Sundby, der als SS-Rottenführer bei der Flak-Abteilung 5, 1. Kompanie, diente.

SS-Flak-Abt. 5 somewhere in the Ukraine.

SS-Flak-Abt. 5 in der Ukraine.

Advancing towards the Caucasus.

Vorstoß in den Kaukasus.

Drawing by the Norwegian war correspondent Finn Wigfors.

Eine Zeichnung des norwegischen Kriegsberichters Finn Wigfors.

Flak positions were clearly marked to avoid being bombed by their own troops.

Die Flakstellungen wurden deutlich gekennzeichnet um das Bombardieren durch die eigenen Truppen zu vermeiden.

Heimkehr der Division "Wiking" | *Division 'Wiking'* returns home

After his return from the front, Fredrik Kaatorp stayed in Graz, waiting to be discharged.

Nach seiner Rückkehr von der Front wartet Fredrik Kaatorp in Graz auf seine Entlassung.

An unknown Norwegian waiting to be discharged in Graz.

Ein unbekannter Norweger wartet auf seine Entlassung in Graz.

From the left, Johannes Knutzen and Fredrik Kaatorp. The rest are unknown.

Von links: Johannes Knutzen und Fredrik Kaatorp. Die anderen sind unbekannt.

2

SS-Freiwilligen-Legion Norwegen und 1. Polizeikompanie

Eine Woche nach dem deutschen Angriff auf die Sowjetunion erhielt NS-Führer Vidkun Quisling die telegrafische Bewilligung zur Aufstellung einer norwegischen Einheit an der Ostfront, und berief eine Sitzung mit den norwegischen Offizieren Carl Langli, Finn Kjelstrup, Henrik Bjerkelund und Jørgen Bakke ein, um den Aufbau der neuen Einheit zu diskutieren.

Im Juli 1941 wurde es in den Zeitungen veröffentlicht, dass der NS-Führer die Freiwilligen-Legion Norwegen zum Einsatz an der Ostfront gegründet hatte. Pressemitteilungen und Aussagen norwegischer Offiziere zufolge sollte die Einheit unter ausschließlich norwegischer Führung an der finnischen Front eingesetzt werden, mit norwegischen Offizieren und norwegischer Kommandosprache.

In Oslo wurde der Regimentsstab unter Leitung von Major Finn Hannibal Kjelstrup aufgestellt. Die Freiwilligen-Legion Norwegen wurde an der Bjølsener Schule in Oslo, und später im Lager Gulskogen bei Drammen aufgestellt. Hier wurde die Ausbildung intensiviert, bevor die Einheit zum Truppenübungsplatz Fallingbostel in Deutschland verlegt wurde, wo die militärische Ausbildung hinsichtlich Zug, Kompanie und Bataillon fortgesetzt wurde.

Als Bataillonskommandeur wird Hauptmann Jørgen Bakke ernannt und zum Major befördert, mit dem deutschen Dienstgrad Legions-Sturmbannführer. Die Unzufriedenheit mit den Deutschen, und was auf der norwegischen Seite als Wortbruch bezeichnet wird, verbreitet sich während des Aufenthalts in Fallingbostel. Auf norwegischer Seite wird behauptet, dass die Ausbildung ursprünglich in Norwegen stattfinden sollte, mit norwegischen Waffen, Uniformen und norwegischer Kommandosprache. Während der Vereidigung meldet das Oslo-Büro, dass der Leiter der Abteilung, Oberst Kjelstrup, verhindert sei, an der Vereidigung im September 1941 teilzunehmen. Nach mehrfachen Besprechungen mit SS-Gruppenführer Hans Jüttner, Major Bakke und Oberst Kjelstrup in Berlin wird Bakke abgelöst, und der frühere Rittmeister Arthur Qvist als neuer Bataillonskommandeur eingesetzt.

Mitte Februar 1942 erhält die SS-Freiwilligen-Legion Norwegen plötzlich den Befehl zur Verlegung an die Ostfront. Das Ziel ist unbekannt, und das Bataillon wird mit Junkers Ju 52 Flugzeugen an den Bestimmungsort abtransportiert. Das Ziel ist aber nicht Finnland, sondern die Gegend südlich von Leningrad. Hier geht die SS-Frw.-Legion Norwegen am 18. Februar 1942 in Stellung, und wird der Kampf gruppe Jeckeln unter dem Kommando von SS-Brigadeführer Friedrich Jeckeln unterstellt. Die Kämpfe an der Front südlich von Leningrad hatten sich allmählich beruhigt, und die Situation erinnerte an die Schützengräben des 1. Weltkriegs. Die Russen hielten ihre Stellungen vor Leningrad, und die SS-Frw.-Legion Norwegen, zusammen mit Einheiten der Wehrmacht und später der SS-Frw.-Legion "Niederlande", legten einen eisernen Ring um die Stadt.

Beide kämpfenden Seiten führten Aufklärungs- und Stoßtrupps gegen feindliche Stellungen durch und machten Gefangene. Die Russen unternahmen eine Reihe von größeren Angriffen, die aber nur wenig erfolgreich waren. Mit der Aufgabe, Bunker zu zerstören und Gefangene zu den eigenen Linien zurückzubringen, hoffte der Leg.-Hauptsturmführer der 4. Kompanie, Ragnar Berg, in der Nacht zum 16. April 1942 mit einem größeren Stoßtrupp in die russischen Stellungen bei Urizk südwestlich von Leningrad einzudringen. Der Versuch scheiterte als der Stoßtrupp in ein Minenfeld gelang und schwere Verluste an Gefallenen und Verwundeten erlitt, darunter auch Leg.-Hauptsturmführer Berg. Im Juli 1942 unternahmen die Russen eine Großoffensive gegen die Stellungen der SS-Frw.-Legion "Niederlande", und ein Zug unter dem Kommando von Leg.-Hauptscharführer Arnfinn Vik, 14. (Pak-) Kompanie der SS-Frw.-Legion Norwegen, wurde eingesetzt. Der Angriff wurde zurückgeschlagen.

Die Kompanien wechselten einander beim Einsatz an der Hauptkampflinie ab. Der Bataillonsstab befand sich etwas hinter der Front, und das Bataillon wurde bei Pulkowo und Ladoga eingesetzt. Ersatzmannschaften aus Norwegen wurden erst bei dem Ersatzbataillon in Holmestrand, und danach in Mitau, Litauen, ausgebildet. Die meisten der Gefallenen wurden auf dem Soldatenfriedhof in Krasnoje Selo beerdigt.

Im Februar 1943 wurde das Bataillon aus den Stellungen gezogen und nach Mitau verlegt, wo Reichsführer-SS Himmler die Männer in einer ermahnenden Rede aufforderte, sich bei dem neuaufgestellten Regiment "Norge" anwerben zu lassen. Alle, die sich zum Dienst bei der neuen Einheit meldeten, erhielten Urlaub in Norwegen, und die gesamte SS-Frw.-Legion Norwegen wurde im März 1943 nach Grafenwöhr in Bayern verlegt. Hier blieb die Einheit, bis sie im Mai 1943 zurück nach Norwegen geschickt wurde und die Mannschaften am 10. Mai 1943 in Oslo entlassen wurden.

2

SS-Freiwilligen-Legion Norwegen and *1. Polizeikompanie*

A week after the German attack on the Soviet Union on 29 June 1941, NS-leader Vidkun Quisling received telegraphic consent to establish a Norwegian unit to be deployed on the Eastern Front. Four Norwegian officers – Carl Langli, Finn Kjelstrup, Henrik Bjerkelund and Jørgen Bakke – were summoned to a meeting with Quisling to discuss how to set up the new unit.

In early July 1941, the press announced that the NS-leader had founded the Norwegian Volunteer Legion for deployment on the Eastern Front. Press coverage and statements by officers indicated that the unit would be sent to the Finnish Front under the exclusive leadership of Norwegian officers, using Norwegian as the command language.

In Oslo, a regimental office was established under the command of Major Finn Hannibal Kjelstrup. The *Norwegian Legion* was based at Bjølsen School in Oslo, and eventually moved to Gulskogen camp near Drammen. Here the unit's training regime was stepped up, before the men were moved to Fallingbostel in Germany in August 1941 for further platoon, company and battalion training.

Captain Jørgen Bakke was appointed as battalion commander by NS-leader Quisling, and promoted to major with the German rank of *Legions-Sturmbannführer*. At Fallingbostel, an increasing amount of dissatisfaction with the Germans made itself felt, and rumours of what the Norwegian volunteers considered to be broken promises spread throughout the camp. A number of Norwegian volunteers claim that they had been promised training in Norway, with Norwegian weapons, uniforms and native speakers giving commands. The conflict culminated during the swearing-in ceremony in September 1941, when the Oslo office under Colonel Kjelstrup gave notification of their absence from the ceremony. After several meetings with *SS-Gruppenführer* Hans Jüttner, Major Bakke and Colonel Kjelstrup in Berlin, Bakke was dismissed as battalion commander in favour of former cavalry captain Arthur Qvist.

In mid-February 1942, the *Norwegian Legion* was suddenly ordered to be transferred to the Eastern Front. The destination was still unknown to most, and the battalion was transported by *Junkers Ju 52* transport aircraft. Instead of Finland, they were sent to an area south of Leningrad. Here the *Norwegian Legion* set up a position on or around 18 February 1942, and was attached to the fighting group Jeckeln under the leadership of *SS-Brigadeführer* Friedrich Jeckeln. The front south of Leningrad had at this time quietened down and developed into trench warfare similar to that in the First World War. The Russians maintained their positions outside Leningrad, and the *Norwegian Legion*, together with units of the *Wehrmacht* and the *SS-Freiwilligen Legion 'Niederlande'* (Dutch volunteer legion), encircled the city with an 'iron ring'.

Both sides conducted reconnaissance patrols and raids on opposing positions and took prisoners. The Russians launched a number of major attacks, but only with marginal results. On the night of 16 April 1942, *Leg.-Hauptsturmführer* Ragnar Berg of *4. Company* led a major assault on Russian positions at Uritsk, south-west of Leningrad, attempting to destroy bunkers and bring prisoners back to their own lines. The mission was an utter failure and the men happened upon a minefield, resulting in many casualties and wounded, including *Leg.-Hauptsturmführer* Berg. In July 1942, the Russians attempted an attack on the positions of the *SS-Frw.-Legion 'Niederlande'*, but the *14. (PAK) Company* of the *Norwegian Legion*, under the leadership of *Leg.-Hauptscharführer* Arnfinn Vik, was able to repulse the assault.

The various companies took turns defending the main line of resistance. The battalion staff was located some way behind the front, and the battalion was inserted at Pulkovo and Ladoga. Replacement troops from Norway were brought in after first having received training at the replacement battalion's HQ in Holmestrand, and later at Mitau in Latvia. Most of the unit's fallen were buried at the battalion's cemetery at Krasnoye Selo.

In February 1943, the battalion retreated and was relocated to Mitau, where *Reichsführer-SS* Himmler gave an admonishing speech and urged the men to sign up for the newly activated *Regiment 'Norge'*. All who enlisted were immediately granted leave in Norway, and in early March 1943 the *Norwegian Legion* was transferred to Grafenwöhr in Bavaria as a single outfit. Here they remained until May 1943, when the men were sent back to Norway and discharged on 10 May in Oslo.

Abreise zur SS-Frw. Legion Norwegen | Leaving for the *Norwegian Legion*

Ragnar Berg attending a course arranged by the Norwegian SS at Kongsvinger Fortress. Nearly all of the course participants volunteered for the *Norwegian Legion*.

Ragnar Berg bei einem Lehrgang der norwegischen SS auf der Festung Kongsvinger. So gut wie alle Teilnehmer meldeten sich als Freiwillige zur SS-Frw.-Legion Norwegen.

The *Norwegian Legion* gathered at University Square in Oslo on 4 July 1941. Quisling reiterated the fact that the *Norwegian Legion* had been established to support Finland and aid in recapturing the territories that had been seized in 1940. The motto 'Help our brothers in Finland' convinced many, not just NS-members, to enlist for service. During the summer of 1941, about 1,700 men had signed up for the *Norwegian Legion*, and the number soon increased to over 1,900 volunteers.

Versammlung der SS-Frw.-Legion Norwegen auf dem Universitätsplatz in Oslo, 4. Juli 1941. Quisling wiederholte in seiner Rede, dass die Legion zur Unterstützung des finnischen Brudervolks gegründet sei, und die Wiedereroberung der Landgebiete, die 1940 von den Russen erobert worden waren, ermöglichen sollte. Das Motto "Hilf unseren Brüdern in Finnland" überzeugte viele, sich als Freiwillige zu melden, darunter auch etliche, die nicht Mitglied der NS waren. Während des Sommers 1941 meldeten sich 1,700 Freiwillige zur norwegischen Legion, und kurz darauf war die Zahl auf 1,900 gestiegen.

The first volunteers to the Legion line up for inspection for the first time, having arrived at Bjølsen School and received their uniforms.

Die ersten Freiwilligen haben sich in der Schule in Bjølsen eingefunden. Sie erhalten neue Uniformen und stellen sich zum ersten Mal zur Besichtigung auf.

Legion-Sturmbannführer Jørgen Bakke, left, the Legion's first commander, and *Legion-Hauptsturmführer* Henrik Brun, company commander of *1. Company*. The picture was taken during the inauguration of the Legion.

Von links: Leg.-Sturmbannführer Jørgen Bakke, der erste Kommandeur der Legion, und Leg.-Hauptsturmführer Henrik Brun, Kompanieführer der 1. Kompanie.

From the left: Bjarne T. Foss, Karl Johan Nabeit and Leif Knutsen at Bjølsen School in Oslo.

Von links: Bjarne T. Foss, Karl Johan Nabeit und Leif Sylvan Knutsen an der Schule in Bjølsen.

Volunteers from the Norwegian SS who had signed up for the Legion. Almost all Norwegian SS members joined the Legion.

Mitglieder der norwegischen SS die sich zur Frw.-Leg. Norwegen gemeldet haben.

The Legion moved from Bjølsen School in Oslo to Gulskogen near Drammen, south of Oslo.

Die Freiwilligen-Legion Norwegen nach der Verlegung von Bjølsen nach Gulskogen bei Drammen südlich von Oslo.

The first battalion line-up of *Viken Battalion* was filmed and used as propaganda for Legion recruitment.

Die erste Bataillonsaufstellung des "Viken-Bataillons" wurde gefilmt und als Propaganda zur Anwerbung Freiwilliger benutzt.

Taking a break while handing out uniforms at Gulskogen.

Eine Pause während der Verteilung von Uniformen in Gulskogen.

A platoon marching near Gulskogen.

Eine Zug marschiert in der Nähe von Gulskogen.

At the training camp at Torpo, Hallingdal, are Sverre Kjelstrup, left, and Wilhelm Fergestad.

Truppenübungsplatz in Torpo, Hallingdal. Von links: Sverre Kjelstrup und Wilhelm Fergestad.

Leaving Norway by boat for training in Germany.

Von Norwegen mit dem Boot zur Ausbildung in Deutschland.

Another view of men leaving Norway by boat for training in Germany.

Von Norwegen mit dem Boot zur Ausbildung in Deutschland.

From the left: company commander *Leg. Hauptsturmführer* Aslak Nesheim, battalion physician *Leg. Obersturmführer* August Ingier and company commander *Leg. Hauptsturmführer* Sverre Wraal.

Von links: Kompanieführer Leg.-Hauptsturmführer Aslak Nesheim, Bataillonsarzt Leg.-Obersturmführer August Ingier und Kompanieführer Leg.-Hauptsturmführer Sverre Wraal.

From the left: platoon leader *Leg. Hauptscharführer* Bjørn Østring, war correspondent *Leg. Oberscharführer* Oscar Bang, unknown, Legion commander Jørgen Bakke and Sven E. Rolf.

Von links: Zugführer Leg.-Hauptscharführer Bjørn Østring, Kriegsberichter Leg.-Oberscharführer Oscar Bang, ein Unbekannter, Legionskommandeur Jørgen Bakke und Sven E. Rolf.

Captain Henry Brun, left, and Major Jørgen Bakke.

Von links: Hauptmann Henrik Brun und Major Jørgen Bakke.

Der Stab der SS-Freiwilligen-Legion Norwegen während der Ausbildung in Fallingbostel | The staff of the *Norwegian Legion* during training in Fallingbostel

Barracks of the Legion's HQ company.

Kaserne der Stabskompanie, SS-Frw.-Legion Norwegen.

Unknown staff officer during riding lessons in Fallingbostel.

Unbekannter Stabsoffizier während der Reitausbildung in Fallingbostel.

Leg.-Unterscharführer Sophus Noreger, right, and *Leg.-Unterscharführer* Bjørn Noreger were father and son, and had both enlisted in the Legion.

Von rechts: Leg.-Unterscharführer Sophus Noreger und Leg.-Unterscharführer Bjørn Noreger, Vater und Sohn. Beide hatten sich zur SS-Frw.-Legion Norwegen gemeldet.

Norwegian Christmas celebration in Fallingbostel, with Norwegian drawings and decorations on the barrack walls.

Weihnachten in Fallingbostel mit norwegischen Zeichnungen und Dekorationen an den Wänden der Kaserne.

A Christmas tree was also in place in Fallingbostel.

Für einen Weihnachtbaum war in Fallingbostel auch gesorgt.

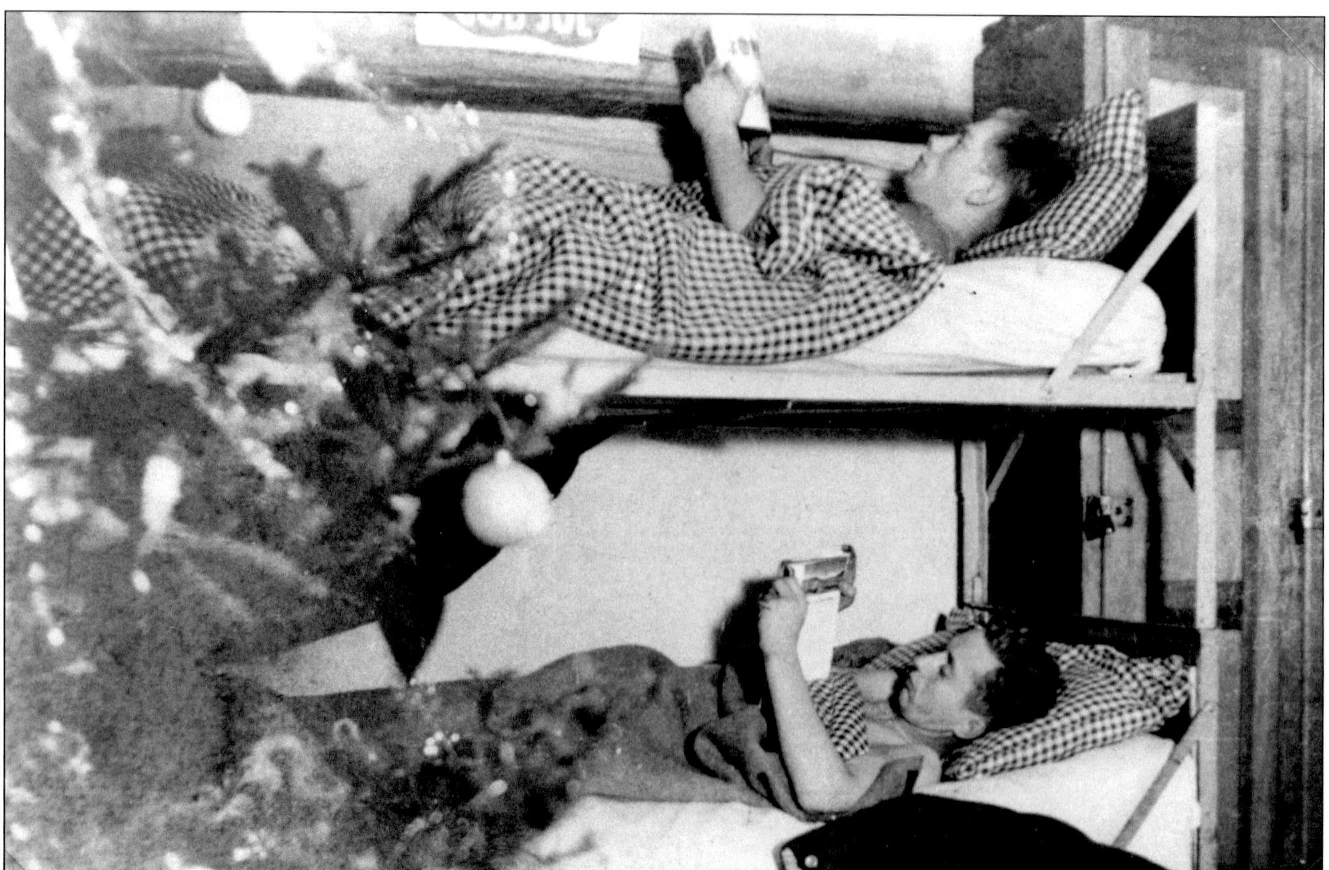

The personnel rooms at Fallingbostel.

Zimmer der Mannschaft in Fallingbostel.

Photo taken during an officer course in Lauenburg for Danish, Dutch and Norwegian officers. Front row, 11th from left, Arthur Qvist; 12th, Sverre Wraal; 13th, Ragnar Berg; 14th, Kristopher Budde Kahrs; 15th, Rolf Falk Muus. Second row, 1st from left, Johan Arnt Johannessen; 2nd, Henrik Stenberg; 3rd, Knut Westad; 5th, Oskar Waldemarsen; 6th, Bernt Anker; 7th, Hans Georg Holter; 11th, Ralf Wirum; 12th, Konrad Rodal; 17th, Steinar Brenna. Third row, 2nd from left, Harald Hervik; 6th, Jens Grønnerød; 18th, John Nygaard. All the rest are unknown.

Offizierslehrgang in Lauenburg mit dänischen, niederländischen und norwegischen Offizieren. Erste Reihe von links: Nr. 11 Arthur Qvist, Nr. 12 Sverre Wraal, Nr. 13 Ragnar Berg, Nr. 14 Kristoffer Budde Kahrs, Nr. 15 Rolf Falk Muus. Zweite Reihe von links: Nr. 1 Johan Arnt Johannessen, Nr. 2 Henrik Stenberg, Nr. 3 Knut Westad, Nr. 5 Oskar Waldemarsen, Nr. 6 Bernt Anker, Nr. 7 Hans Georg Holter, Nr. 11 Rolf Wirum, Nr. 12 Konrad Rodal, Nr. 17 Steinar Brenna. Dritte Reihe von links: Nr. 2 Harald Hervik, Nr. 6 Jens Grønnerød, Nr. 18 John Nygaard.

Quisling visits the Legion during the swearing-in ceremony. From the left: *SS-Brigadeführer* Paul Wegener, Vidkun Quisling, *SS-Hauptsturmführer* Felix Hartmann, *SS-Brigadeführer* Hans Jüttner, unknown and *Leg.-Sturmbannführer* Jørgen Bakke.

Quisling zu Besuch bei der SS-Frw.-Legion Norwegen während der Vereidigung. Von links: SS-Brigadeführer Paul Wegener, Vidkun Quisling, SS-Hauptsturmführer Felix Hartmann, SS-Brigadeführer Hans Jüttner, ein Unbekannter und Leg.-Sturmbannführer Jørgen Bakke.

Bjarne, right, and Gunnar Stake were father and son, and had both joined the Legion.

Von rechts: Bjarne und Gunnar Stake, Vater bzw. Sohn in der SS-Frw.-Legion Norwegen.

Swearing-in ceremony with the German advisors in the foreground. Third from the left is *SS-Untersturmführer* Dieter Radbruch.

Vereidigung mit den deutschen Beratern im Vordergrund. Nr. 3 von links: SS-Untersturmführer Dieter Radbruch.

From the left: *Leg.-Sturmbannführer* Jørgen Bakke, *SS-Brigadeführer* Hans Jüttner and Vidkun Quisling.

Von links: Leg.-Sturmbannführer Jørgen Bakke, SS-Brigadeführer Hans Jüttner und Vidkun Quisling.

From the left: *Leg.-Obersturmführer* Karsten Sveen, *Leg.-Sturmbannführer* Jørgen Bakke, *Leg.-Obersturmführer* John Braset and *Leg.-Hauptsturmführer* Sverre Wraal.

Von links: Leg.-Obersturmführer Karsten Sveen, Leg.-Sturmbannführer Jørgen Bakken, Leg.-Obersturmführer John Braset und Leg.-Hauptsturmführer Sverre Wraal.

Legion commander *Leg.-Sturmbannführer* Jørgen Bakke, left, and *Leg.-Hauptsturmführer* Walter Fürst, commander of the Legion's war correspondent unit.

Von links: Legionskommandeur Leg.-Sturmbannführer Jørgen Bakke und Leg.-Hauptsturmführer Walter Fürst, Leiter des Kriegsberichter-Zugs der SS-Frw.-Legion Norwegen.

Die SS-Frw. Legion Norwegen – Ausbildung in Fallingbostel, 1. Kompanie | The *Norwegian Legion* – training in Fallingbostel, *1. Company*

Leg.-Obersturmführer Olaf Lindvig was company commander of the Legion's *1. Company*.

Leg.-Obersturmführer Olaf Lindvig war Kompanieführer der 1. Kompanie der SS-Frw.-Legion Norwegen.

From the left: *Leg.-Hauptscharführer* Bjørn Østring, *Leg.-Hauptsturmführer* Henrik Brun, *Leg.-Hauptscharführer* Hans Ode Fey and *Leg.-Hauptscharführer* Per Wang.

Von links: Leg.-Hauptscharführer Bjørn Østring, Leg.-Hauptsturmführer Henrik Brun, Leg.-Hauptscharführer Hans Ode Fey und Leg.-Hauptscharführer Per Wang.

Swearing-in ceremony at *1. Company.* Second from the left is Arne Nilsen.

Vereidigung der 1. Kompanie. Nr. 2 von links: Arne Nilsen.

Inside the barracks of *1. Company* in Fallingbostel.

In der Kaserne der 1. Kompanie in Fallingbostel.

From the right: *Leg.-Unterscharführer* Arne Nilsen, *Leg.-Hauptscharführer* Bjarne Larsen and *Leg.-Hauptscharführer* Per Wang.

Von rechts: Leg.-Unterscharführer Arne Nilsen, Leg.-Hauptscharführer Bjarne Larsen und Leg.-Hauptscharführer Per Wang.

One of the barracks' sleeping rooms in Fallingbostel.

Ein Schlafraum der Kaserne in Fallingbostel.

Leg.-Hauptsturmführer Henrik Brun was the first company commander of the *Norwegian Legion*'s *1. Company*.

Leg.-Hauptsturmführer Henrik Brun war der erste Kompanieführer der 1. Kompanie der SS-Frw.-Legion Norwegen.

Die SS-Frw. Legion Norwegen – Ausbildung in Fallingbostel, 2. Kompanie | The *Norwegian Legion* – training in Fallingbostel, *2. Company*

From the left: *Leg.-Unterscharführer* Per Zingstad Nilsen, *Leg.-Hauptscharführer* Harald Hervik and *Leg.-Unterscharführer* Arvid Fosse. All were NCOs in *2. Company*.

Von links: Leg.-Unterscharführer Per Zingstad Nilsen, Leg.-Hauptscharführer Harald Hervik und Leg.-Unterscharführer Arvid Fosse, drei Unteroffiziere der 2. Kompanie.

All officers had to learn to ride horseback, as seen in this riding lesson.

Sämtliche Offiziere mussten reiten lernen. Hier ein Bild von der Reitausbildung.

Training in Fallingbostel. From the left: *Leg.-Unterscharführer* Olav Kjølberg, two unknowns and *Leg.-Untersturmführer* Walter Steen in the middle of the picture. Steen was a veteran of the Winter War in Finland.

Ausbildung in Fallingbostel. Von links: Leg.-Unterscharführer Olav Kjølberg, zwei Unbekannte und Leg.-Untersturmführer Walter Steen in der Mitte des Bildes. Er hatte am Winterkrieg in Finnland teilgenommen.

2. Company field exercise.

Feldübung der 2. Kompanie.

2. Company field exercise.

Feldübung der 2. Kompanie.

Karsten Sveen on the right during the swearing-in ceremony in Fallingbostel.

Rechts Karsten Sveen bei der Vereidigung in Fallingbostel.

The Legion marches in front of Vidkun Quisling during the swearing-in ceremony in Fallingbostel.

Die SS-Frw.-Legion Norwegen marschiert vor Quisling während der Vereidigung in Fallingbostel.

Another view of the Legion marching past Vidkun Quisling during the swearing-in ceremony in Fallingbostel.

Die SS-Frw.-Legion Norwegen marschiert vor Quisling während der Vereidigung in Fallingbostel.

Die SS-Frw. Legion Norwegen – Ausbildung in Fallingbostel, 3. Kompanie | The *Norwegian Legion* – training in Fallingbostel, *3. Company*

An unknown NCO of *3. Company.*

Ein unbekannter Unteroffizier der 3. Kompanie.

At the firing range are, from the left, Olav Haavarsholmen, *Leg.-Hauptscharführer* Thomas Gysler and *Leg.-Oberscharführer* Knut Schjefstad.

Am Schießplatz. Von links: Olav Haavarsholmen, Leg.-Hauptscharführer Thomas Gysler und Leg.-Oberscharführer Knut Schjefstad.

Christmas celebration of *3. Company*.

Weihnachtsfeier der 3. Kompanie.

The Legion commander inspects *3. Company*. From the left: *Leg.-Sturmbannführer* Jørgen Bakke, unknown and *Leg.-Obersturmführer* John Braset, *3. Company* commander.

Der Legionskommandeur inspiziert die 3. Kompanie. Von links: Leg.-Sturmbannführer Jørgen Bakke, ein Unbekannter und Leg.-Obersturmführer John Braset, Kompanieführer der 3. Kompanie.

The barracks of *3. Company*.

Kaserne der 3. Kompanie.

Die SS-Frw. Legion Norwegen – Ausbildung in Fallingbostel, 4. Kompani | The *Norwegian Legion* – training in Fallingbostel, *4. Company*

4. Company. First row, from the left: *Leg.-Untersturmführer* Rolf Wirum, *Leg.-Obersturmführer* Njål Reppen and *Leg.-Untersturmführer* Charles Westberg.

4. Kompanie. Erste Reihe von links: Leg.-Untersturmführer Rolf Wirum, Leg.-Obersturmführer Njål Reppen und Leg.-Untersturmführer Charles Westberg.

4. Company field exercise.

Feldübung der 4. Kompanie.

From the left: two unknowns, Hermann Bay and Rolf Torp.

Von links: zwei Unbekannte, Hermann Bay und Rolf Torp.

On the left is *Leg.-Hauptscharführer* Mathias Østhassel.

Nr. 1 von links: Leg.-Hauptscharführer Mathias Østhassel.

Mortar practice.

Granatwerfer-Übung.

Practice with an SMG (heavy machine gun).

Übung mit einem schweren Maschinengewehr (SMG).

4. Company commander Ragnar Berg gives orders.

Der Kompanieführer der 4. Kompanie, Ragnar Berg, erteilt einen Befehl.

Christmas celebration at *4. Company*. The officer in the picture is *Leg.-Untersturmführer* Knut Westad from Stange, southern Norway.

Weihnachtsfeier der 4. Kompanie. Der Offizier im Bild ist Leg.-Untersturmführer Knut Westad aus Stange, Südnorwegen.

Another view of the Christmas celebration at *4. Company*. The officer in the picture is *Leg.-Untersturmführer* Knut Westad from Stange, southern Norway.

Weihnachtsfeier der 4. Kompanie. Der Offizier im Bild ist Leg.-Untersturmführer Knut Westad aus Stange, Südnorwegen.

From the right: *Leg.-Hauptsturmführer* Ragnar Berg and *Leg.-Obersturmführer* Njål Reppen. The rest are unknown.

Von rechts: Leg.-Hauptsturmführer Ragnar Berg und Leg.-Obersturmführer Njål Reppen. Die anderen sind unbekannt.

Die SS-Frw. Legion Norwegen – Ausbildung in Fallingbostel, 14. Kompanie | The *Norwegian Legion* – training in Fallingbostel, *14. Company*

In front from left: *Leg.-Hauptsturmführer* Finn Finson, commander of *14. Company*, and his second in command, *Leg.-Obersturmführer* Kåre Opsahl.

Vorne von links: Leg.-Hauptsturmführer Finn Finson, Kompanieführer der 14. Kompanie, und sein Stellvertreter Leg.-Obersturmführer Kåre Opsahl.

14. Company filing out.

Ausmarsch der 14. Kompanie.

Sign on the barracks of *14. Company.*

Das Schild an der Kaserne der 14. Kompanie.

At a funeral in Fallingbostel are *Leg.-Hauptsturmführer* Finn Finson, front, left, commander of *14. Company*, and his second in command, *Leg.-Obersturmführer* Kåre Opsahl.

Eine Beerdigung in Fallingbostel. Vorne von links: Leg.-Hauptsturmführer Finn Finson, Kompanieführer der 14. Kompanie, und sein Stellvertreter Leg.-Obersturmführer Kåre Opsahl.

Food queue at the field kitchen.

Warteschlange vor der Feldküche.

Commissioned officers of *14. Company*. From the left: *Leg.-Hauptscharführer* Arnfinn Vik, *Leg.-Unterscharführer* Thomas Hvistendahl, *Leg.-Unterscharführer* Roy Wentzel Larsen, *Leg.-Unterscharführer* Reidar Holst and *Leg.-Hauptscharführer* Åge Holst. Reidar and Åge were brothers, and had two more brothers who had also volunteered. One of them was in *'Wiking'*, the other in the Legion.

Unteroffiziere der 14. Kompanie. Von links: Leg.-Hauptscharführer Arnfinn Vik, Leg.-Unterscharführer Thomas Hvistendahl, Leg.-Unterscharführer Roy Wentzel Larsen, Leg.-Unterscharführer Reidar Holst und Leg.-Hauptscharführer Åge Holst. Reidar und Åge waren Brüder und hatten zwei weitere Brüder die als Freiwillige dienten, der eine bei "Wiking", der andere bei der SS-Frw.-Legion Norwegen.

A gun crew from *14. Company*.

Eine Pak-Bedienung der 14. Kompanie.

Shooting at moving targets was an important part of the training.

Das Schießen auf bewegliche Ziele war ein wichtiger Teil der Ausbildung.

Die SS-Freiwilligen-Legion Norwegen in Stettin | The *Norwegian Legion* in Szczecin (Stettin)

Taking the oath in Stettin. First from the left is *Leg.-Hauptscharführer* Arnfinn Vik.

Vereidigung in Stettin. Nr. 1 von links ist Leg.-Hauptscharführer Arnfinn Vik.

Minister of Justice Sverre Riisnæs attending the swearing-in ceremony. From the left: unknown, Sverre Riisnæs, *Leg.-Hauptsturmführer* Brynjulf Gottenborg and *Leg.-Sturmbannführer* Arthur Quist.

Justizminister Riisnæs bei der Vereidigungszeremonie. Von links: ein Unbekannter, Sverre Riisnæs, Leg.-Hauptscharführer Brynjulf Gottenborg und Leg.-Sturmbannführer Arthur Qvist.

Die SS-Freiwilligen-Legion Norwegen an der Front – der Bataillonsstab | The *Norwegian Legion* at the front – HQ personnel

Battalion commander *Leg.-Sturmbannführer* Arthur Qvist on the plane ride to the front.

Bataillonskommandeur Leg.-Sturmbannführer Arthur Qvist im Flugzeug auf dem Weg zur Front.

Refurbishing a bunker at the front.

Bunkerbau an der Front.

A group from HQ near a defeated Russian tank. First on the right is Oscar Bang. He was head of the Legion's war correspondence unit.

Mitglieder des Bataillonsstab vor einem vernichteten russischen Panzer. Der Erste von rechts ist Oscar Bang, der die Kriegsberichter-Abteilung der SS-Frw.-Legion Norwegen leitete.

Bjørn Noreger on the right; the rest are unknown.

Von rechts: Bjørn Noreger. Die anderen sind unbekannt.

At a funeral are, from the left: *Leg.-Sturmbannführer* Arthur Qvist, unknown, field priest *Leg.-Hauptsturmführer* Knut Jarle Geelmuyden and an unknown officer.

Eine Beerdigung. Von links: Leg.-Sturmbannführer Arthur Qvist, ein Unbekannter, Feldpfarrer Leg.-Hauptsturmführer Knut Jarle Geelmuyden und ein unbekannter Offizier.

Dead soldiers are swathed before being buried in rows.

Die Toten werden eingehüllt und in Reihen beerdigt.

The Legion's cemetery in Krasnoye Selo. Today this spot is used as garden plot. Most Norwegians were disinterned and reburied in another cemetery.

Der Soldatenfriedhof in Krasnoje Selo. Hier liegen heute Gartenparzelle. Die meisten der Gefallenen wurden auf einem neuen Friedhof begraben.

Norwegian nurses lay down a wreath and decorate the graves of fallen Legionaries.

Norwegische DRK-Schwestern dekorieren die Gräber gefallener Legionäre.

Battalion physician *Leg.-Obersturmführer* August Ingier in front of his bunker.

Der Bataillonsarzt Leg.-Obersturmführer August Ingier vor seinem Bunker.

Physician and *Leg.-Hauptscharführer* Kjell Quist Christiansen, left, together with two staff colleagues some distance behind the front.

Ganz links: Bataillonsarzt Leg.-Hauptscharführer Kjell Quist Christiansen zusammen mit zwei Kameraden aus dem Stab hinter der Front.

A medical bunker at the front. Here all the wounded were transported and treated before being sent back from the front lines to a hospital.

Der Sanitätsbunker an der Front wo die Verwundeten vor dem Transport ins Lazarett behandelt wurden.

A wounded soldier receives treatment inside the bunker.

Ein Verwundeter wird im Bunker behandelt.

Norske Soldater i Kamp

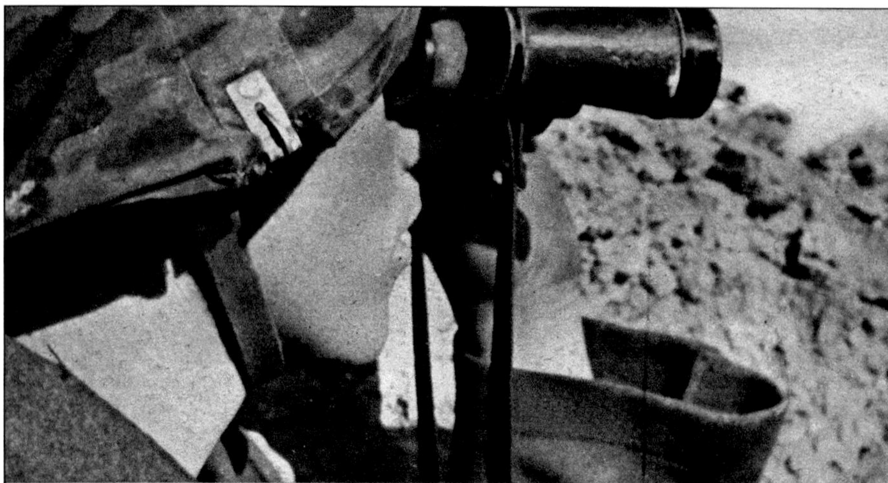

Oppmerksomt følges hver en bevegelse hos fienden.
Aufmerksam wird jede einzelne Bewegung beim Feinde beobachtet.

Også her heter det: „Spar på vannet!"
Auch hier heisst es: „Spare mit dem Wasser!"

Alltid beredt! — Immer bereit!

Dette er resultatet av et 10 min. regnskyll.
Das ist das Ergebnis eines zehnminütigen Regenshauers.

Mathenteren er endelig kommet. — Der Essenholer ist endlich gekommen.

Munin.

Tilvenstre: En fortjent hvil foran „Hotell Ringebu".

Links: Eine verdiente Ruhepause vor dem „Hotel Ringebu".

Et bilde som taler for seg selv.

Ein Bild, welches für sich selbst spricht.

En „melder" er startklar.

Ein Melder ist klar zum Start.

Foto: Christiansen (5) — Rolf Holm (1) — Nussbaumer (1) — Wiesebach (1) — Østring (2).

Munin.

Soldiers from HQ with one of their vehicles behind the front. The officer standing by the car, *SS-Obersturmführer* Vogel, was supply officer for the *Norwegian Legion*.

Soldaten des Bataillonsstabs mit dem Fahrzeug hinter der Front. Der Offizier am Auto, SS-Obersturmführer Vogel, war der Verpflegungsoffizier der SS-Frw.-Legion Norwegen.

Food is handed out to the people of Krasnoye Selo.

Lebensmittel werden an die Einwohner von Krasnoje Selo verteilt.

From the left: NCOs Jan Henrik Henriksen, Bjørn Noreger and an unknown *Hauptscharführer*.

Von links: Unteroffiziere Jan Henrik Henriksen, Bjørn Noreger und ein unbekannter Hauptscharführer.

Driver Ernst Hillgård surveys the Russian positions with a scissor scope.

Der Fahrer Ernst Hillgård beobachtet die russischen Stellungen mit einem Scherenfernrohr.

Photo taken through a scissor scope.

Eine Aufnahme durch das Scherenfernrohr.

Battalion commander *Leg.-Sturmbannführer* Arthur Qvist with his staff behind the front. From the right: *SS-Obersturmführer* Dieter Radbruch, *Leg.-Sturmbannführer* Qvist and *Leg.-Untersturmführer* Sophus Kahrs. The rest are unknown.

Bataillonskommandeur Leg.-Sturmbannführer Arthur Qvist mit seinem Stab hinter der Front. Von rechts: SS-Obersturmführer Dieter Radbruch, Leg.-Sturmbannführer Qvist und Leg.-Untersturmführer Sophus Kahrs. Die anderen sind unbekannt.

Leg.-Obersturmführer Ole Hafstad was the Legion officer responsible for the improvement of positions and bunkers.

Leg.-Obersturmführer Ole Hafstad war der Stellungsoffizier der SS-Frw.-Legion Norwegen, verantwortlich für den Ausbau von Bunkern und Schützengräben.

Leg.-Hauptsturmführer Brynjulf Gottenborg in his office behind the front.

Leg.-Hauptsturmführer Brynjulf Gottenborg in seinem Arbeitszimmer hinter der Front.

Leg.-Obersturmführer Sophus Kahrs, left, and *SS-Obersturmführer* Dieter Radbruch behind the front, studying a map.

Von links: Leg.-Obersturmführer Sophus Kahrs und SS-Obersturmführer Dieter Radbruch studieren eine Heereskarte hinter der Front.

NS-leader Vidkun Quisling paying a visit to the Legion and inspecting Legionaries who have received the Iron Cross 2nd Class.

NS-Führer Vidkun Quisling während eines Besuches bei der SS-Frw.-Legion Norwegen. Hier inspiziert er Legionäre die das Eiserne Kreuz 2. Klasse erhalten haben.

Leg.-Sturmbannführer Arthur Qvist, commander of the *Norwegian Legion*, at the front.

Leg.-Sturmbannführer Arthur Qvist, Kommandeur der SS-Frw.-Legion Norwegen, an der Front.

Soldiers from HQ driving a motorcycle. Sitting in the sidecar is Leif Sylvan Knutsen.

Soldaten des Bataillonsstabs fahren ein Beiwagenkrad. Im Beiwagen Leif Sylvan Knutsen.

War correspondent *Leg.-Oberscharführer* Oscar Bang drawing a propaganda picture.

Kriegsberichter Leg.-Oberscharführer Oscar Bang zeichnet ein Propagandabild.

War correspondents working on their reports behind the front. From the left: Arne Ormstad and Bjarne Sem.

Kriegsberichter bei der Arbeit an ihren Reportagen hinter der Front. Von links: Arne Ormstad und Bjarne Sem.

Author and war correspondent *Leg.-Unterscharführer* Karl Holter in Krasnoye Selo.

Der Verfasser und Kriegsberichter Leg.-Unterscharführer Karl Holter in Krasnoje Selo.

Two unknown Norwegian NCOs.

Zwei unbekannte norwegische Unteroffiziere.

Journey from the front to Mitau, now Jelgava, in Latvia. Standing in front from the left: unknown and Leif Sylvan Knutsen.

Die Fahrt von der Front nach Mitau, jetzt Jelgava, Lettland. Stehend vorne von links: ein Unbekannter und Leif Sylvan Knutsen.

The train ride from the front to Mitau.

Die Zugfahrt von der Front nach Mitau.

Die SS-Freiwilligen-Legion Norwegen an der Front – 1. Kompanie | The *Norwegian Legion* at the front – *1. Company*

1. Company arrives by plane at the front. Arne Nilsen is to the left.

Die 1. Kompanie bei der Ankunft mit dem Fleugzeug an der Front. Links Arne Nilsen.

A group from *1. Company* in their trench.

Eine Gruppe der 1. Kompanie im Schützengraben.

Platoon leader in *1. Company*, *Leg.-Oberscharführer* Kjell Kracht, received both the Iron Cross and the War Merit Cross 2nd Class.

Zugführer in der 1. Kompanie, Leg.-Oberscharführer Kjell Kracht, erhielt sowohl das Eiserne Kreuz als auch das Kriegsverdienstkreuz 2. Klasse.

Arne Eriksrud, an enlisted soldier of *1. Company*, at the front.

Arne Eriksrud, ein Legionsschütze der 1. Kompanie an der Front.

Leg.-Oberscharführer Einar Grill Fasting, a platoon leader in *1. Company*.

Leg.-Oberscharführer Einar Grill Fasting, Zugführer in der 1. Kompanie.

Husker DU?

En beretning i bilder fra Den norske Legions innsats.

II

Erinnerst du dich?

Ein Bildbericht von der Norwegischen Legion, ihrer Errichtung, Ausbildung und ihrem Einsatz

Ankomst til Krassnoe Sselo. Bagasjen losses

Die Reise von Riga nach Krassnoe Sselo ist beendet. Das Gepäch wird versteut

En gruppefører på observasjonspost i en utsatt stilling

Ein Gruppenführer auf Beobachtungsposten in einer vorgeschobenen Stellung

Panserallarm foran Leningrad

Panzeralarm vor Leningrad

Vinterstemning over de norske stillingene ved Leningrad

↓ Winterstimmung über den norwegischen Stellungen bei Leningrad

Motorsykkelmelder på sølete veger

Kradmelder auf verschlammten Wegen

Munin.

En norsk skipatrulje drar ut — Eine Norwegische Schipatrouille zieht aus

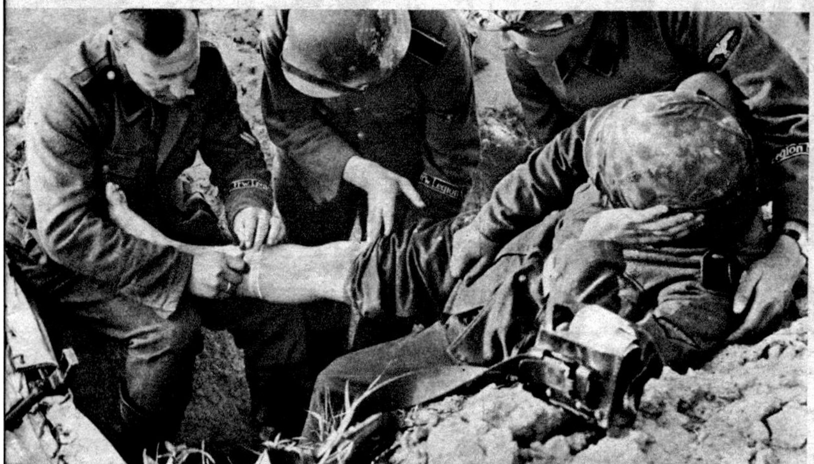

En splint — et sår — en rask forbinding og kampen går videre

Ein Splitter — eine Wunde — ein schneller Verband um diese — und schon geht der Kampf weiter

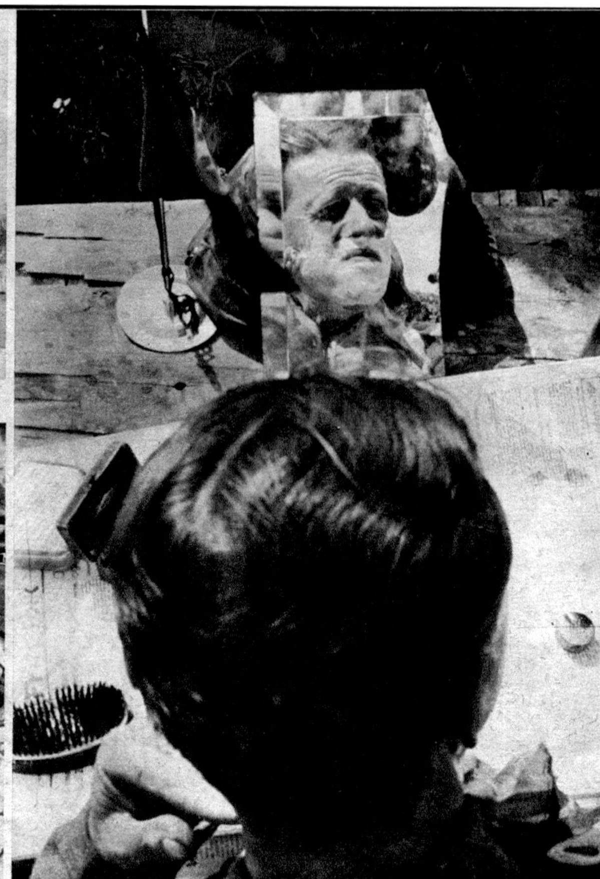

«Rittmester'n» gjør sitt morgentoalett i friluft

Der »Rittmeister« bei der Morgentoilette in frischer Luft

Vidkun Quisling hilser på sine soldater foran Leningrad

Vidkun Quisling begrüsst seine vor Leningrad befindlichen Soldaten

Fortsettes i neste nummer

Foto: Christiansen, Thur og Eines

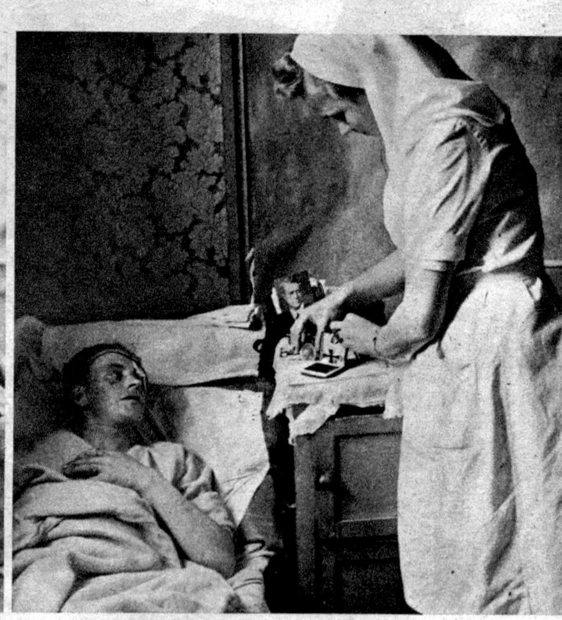

Morgenen etter «Støttropp Berg». — Det hviler en saga bak dette jernkorset og såretmerket i gull

Am Morgen nach dem Unternehmen: Stosstrupp »Berg«
Es schwebt etwas fast Sagenhaftes um dieses Eiserne Kreuz und das Verwundetenabzeichen in Gold

⟶

På marsj fra Krasnojwardejsk til Leningrad. — Sitt ned og vent, far, det kommer snart en bil

Auf dem Marsch von Krasnojwardejsk nach »Petersburg«
Setz dich ein Weilchen nieder, mein Lieber, es kommt bald ein Auto!

Munin.

Leg.-Untersturmführer, and later *SS-Hauptsturmführer*, Olaf T. Lindvig, company commander of *1. Company* and later also commander of *1. Company, Regiment 'Norge'*. He was an extremely popular officer. Lindvig had attended the Norwegian Officer Candidate School before the war and took part in the fighting against the Germans in 1940.

Leg.-Untersturmführer und später SS-Hauptsturmführer Olaf T. Lindvig, Kompanieführer der 1. Kompanie und später auch Führer der 1. Kompanie des Regiments "Norge". Lindvig, ein äußerst beliebter norwegischer Offizier, nahm 1940 am Feldzug gegen die deutschen Truppen in Norwegen teil.

Leg.-Hauptscharführer Bjørn Østring was a platoon leader in *1. C*ompany and a prominent figure in the Norwegian National Socialist youth organisation NSUF. After the war, he became well known as a spokesman for former Norwegian front line fighters.

Leg.-Hauptscharführer Bjørn Østring war Zugführer in der 1. Kompanie und eine leitende Figur im nationalsozialistischen norwegischen Jugendverband NSUF. Nach dem Krieg wurde er als Fürsprecher der ehemaligen norwegischen Frontkämpfer bekannt.

Leg.-Hauptscharführer Arne Nilsen was one of the first Norwegians to receive the Iron Cross 1st Class. He was a platoon leader in *1. Company*. After his time with the Legion, he served as an instructor for the Norwegian NS youth organisation *Unghirdmarinen*.

Leg.-Hauptscharführer Arne Nilsen war einer der ersten Norweger denen das Eiserne Kreuz 1. Klasse verliehen wurde. Er war Zugführer in der 1. Kompanie. Nach seinem Fronteinsatz diente er als Berater bei der NS-Jugendorganisation *Unghirdmarinen* in Norwegen.

Leg.-Unterscharführer Håkon Belgonen was a squad leader in *1. Company*. He later signed up for the *SS-Schijäger Battalion 'Norge'* and was killed on 25 June 1944 at Hasselmann Hill in Karelia.

Leg.-Unterscharführer Håkon Belgonen war Gruppenführer bei der 1. Kompanie. Später meldete er sich zum SS-Schijäger-Bataillon "Norge", und fiel am 25.06.44 auf der Hasselmannhöhe in Karelien.

Minister of Justice Sverre Riisnæs visits the Legion. Bjørn Østring is to the left.

Justizminister Sverre Riisnaes zu Besuch bei der SS-Frw.-Legion Norwegen. Links Bjørn Østring.

Minister of Justice Sverre Riisnæs in conversation with Legionaries. To his right is Bjørn Østring.

Justizminister Sverre Riisnaes im Gespräch mit Legionären. Zu seiner Rechten Bjørn Østring.

A funeral. First row from the left: Bjørn Østring, unknown and Kjell Tønnesen.

Eine Beerdigung. Erste Reihe von links: Bjørn Østring, ein Unbekannter und Kjell Tønnesen.

The graves of Per Wang and Trond Aspesletten.

Die Gräber von Per Wang und Trond Aspesletten.

An honour guard at the Legion's cemetery in Krasnoye Selo.

Ehrenwache am Soldatenfriedhof Krasnoje Selo.

Legionaries waiting to be awarded the Iron Cross. From the left: unknown, *Leg.-Sturmbannführer* Arthur Qvist, *Leg.-Hauptsturmführer* Brynjulf Gottenborg, *Leg.-Obersturmführer* John Braset and *Leg.-Hauptscharführer* Bjørn Østring.

Legionäre sind zur Verleihung des Eisernen Kreuzes angetreten. Von links: ein Unbekannter, Leg.-Sturmbannführer Arthur Qvist, Leg.-Hauptsturmführer Brynjulf Gottenborg, Leg.-Obersturmführer John Braset und Leg.-Hauptscharführer Bjørn Østring.

An anti-aircraft position of *1. Company.*

Eine Flakstellung der 1. Kompanie.

Front row, from the left: Andreassen, Kåre Husum, Arne Nilsen, Roald Bjørnstad, Kjell Kracht, Bjarne Sem and unknown. Second row, from the left: Einar Grill Fasting, three unknowns and John Kristiansen.

Erste Reihe von links: Andreassen, Kåre Husum, Arne Nilsen, Roald Bjørnstad, Kjell Kracht, Bjarne Sem und ein Unbekannter. Zweite Reihe von links: Einar Grill Fasting, drei Unbekannte und John Kristiansen.

A quiet moment at the front while writing letters and relaxing in the sun.

Ein ruhiger Augenblick an der Front beim Briefe schreiben und Entspannen in der Sonne.

MG maintenance in *1. Company*'s trench.

MG-Reinigung im Schützengraben der 1. Kompanie.

Leg.-Hauptscharführer Roald Bjørnstad was first sergeant at *1. Company*, responsible for provisions and equipment.

Leg.-Hauptscharführer Roald Bjørnstad war Spieß der 1. Kompanie. Er hatte für die Verpflegung und Ausrüstung der 1. Kompanie zu sorgen.

Inside Bjørn Østring's bunker. From the left: *Leg.-Oberscharführer* Arne Nilsen, Erik Bratlien, Leg.-*Hauptscharführer* Bjørn Østring, *Leg.-Unterscharführer* Oddvar Engen, *Leg.-Unterscharführer* Henrik Pedersen and *Leg.-Unterscharführer* Einar Grill Fasting.

Im Bunker von Bjørn Østring. Von links: Leg.-Oberscharführer Arne Nilsen, Erik Bratlien, Leg.-Hauptscharführer Bjørn Østring, Leg.-Unterscharführer Oddvar Engen, Leg.-Unterscharführer Henrik Pedersen und Leg.-Unterscharführer Einar Grill Fasting.

The Quisling government's Minister of Culture, Rolf Jørgen Fuglesang, visits the Legion. From the right: *Leg.-Unterscharführer* Einar Grill Fasting, Fuglesang and Arthur Qvist.

Der Kulturminister der Quisling-Regierung, Rolf Jørgen Fuglesang besucht die SS-Frw.-Legion Norwegen. Von rechts: Leg.-Unterscharführer Einar Grill Fasting, Fuglesang und Arthur Qvist.

A group of Legionaries on leave behind the front.

Ein Gruppe Legionäre auf Urlaub hinter der Front.

Handing out awards to Legionaries, *Leg.-Untersturmführer* Sophus Kahrs, left, and *Leg.-Sturmbannführer* Arthur Qvist.

Verleihung von Auszeichnungen an die Legionäre. Von links: Leg.-Untersturmführer Sophus Kahrs und Leg.-Sturmbannführer Arthur Qvist.

Ready to depart for Mitau from the front. From the left: *SS-Obersturmführer* Dieter Radbruch, *Leg.-Obersturmführer* Kåre Opsahl, *Leg.-Hauptscharführer* Roald Bjørnstad and unknown.

Klar zum Abtransport von der Front nach Mitau. Von links: SS-Obersturmführer Dieter Radbruch, Leg.-Obersturmführer Kåre Opsahl, Leg.-Hauptscharführer Roald Bjørnstad und ein Unbekannter.

Before their departure from the front, the Legionaries held a farewell ceremony at the Legion's cemetery. The oldest member of the Legion, author and *Leg.-Unterscharführer* Karl Holter, read out the names of all the men who had fallen.

Vor dem Abmarsch von der Front hielten die Legionäre eine Abschiedszeremonie am Soldatenfriedhof. Der Legionsälteste, Verfasser und Leg.-Unterscharführer Karl Holter, verlas die Namen der Gefallenen.

Departure for Mitau.

Abmarsch nach Mitau.

Die SS-Freiwilligen-Legion Norwegen an der Front – 2. Kompanie | The *Norwegian Legion* at the front – *2. Company*

2. Company arrives at the front by plane from Riga.

Die 2. Kompanie kommt mit dem Flugzeug aus Riga an der Front an.

The equipment is loaded into trucks to be moved to forward positions.

Die Ausrüstung wird in Lastwagen geladen und zu den Stellungen gebracht.

A patrol in the trench of *2. Company*. Hand-grenades lie ready in case the Russians attack.

Eine Streife im Graben der 2. Kompanie. Die Handgranaten liegen bereit, falls die Russen angreifen sollten.

A road junction in Krasnoye Selo, only 29 kilometres (18 miles) outside Leningrad.

Eine Wegkreuzung in Krasnoje Selo, nur 29 Kilometer von Leningrad.

View from the trenches towards Leningrad.

Blick auf Leningrad aus dem Schützengraben.

A mortar in the trench of *2. Company* is used to strike enemy positions.

Mit dem Granatwerfer werden die Stellungen des Feindes angegriffen.

No man's land, with chevaux-de-frise to stop enemy tanks.

Niemandsland mit Spanischen Reitern zur Abwehr feindlicher Panzer.

Legionaries in conversation with Russian deserters. Some of the Legionaries had Russian parents and spoke Russian well.

Legionäre im Gespräch mit russischen Überläufern. Einige der Legionäre waren russischer Abstammung und sprachen daher gut Russisch.

Lookout post in a tree. This was a dangerous place to be because of snipers.

Beobachtungsposten auf einem Baum. Aufgrund von Scharfschützen war es gefährlich, hier Position einzunehmen.

Leg.-Unterscharführer Bjarne Glemmestad, left, and *Leg.-Unterscharführer* Jens Grini at the front.

Von links: Leg.-Unterscharführer Bjarne Glemmestad und Leg.-Unterscharführer Jens Grini an der Front.

Clearing snow from the trenches was a major part of daily life in winter. Temperatures could fall as low as minus 50° Celsius (-60°F).

Schneeschaufeln war eine der wichtigsten Aufgaben im Winter. Die Temperatur konnte auf minus 50 Grad sinken.

One of *2. Company*'s bunkers in the first line of defence.

Ein Bunker der 2. Kompanie an der vordersten Frontlinie.

A bunker right behind the front, winter 1942.

Ein Bunker hinter der Front im Winter 1942.

Munin
STORGATA
NR. 17-18 • 2. ÅRG.
DESEMBERHEFTE 1943
PRIS I KRONE

Munin.

Fr.Gunvor Tvengsberg
A/S Oslo Sporveier
Underhaugsv.5
O s l o 30.
RAHMER

Munin.

Leg.-Hauptscharführer Harald Hervik at the castle in Uritsk.

Leg.-Hauptscharführer Harald Hervik am Schloss in Urizk.

The Legionaries' equipment at the front also included skis. Often these were used by messengers to expedite delivery of dispatches.

Skier gehörten mit zur Ausrüstung der Legionäre an der Front. Die Skier wurden oft von Meldern benutzt, um Mitteilungen rasch zustellen zu können.

Legion commander *Leg.-Sturmbannführer* Arthur Qvist, with *Leg.-Hauptsturmführer* Brynjulf Gottenborg in the background. The picture shows his office in Uritsk.

Legionskommandeur Leg.-Sturmbannführer Arthur Qvist mit Leg.-Hauptsturmführer Brynjulf Gottenborg im Hintergrund. Das Foto zeigt sein Büro in Urizk.

Leg.-Hauptsturmführer Karsten Sveen was company commander of *2. Company* and very popular with his troops. Sveen had fought against the Germans in 1940 at, among others, Midtskogen and in Gudbrandsdal.

Leg.-Hauptsturmführer Karsten Sveen war Kompanieführer der 2. Kompanie. Er war sehr beliebt bei seinen Soldaten. Sveen hatte 1940 am Feldzug gegen die deutschen Truppen in Norwegen teilgenommen, und unter anderem bei Midtskogen und in Gudbrandsdalen gegen deutsche Fallschirmjäger gekämpft.

Leg.-Unterscharführer Nils Lande received the Iron Cross 1st Class posthumously for several successful campaigns against Russian positions. During one of the attacks, 34 enemy soldiers were killed and six were taken prisoner. One heavy mounted machine gun, three machine guns and 30 rifles were captured as well. Lande had also participated in the Winter War in Finland in 1939–40. He died on 13 January 1943 at a field hospital in Krasnogvardeysk.

Leg.-Unterscharführer Nils Lande wurde nach seinem Tod mit dem Eisernen Kreuz 1. Klasse ausgezeichnet, nachdem er mehrmals erfolgreich russische Stellungen mit Stoßtrupps angegriffen hatte. Während einem dieser Angriffe wurden 34 russische Soldaten getötet und sechs gefangengenommen. Dabei wurden ein SMG, drei Maschinenpistolen und 30 Gewehre erbeutet. Lande hatte 1939–40 am Winterkrieg in Finnland teilgenommen. Er starb am 13.01.43 in einem Lazarett in Krasnogwardeisk.

From the left: NCOs *Leg.-Unterscharführer* Per Zingstad Nilsen, *Leg.-Hauptscharführer* Harald Hervik and *Leg.-Unterscharführer* Knud Rønneberg. All were members of *2. Company*.

Von links: die Unteroffiziere Leg.-Unterscharführer Per Zingstad Nilsen, Leg.-Hauptscharführer Harald Hervik und Leg.-Unterscharführer Knud Rønneberg. Alle drei gehörten zur 2. Kompanie.

A group of soldiers from *2. Company* in their trench. From the left: *Leg.-Unterscharführer* Ove Bruun, unknown, *Leg.-Hauptscharführer* Harald Hervik, Lars Gran and Berg.

Ein Gruppe Soldaten der 2. Kompanie im Schützengraben. Von links: Leg.-Unterscharführer Ove Bruun, ein Unbekannter, Leg.-Hauptscharführer Harald Hervik, Lars Gran und Berg.

Inside a bunker, planning an attack.

Vorbereitungen eines Stoßtrupps in einem Bunker.

Handing out awards. From the left: *Leg.-Untersturmführer* Sophus Kahrs, *Leg.-Sturmbannführer* Arthur Qvist and *Leg.-Unterscharführer* Karl Svenningsen.

Verleihung von Auszeichnungen. Von links: Leg.-Untersturmführer Sophus Kahrs, Leg.-Sturmbannführer Arthur Qvist und Leg.-Unterscharführer Karl Svenningsen.

Hand-grenades are thrown at enemy positions. From the left: Kristiansen, *Leg.-Scharführer* Bjarne Sveen and *Leg.-Hauptscharführer* Harald Hervik.

Handgranaten werden auf feindliche Stellungen geworfen. Von links: Kristiansen, Leg.-Scharführer Bjarne Sveen und Leg.-Hauptscharführer Harald Hervik.

Uritsk, 1 May 1942. From the left: *Leg.-Unterscharführer* Kristian Larsen, Leopold Welde, Arne Torgersen, Alfred Olsen and unknown.

Urizk, 01.05.42. Von links: Leg.-Unterscharführer Kristian Larsen, Leopold Welde, Arne Torgersen, Alfred Olsen und ein Unbekannter.

Knut Gamborg Nilsen is exhausted after fighting back a Russian attack at Uritsk with his troop.

Knut Gamborg Nilsen ist völlig erschöpft nachdem er mit seiner Truppe einen russischen Angriff bei Urizk abwehren konnte.

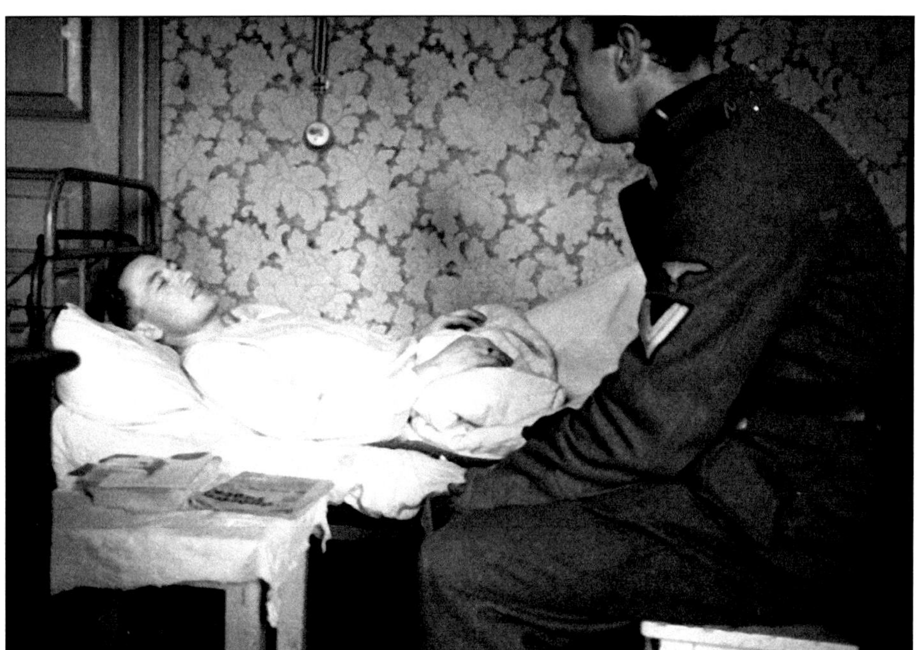

A soldier visits his wounded comrade at a field hospital.

Ein Soldat besucht seinen verwundeten Kameraden im Lazarett.

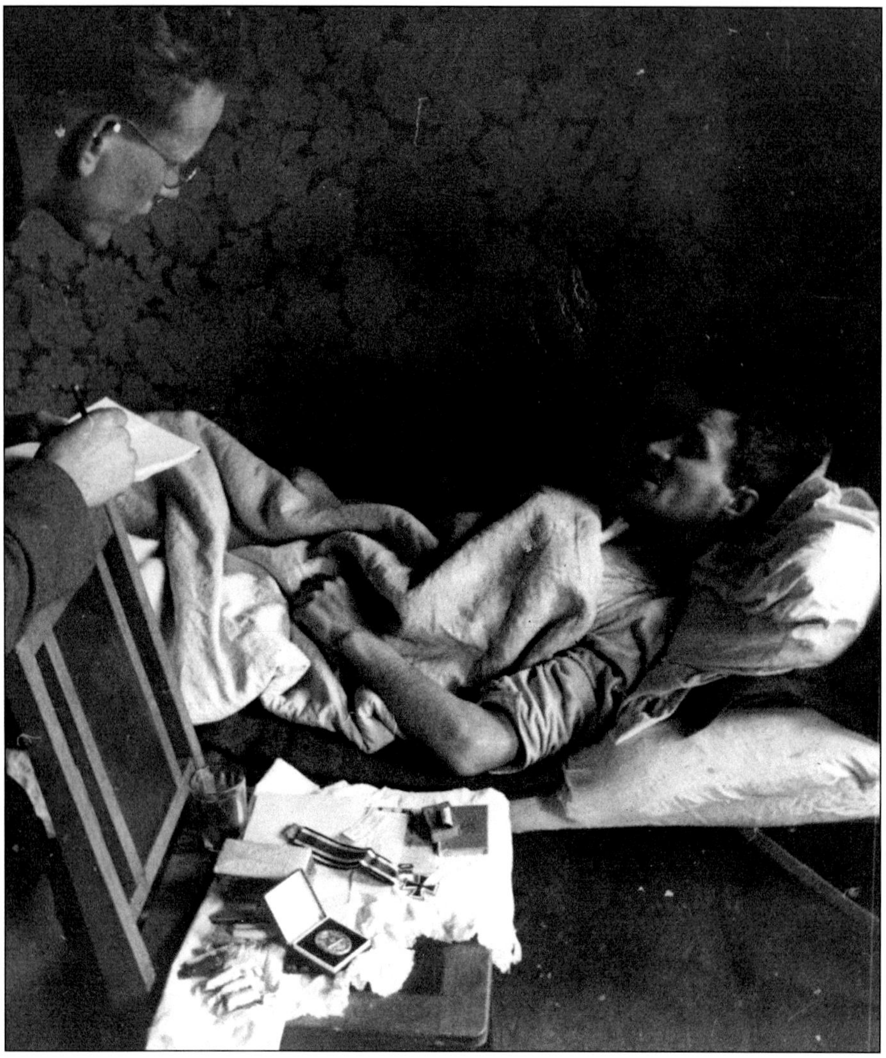

War correspondent Bjarne Sem interviews a wounded Legionary at a field hospital.

Der Kriegsberichter Bjarne Sem interviewt einen verwundeten Legionär im Lazarett.

From the left: *Leg.-Unterscharführer* Dagfinn Gjertsen, *Leg.-Unterscharführer* Arvid Fosse, *Leg.-Hauptscharführer* Henrik Stenberg and *Leg.-Oberscharführer* Osvald Kristoffersen preparing to depart for Mitau.

Von links: Leg.-Unterscharführer Dagfinn Gjertsen, Leg.-Unterscharführer Arvid Fosse, Leg.-Hauptscharführer Henrik Stenberg und Leg.-Oberscharführer Oswald Kristoffersen bereiten sich auf die Abreise nach Mitau vor.

Die SS-Freiwilligen-Legion Norwegen an der Front – 3. Kompanie | The *Norwegian Legion* at the front – *3. Company*

Soldiers from *3. Company* with a Russian deserter.

Soldaten der 3. Kompanie zusammen mit einem russischen Überlaufer.

Krasnoye Selo in the winter of 1942.

Krasnoje Selo, Winter 1942.

Leg.-Oberscharführer Knut Schjefstad inspects the trench of *3. Company*.

Leg.-Oberscharführer Knut Schjefstad inspiziert den Schützengraben der 3. Kompanie.

Leg.-Unterscharführer Magne Falkum collects firewood for the bunker.

Leg.-Unterscharführer Magne Falkum holt Brennholz für den Bunker.

Knut Schjefstad with a Russian deserter.

Knut Schjefstad zusammen mit einem russichen Überläufer.

Three officers from *3. Company*. From the left: platoon leader *Leg.-Untersturmführer* Jørgen Høve, company commander *Leg.-Obersturmführer* John Braset and an unknown colleague.

Drei Offiziere der 3. Kompanie. Von links: Zugführer Leg.-Untersturmführer Jørgen Høve, Kompanieführer Leg.-Obersturmführer John Braset und ein Unbekannter.

A light mortar is used to strike enemy positions.

Ein leichter Granatwerfer wird gegen feindliche Stellungen eingesetzt.

Leg.-Unterscharführer Peter Pettersen manning an anti-aircraft machine gun.

Leg.-Unterscharführer Petter Pettersen an einem Flak-MG.

Platoon leader Einar Høve at his position. He was killed on 14 February 1943 during an attack on Russian positions.

Zugführer Leg.-Untersturmführer Einar Høve in seiner Stellung. Er fiel am 14.02.43 während eines Stoßtruppangriffs auf russische Stellungen.

Distinguished visitors from Norway. From the left: *Höherer SS-und Polizeiführer Nord* Wilhelm Rediess, *Reichskommissar* Josef Terboven and Friedrich August Jeckeln, commander of the unit to which the Legion was attached.

Hoher Besuch aus Norwegen. Von links: Höherer SS-und Polizeiführer Nord Wilhelm Redieß, Reichskommissar Josef Terboven und Friedrich August Jeckeln. Letzterer war Kommandeur der Einhet, der die SS-Frw.-Legion Norwegen unterlag.

The Legion cemetery in Krasnoye Selo. Legion commander Qvist has his back to the camera.

Soldatenfriedhof in Krasnoje Selo. Legionskommandeur Qvist mit dem Rücken zur Kamera.

The Legion cemetery in Krasnoye Selo.

Soldatenfriedhof in Krasnoje Selo.

Spring was troublesome for the Legion, as they struggled to keep the water out of the trenches.

Der Frühling war gekommen, und man hatte große Schwierigkeiten, das Wasser aus den Schützengräben fernzuhalten.

Keeping the water out of the trenches was a time-consuming task.

Es war sehr zeitaufwendig, das Wasser aus den Schützengraben zu entfernen.

Munin.

Minister Fuglesang nedlegger blomster på de falnes graver.

Minister Fuglesang legt Kränze an den Gräbern der Gefallenen nieder.

HOS GUTTENE I DEN NORSKE LEGION

Bei den Männern der norwegische Legion.

En aldri så liten blund foran bunkeren.

Ein ganz kurzes Schläfchen vor dem Bunker.

Morgentoilett.

Morgentoilette.

Munin.

Minister Fuglesang besøker de forreste linjer.

Minister Fuglesang besucht die vordersten Linien.

Maten må fram.

Mit Handkarren wird die Verpflegung von der Ausgabestelle zur Kompanie gefahren.

Norske legionærer arbeider på russisk jord.

Norwegische Legionäre arbeiten auf russischer Erde.

Matutdeling.

Essenausgabe bei den Männern der norwegischen Legion.

Foto: SS-PK Christiansen (6), SS-PK Nussbaumer (1).

Munin.

Leg.-Rottenführer Dyre Halse on patrol.

Leg.-Rottenführer Dyre Halse auf Streifwache.

A bunker of *3. Company*.

Ein Bunker der 3. Kompanie.

Company commander *Leg.-Obersturmführer* John Braset, on the right, at his command post.

Rechts Kompanieführer Leg.-Obersturmführer John Braset in seinem Gefechtsstand.

3. Company position, with two unknown Legionaries.

Stellung der 3. Kompanie. Zwei unbekannte Legionäre.

Preparing food in the trenches.

Essenszubereitung im Schützengraben.

A platoon from *3. Company* takes a break at a Russian house that was hit by artillery.

Ein Zug der 3. Kompanie ruht sich vor einem russischen Haus aus, das von Artilleriefeuer getroffen wurde.

Brothers Svein, left. and Dyre Halse. Svein was with *14. Company*, while Dyre was with *3. Company*.

Von links: die Brüder Svein und Dyre Halse. Svein war bei der 14. Kompanie, Dyre bei der 3. Kompanie.

From the left: *Leg.-Hauptscharführer* Olaf Røed, *Leg.-Untersturmführer* Rolf Wirum and Dyre Halse.

Von links: Leg.-Hauptscharführer Olaf Røed, Leg.-Untersturmführer Rolf Wirum und Dyre Halse.

From the left: Dyre Halse, *Leg.-Untersturmführer* Rolf Wirum and *Leg.-Unterscharführer* Peter Pettersen.

Von links: Dyre Halse, Leg.-Untersturmführer Rolf Wirum und Leg.-Unterscharführer Peter Pettersen.

Leg.-Oberscharführer Knut Schjefstad began as a radio operator in the Legion, was promoted to platoon leader and later became a war correspondent. Schjefstad was killed on 1 March 1943 during the bombing of Berlin.

Leg.-Oberscharführer Knut Schjefstad war erst Funker bei der SS-Frw.Legion Norwegen, dann Zugführer und später Kriegsberichter. Schjefstad fiel am 01.03.43 in Berlin während des Fliegerangriffs der Alliierten.

Dyre Halse, left, and *Leg.-Unterscharführer* Peter Pettersen.

Von links: Dyre Halse und Leg.-Unterscharführer Peter Pettersen.

Dyre Halse, left, and an unknown soldier enjoying the spring sun in the trenches.

Von links: Dyre Halse und ein Unbekannter genießen die Frühlingssonne im Schützengraben.

A group of soldiers on leave behind the front.

Ein Gruppe beurlaubter Soldaten hinter der Front.

Die SS-Freiwilligen-Legion Norwegen an der Front – 4. Kompanie | The *Norwegian Legion* at the front – *4. Company*

4. Company arrives at the front by plane.

Die 4. Kompanie bei der Ankunft mit dem Flugzeug an der Front.

From the left: *Leg.-Scharführer* Bjørn Noreger, *Leg.-Oberscharführer* Odd Meidell Ljungberg (KIA) and *Leg.-Unterscharführer* Robert William Hagelin, who died of tuberculosis on 5 August 1943.

Von links: Leg.-Scharführer Bjørn Noreger, Leg.-Oberscharführer Odd Meidell Ljungberg (gefallen) und Leg.-Unterscharführer Robert William Hagelin, der am 05.08.43 an Tuberkulose starb.

In position are *Leg.-Scharführer* Bjørn Noreger, left, and two unknown comrades.

In Stellung. Von links: Leg.-Scharführer Bjørn Noreger und zwei Unbekannte.

Bombarding Russian positions with heavy mortar fire.

Schwere Granatwerfer beschießen die russischen Stellungen.

Platoon leader *Leg.-Hauptscharführer* Sverre Kjelstrup, left, and company commander *Leg.-Hauptsturmführer* Ragnar Berg.

Von links: Zugführer Leg.-Hauptscharführer Sverre Kjelstrup und Kompanieführer Leg.-Hauptsturmführer Ragnar Berg.

A light machine gun (LMG) in place with *4. Company*.

Leichtes MG der 4. Kompanie.

A *4. Company* mortar position. This was a heavily armed company with mounted machine guns (SMGs) and heavy mortars.

Ein Granatwerferstellung der 4. Kompanie, eine schwer bewaffnete Kompanie mit SMGs und schweren Granatwerfern.

The position is camouflaged with snow.

Die Stellung wird mit Schnee getarnt.

Husker DU?

Den faste meldevegen gjennom «Kløfta»
Auf festem Meldeweg durchs Gelände

Felix Hartmann på lovlige veger
Felix Hartmann auf dem richtigen Weg

Erinnerst du dich?

III

→

En såret bringes tilbake gjennom løpegraven til 1. kp.
Ein Verwundeter wird im Laufgraben zurückgebracht

←

Pussen sitter i blodet, og en rolig dag innbyr til ekstrapuss
Das Putzen liegt im Blute. Ein ruhiger Tag ladet zum Extraputz

Den russiske hjelpeskredderen prøver den nye jakken
Ein russischer Hilfsschneider bei der Legion prüft den neuen Rock

↓

En såret kjemper på frontsykehuset
Ein verwundeter Kämpfer im Frontlazarett

↓

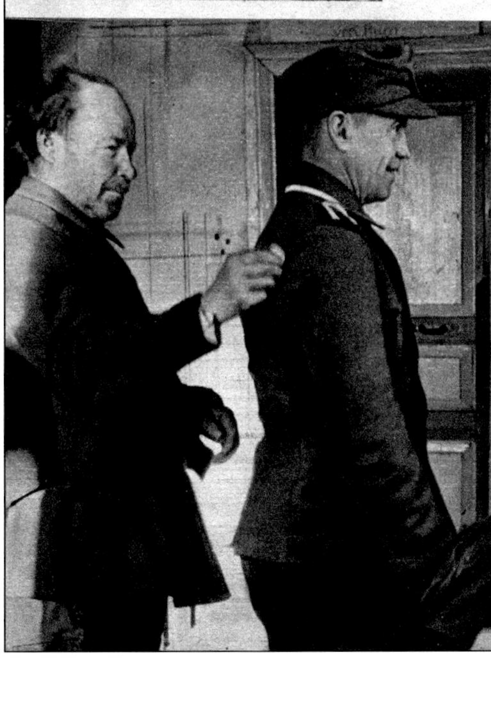

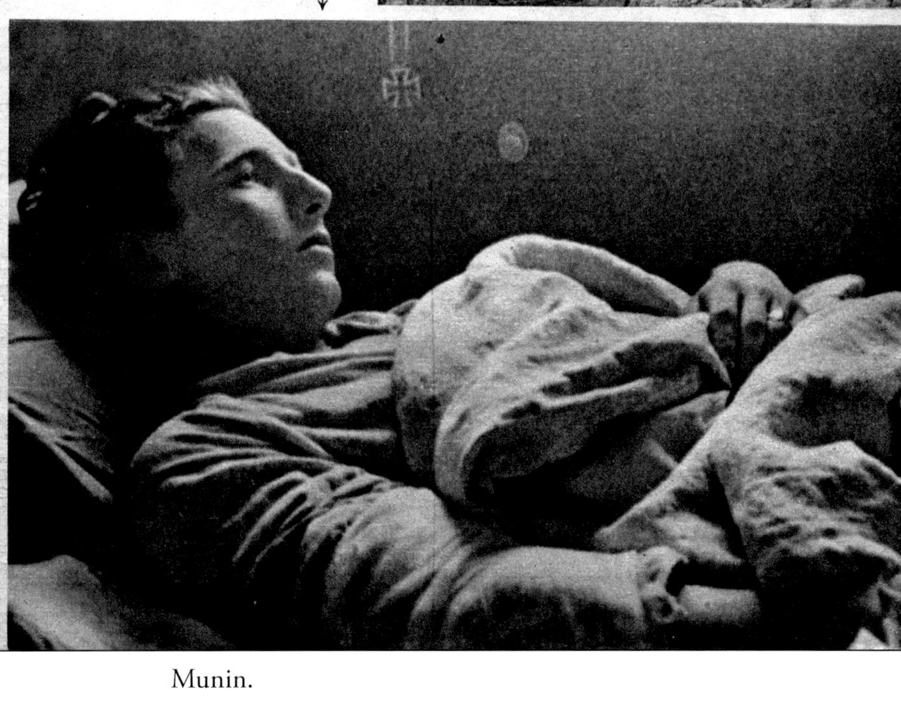

Munin.

Tannlægen «opererer» helt i forreste linje med sitt transportable utstyr
Der Zahnarzt «operiert» in vordester Linie mit seiner fahrbaren Ausrüstung

På post ved den heimelagede «kikkerten
Auf geschütztem Ausguckposten

Idyll i «Riegelstellung» påsken 1942 — Idyll in der «Riegelstellung» Ostern 1942

Reichsführer SS inspiserer avdelinger av Legionen etter endt frontinnsats
Reichsführer der SS Himmler besichtigt Abteilungen der Legion

Foto: Christiansen og Thur

Våpenpuss
Waffenputzen

Munin.

Motorcycle orderly Ernst Hillgaar with a captured Russian machine gun of type PPSh.

Der Kradmelder Ernst Hillgaar, hier mit einer eroberten russischen Maschinenpistole vom Typ PPSch.

Ernst Hillgaar on his motorcycle with sidecar (*B-Krad*).

Ernst Hillgaar auf seinem Beiwagenkrad.

Inside a machine-gun bunker of *4. Company*.

Im SMG-Bunker der 4. Kompanie.

A heavy machine-gun (SMG) emplacement in the winter of 1942.

SMG-Stellung, Winter 1942.

A group from *4. Company* posing near a captured Russian tank. On the far right is field priest *Leg.-Hauptsturmführer* Knut Jarle Geelmuyden.

Ein Gruppe der 4. Kompanie vor einem zerstörten russischen Panzer. Ganz rechts: der Feldpfarrer Leg.-Hauptsturmführer Knut Jarle Geelmuyden.

NCOs *Leg.-Hauptscharführer* Steinar Brenna (KIA), left, and *Leg.-Scharführer* Bjørn Noreger.

Von links: die Unteroffiziere Leg.-Hauptscharführer Steinar Brenna (gefallen) und Leg.-Scharführer Bjørn Noreger.

Sign showing the location of *Leg.-Scharführer* Bjørn Noreger's troop headquarters.

Ein Schild, das die Position des Gefechtsstands von Leg.-Scharführer Bjørn Noreger und seinem Zug anzeigt.

Sophus, left, and Bjørn Noreger during a meeting just behind the front in Krasnoye Selo.

Von links: Sophus und Bjørn Noreger während einer Besprechung hinter der Front in Krasnoje Selo.

From the left: platoon leader *Leg.-Oberscharführer* Tor Arntzen, company commander Njål Reppen and platoon leaders *Leg.-Oberscharführer* Henrik Pedersen and *Leg.-Scharführer* Bjørn Noreger.

Von links: Zugführer Leg.-Oberscharführer Tor Arntzen, Kompanieführer Njål Reppen und die Zugführer Leg.-Oberscharführer Henrik Pedersen und Leg.-Scharführer Bjørn Noreger.

From the left: unknown, *Leg.-Untersturmführer* Rolf Wirum, *Leg.-Obersturmführer* Njål Reppen and two unknowns.

Von links: ein Unbekannter, Leg.-Untersturmführer Rolf Wirum, Leg.-Obersturmführer Njål Reppen und zwei Unbekannte.

Hermann Bay lost a leg during the infamous shock squad raid led by Ragnar Berg. The raid, during which company commander Ragnar Berg and several others were killed, was an utter failure.

Hermann Bay verlor ein Bein bei dem berühmten Stoßtruppangriff Ragnar Bergs, der vollends scheiterte. Kompanieführer Ragnar Berg und mehrere andere sind dabei gefallen.

Severely wounded, Hermann Bay was carried back to his position by *Leg.-Unterscharführer* Carsten Simonsen on 16 April 1942.

Am 16.04.42 trug Leg.-Unterscharführer Carsten Simonsen den schwer verwundeten Hermann Bay zurück zur eigenen Stellung.

Latvian and Norwegian volunteers loading machine-gun belts at the Leningrad Front.

Lettische und norwegische Freiwillige beim Laden von SMG-Gurten an der Leningrader Front.

Armourer Skau bailed out *4. Company* many times and kept all weapons in good condition.

Der Waffenwart Skau rettete die 4. Kompanie etliche Male dadurch, dass er die Waffen in gutem Zustand hielt.

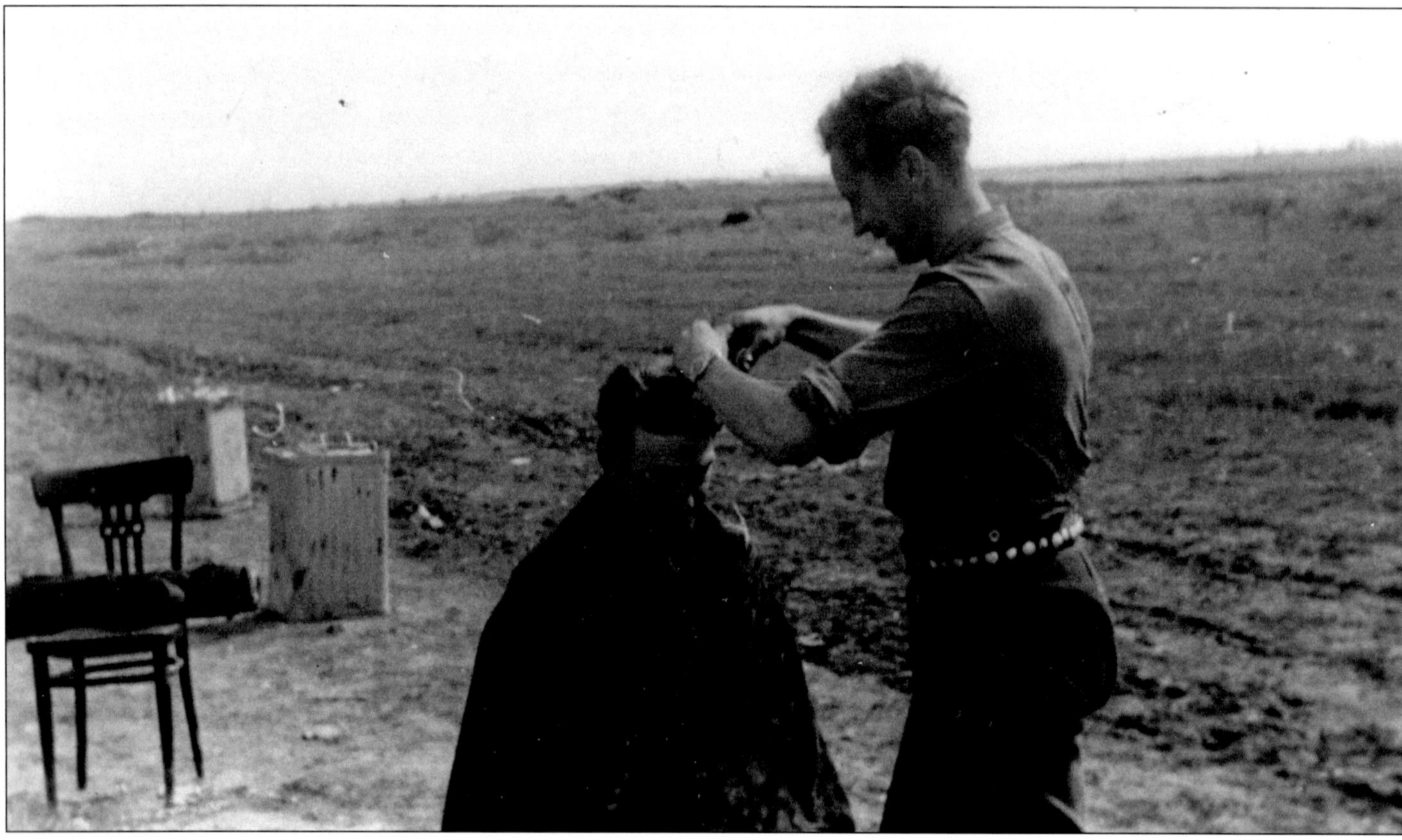

Having a haircut during a quiet moment at the front.

Haare schneiden während eines ruhigen Augenblicks and der Front.

A volunteer of *4. Company* manning a Czech machine gun used as a spare weapon by the company.

Ein Freiwilliger der 4. Kompanie an einem tschechischen MG das von der Kompanie als Reservewaffe benutzt wurde.

A group of NCOs from *4. Company*. First row from the left: *Leg.-Unterscharführer* Reidar Verner, *Leg.-Oberscharführer* Mathias Østhassel and *Leg.-Unterscharführer* Finn Faye Lund. Second row from the left: *Leg.-Unterscharführer* Alf Knutsen, *Leg.-Unterscharführer* Magne Falkum, *Leg.-Unterscharführer* Albert Tuxen Todnem, unknown and *Leg.-Unterscharführer* Torstein Dagestad.

Ein Gruppe Unteroffiziere der 4. Kompanie: Erste Reihe von links: Leg.-Unterscharführer Reidar Verner, Leg.-Oberscharführer Mathias Østhassel und Leg.-Unterscharführer Finn Faye Lund. Zweite Reihe von links: Leg.-Unterscharführer Alf Knutsen, Leg.-Unterscharführer Magne Falkum, Leg.-Unterscharführer Albert Tuxen Todnem, ein Unbekannter und Leg.-Unterscharführer Torstein Dagestad.

A light mortar of *4. Company*.

Leichter Granatwerfer der 4. Kompanie.

From the left: unknown, *Leg.-Obersturmführer* Njål Reppen, *Leg.-Scharführer* Bjørn Noreger and *Leg.-Oberscharführer* Tor Arntzen.

Von links: ein Unbekannter, Leg.-Obersturmführer Njål Reppen, Leg.-Scharführer Bjørn Noreger und Leg.-Oberscharführer Tor Arntzen.

Volunteers from *4. Company*. Seated is *Leg.-Untersturmführer* Jørgen Høve.

Freiwillige der 4. Kompanie. Sitzend: Leg.-Untersturmführer Jørgen Høve.

A hot day at the front.

Ein heißer Tag an der Front.

From the left: Olav Tronerud, Rolf Klemetsrud and Trygve Hangeland.

Von links: Olav Tronerud, Rolf Klemetsrud und Trygve Hangeland.

Die SS-Freiwilligen-Legion Norwegen an der Front – 14. Kompanie | The *Norwegian Legion* at the front – *14. Company*

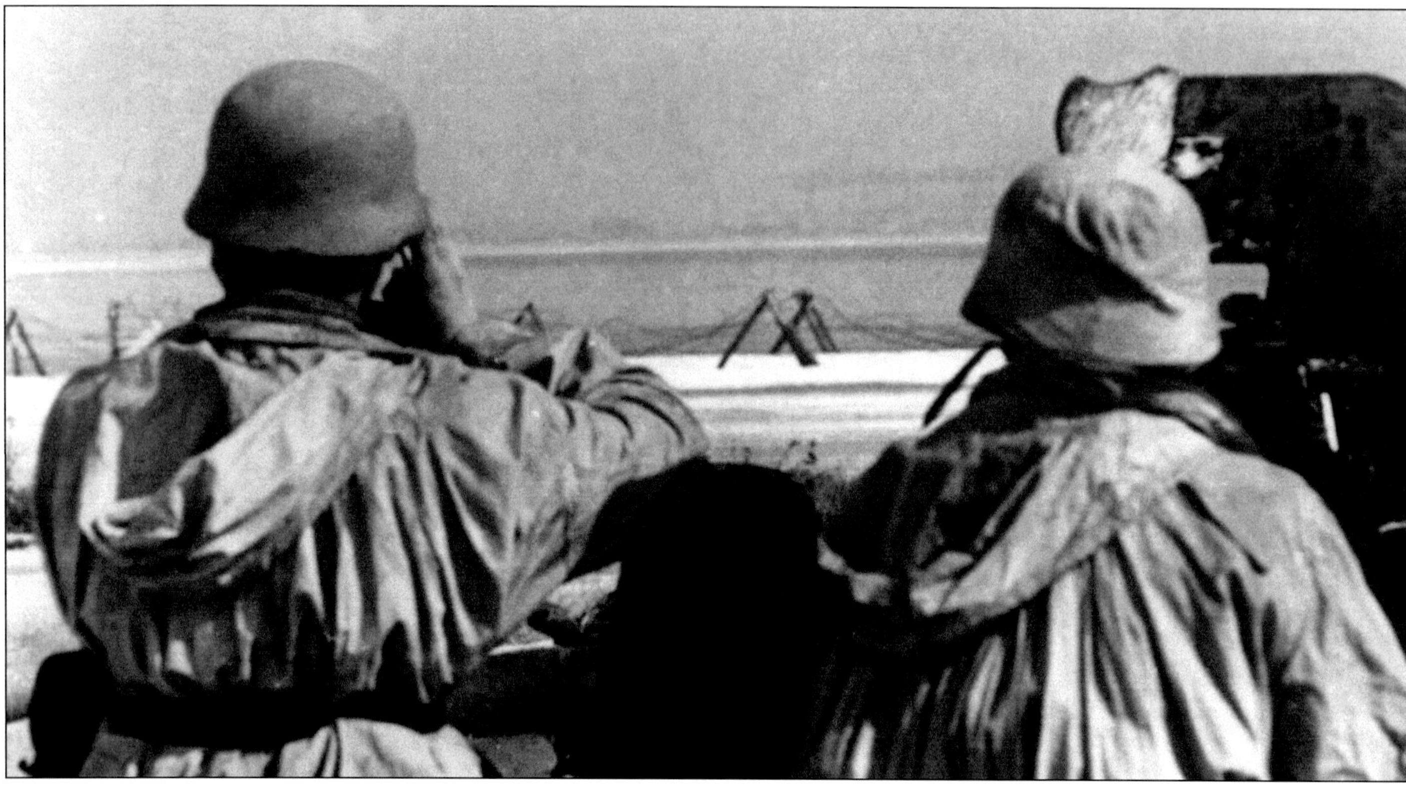

An anti-tank position of *14. Company*. Such positions lay scattered throughout the Legion's operational area to guard against armoured attack.

Ein Pak-Stellung der 14. Kompanie. Solche Stellungen lagen im ganzen Gebiet der Abteilung verteilt, um feindliche Panzerangriffe abzuwehren.

Leg.-Unterscharführer and gun commander Thomas Hvistendahl at his gun.

Leg.-Unterscharführer und Pak-Kommandant Thomas Hvistendahl an seinem Geschütz.

An anti-tank gun is sighted in.

Eine Pak wird eingerichtet.

Anti-tank guns had to be moved frequently to avoid detection and attack by Russians forces.

Pak-Stellungen mussten öfters gewechselt werden, um die Entdeckung und den Angriff durch russische Truppen zu vermeiden.

Three unknown soldiers from *14. Company*.

Drei unbekannte Soldaten der 14. Kompanie.

Leg.-Unterscharführer Per Willy Meidell was a gun commander from *14. Company*. Wounded twice, Meidell was awarded the Iron Cross 1st Class.

Leg.-Unterscharführer Per Willy Meidell war PAK-Kommandant in der 14. Kompanie. Meidell wurde zweimal verwundet und mit dem Eisernen Kreuz 1. Klasse ausgezeichnet.

Leg.-Unterscharführer Per Meidell.

Leg.-Unterscharführer Per Meidell.

A wounded soldier on his way to a field hospital. Due to his relatively light injuries, he was able to make his own way. The label around his neck informed the hospital about his injury and the type of first aid provided by medical staff in the trenches.

Ein verwundeter Soldat auf dem Weg zum Lazarett. Da er nicht schwer verwundet war, konnte er selber gehen. Die Marke um seinen Hals gibt Hinweise über die Verletzung und Erste-Hilfe-Maßnahmen der Sanitätssoldaten im Schützengraben.

Leg.-Hauptscharführer and gun commander Arnfinn Vik at the front.

Leg.-Hauptscharführer und Pak-Kommandant Arnfinn Vik an der Front.

Four unknown soldiers from *14. Company* enjoy the spring sun in the trenches.

Vier unbekannte Soldaten der 14. Kompanie genießen die Sonne im Schützengraben.

Ludvig Lundemoe – platoon leader, *Leg.-Hauptscharführer* and gun commander – was killed on 2 February 1943 at Krasny Bor. He was hit in the hip by machine-gun fire.

Zugführer, Leg.-Hauptscharführer und Pak-Kommandant Ludvig Lundemoe fiel am 12.02.43 bei Krasny Bor. Er wurde von einer MG-Garbe an der Hüfte getroffen.

From the left: Alf Nybakken, platoon leader *Leg.-Hauptscharführer* Åge Holst, *Leg.-Unterscharführer* Arne Olavsen, Erling Borglund, Finn Brekke, *Leg.-Unterscharführer* Egil Bergaust and *Leg.-Unterscharführer* Gunnar Sandved. All belonged to Holst's platoon in *14. Company.*

Von links: Alf Nybakken, Zugführer Leg.-Hauptscharführer Åge Holst, Leg.-Unterscharführer Arne Olavsen, Erling Borglund, Finn Brekke, Leg.-Unterscharführer Egil Bergaust und Leg.-Unterscharführer Gunnar Sandved. Alle waren in Holsts Zug bei der 14. Kompanie.

An anti-tank gun in position.

Eine Pak in Stellung.

An anti-tank gun in position.

Eine Pak in Stellung.

From the left: Arne Nordhagen, Ove Houth (KIA), *Leg.-Hauptscharführer* Åge Holst, Alfred Gasman (KIA), *Leg.-Unterscharführer* Gunnar Sandved, *Leg.-Oberscharführer* Henrik Pedersen and *Leg.-Unterscharführer* Arne Olavsen.

Von links: Arne Nordhagen, Ove Houth (gefallen), Leg.-Hauptscharführer Åge Holst, Alfred Gasmann (gefallen), Leg.-Unterscharführer Gunnar Sandved, Leg.-Oberscharführer Henrik Pedersen und Leg.-Unterscharführer Arne Olavsen.

Leg.-Unterscharführer Ivar Staff, who was killed on 4 December 1942 during heavy fighting while his position was surrounded by Russian soldiers.

Leg.-Unterscharführer Ivar Staff fiel am 04.12.42 unter schweren Kämpfen, während seine Stellung von russischen Soldaten umringt war.

General and commander of the *2. SS-Infantry Brigade (mot.)*, *SS-Brigadeführer* Friedrich Jeckeln, visits a position of *14. Company*. From the right: unknown, *Leg.-Sturmbannführer* Arthur Qvist, unknown and *Leg.-Hauptsturmführer* Finn Finson.

General und Kommandeur der 2. SS-Infanterie-Brigade (mot.), SS-Brigadeführer Friedrich Jeckeln, besucht eine Stellung der 14. Kompanie. Von rechts: ein Unbekannter, Leg.-Sturmbannführer Arthur Qvist, ein Unbekannter und Leg.-Hauptsturmführer Finn Finson.

Company commander *Leg.-Hauptsturmführer* Finn Finson was not particularly well-liked by his soldiers.

Kompanieführer Leg.-Hauptsturmführer Finn Finson war äußerst unbeliebt bei seiner Mannschaft.

Leg.-Unterscharführer Arnof Torstensen. For a while he was also first sergeant of *14. Company*.

Leg.-Unterscharführer Arnolf Torstensen. Eine Zeit lang war er auch Spieß der 14. Kompanie.

First sergeant of *14. Company*, *Leg.-Hauptscharführer* Thomas Gysler.

Leg.-Hauptscharführer Thomas Gysler war Spieß der 14. Kompanie.

Jens Lindhagen was promoted from private to *Leg.-Rottenführer* at the front.

Jens Lindhagen wurde an der Front vom Leg.-Schützen zum Leg.-Rottenführer befördert.

From the left: two Norwegian soldiers, *Leg.-Rottenführer* Asbjørn Dokken, a veteran of the Winter War in Finland 1939–40, and gun commander *Leg.-Unterscharführer* Roy Wentzel Larsen, with members of the German police.

Von links: zwei norwegische Freiwillige, Leg.-Rottenführer Asbjørn Dokken, ein Veteran des finnischen Winterkrieges 1939–40, und Pak-Kommandant Leg.-Unterscharführer Roy Wentzel Larsen. Die anderen sind deutsche Ordnungspolizisten.

Awarding the Iron Cross 2nd Class. From the left: *Leg.-Obersturmführer* Njål Reppen, *Leg.-Rottenführer* Johan Talaasen, Hugo Mørk and *Leg.-Sturmbannführer* Arthur Qvist.

Verleihung des Eisernen Kreuzes 2. Klasse. Von links: Leg.-Obersturmführer Njål Reppen, Leg.-Rottenführer Johan Talaasen, Hugo Mørk und Leg.-Sturmbannführer Arthur Qvist.

German and Norwegian volunteers in the trench of *14. Company*.

Deutsche und norwegische Freiwillige im Schützengraben der 14. Kompanie.

The *Norwegian Legion* leaves the Leningrad Front. In the middle of the picture is deputy Legion commander *Leg.-Hauptsturmführer* Finn Finson. During the ceremony, the Legion bids farewell to its fallen Legionaries.

Die SS-Frw.-Legion Norwegen verlässt die Leningrader Front. In der Mitte der stellvertretende Legionskommandeur, Leg.-Hauptsturmführer Finn Finson. Bei dieser Trauerfeier nimmt die Legion Abschied von ihren Gefallenen.

The farewell ceremony for fallen Legionaries.

Während der Trauerfeier für die gefallenen Legionäre.

Arne Ormstad arrives in Riga on his way to Mitau.

Arne Ormstad kommt während der Fahrt nach Mitau in Riga an.

Ersatzbataillon der SS-Freiwilligen-Legion Norwegen | Replacement battalion for the *Norwegian Legion*

The replacement battalion for the *Norwegian Legion*. As the Legion lost an increasing number of soldiers due to injuries or death on the battlefield, the need for replacements arose. Before joining the Legion, all newcomers received training in Holmestrand. This picture shows a group of new recruits in Holmestrand.

Das Ersatzbataillon der SS-Frw.-Legion Norwegen. Durch die Verluste der Legion an Gefallenen und Verwundeten entstand ein Bedarf an neuen Streitkräften, die in Holmestrand südlich von Oslo ausgebildet wurden. Hier eine Gruppe neuer Rekruten in Holmestrand.

The entrance to Holmestrand camp.

Eingang zum Lager Holmestrand.

Ministers Jonas Lie and Jørgen Fuglesang visit the camp to attend the swearing-in of new recruits. Front row from the left: head of the *Rikshirden* Thorvald Thronsen, Minister Rolf Jørgen Fuglesang, German training officer Heinrich Petersen, Minister Jonas Lie and Lie's adjutant.

Die Minister Jonas Lie und Rolf Jørgen Fuglesang besuchen das Lager, um an der Vereidigung der neuen Rekruten teilzunehmen. Erste Reihe von links: oberster Befehlshaber der *Rikshirden*, Thorvald Thronsen, Minister Rolf Jørgen Fuglesang, Lagerkommandant Heinrich Petersen, Minister Jonas Lie und Lies Adjutant.

During the visit.

Während des Besuchs.

From the left: Jonas Lie, Rolf Jørgen Fuglesang, Lie's adjutant, Heinrich Petersen and Thorvald Thronsen.

Von links: Jonas Lie, Rolf Jørgen Fuglesang, Lies Adjutant, Heinrich Petersen und Thorvald Thronsen.

Swearing-in of soldiers and nurses.

Vereidigung von Soldaten und DRK-Schwestern.

SS-Obersturmbannführer Heinrich Petersen addresses the newly arrived soldiers.

SS-Obersturmbannführer Heinrich Petersen hält eine Rede vor den neuen Soldaten.

Soldiers and nurses leaving the camp after the swearing-in ceremony.

Soldaten und DRK-Schwestern verlassen das Lager nach der Vereidigung.

Lunch break at Holmestrand camp.

Essenspause im Lager Holmestrand.

Leg.-Untersturmführer Jørgen Høve in Holmestrand.

Leg.-Untersturmführer Jørgen Høve in Holmestrand.

Leg.-Untersturmführer Fritjof Georg Henriksen in Holmestrand.

Leg.-Untersturmführer Fritjof Georg Henriksen in Holmestrand.

The recruits march to the Royal Palace in Oslo before leaving for the front. *SS-Hauptsturmführer* Felix Hartmann is leading the group.

Die Rekruten marschieren zum Schloss in Oslo kurz vor der Abreise zur Front. An der Spitze marschiert SS-Hauptsturmführer Felix Hartmann.

Line-up on Palace Square in Oslo. *SS-Obersturmbannführer* Heinrich Petersen, left, *and SS-Obersturmführer* Erich Friedrich Dahm, company commander of the replacement company.

Aufstellung auf dem Schlossplatz in Oslo. Von links: SS-Obersturmbannführer Heinrich Petersen und SS-Obersturmführer Erich Friedrich Dahm, Kompanieführer der Ersatzkompanie.

Die SS-Freiwilligen-Legion Norwegen – Auflösung in Mitau | The *Norwegian Legion* – disbandment in Mitau

The Legion arrived at Mitau to be disbanded. From the left: *Leg.-Hauptscharführer* Arne Nilsen, *Leg.-Hauptscharführer* Kjell Kracht and *Leg.-Hauptscharführer* Roald Bjørnstad.

Die SS-Frw.-Legion Norwegen ist in Mitau angekommen um aufgelöst zu werden. Von links: Leg.-Hauptscharführer Arne Nilsen, Leg.-Hauptscharführer Kjell Kracht und Leg.-Hauptscharführer Roald Bjørnstad.

Company commander of *2. Company*, *Leg.-Hauptsturmführer* Karsten Sveen, left, and platoon leader *Leg.-Obersturmführer* Jens Grønnerød.

Von links: Kompanieführer der 2. Kompanie Leg.-Hauptsturmführer Karsten Sveen und sein Zugführer Leg.-Obersturmführer Jens Grønnerød.

From the right: *Leg.-Oberscharführer* Knud Rønneberg, *Leg.-Hauptscharführer* Harald Hervik, *Leg.-Unterscharführer* Arvid Fosse and *Leg.-Unterscharführer* Erik Eriksen in Mitau.

Von rechts: Leg.-Oberscharführer Knud Rønneberg, Leg.-Hauptscharführer Harald Hervik, Leg.-Unterscharführer Arvid Fosse und Leg.-Unterscharführer Erik Eriksen in Mitau.

Leg.-Hauptsturmführer Frode Halle in Mitau.

Leg.-Hauptsturmführer Frode Halle in Mitau.

Reichsführer-SS Heinrich Himmler visits Mitau to persuade the Legionaries to continue fighting for *Regiment 'Norge'*.

Reichsführer-SS Heinrich Himmler zu Besuch in Mitau, um die ehemaligen SS-Legionäre zu überzeugen, sich beim Regiment "Norge" aufs Neue zu bewerben.

Heinrich Himmler in Mitau with, far left, *Leg.-Untersturmführer* Rolf Wirum.

Heinrich Himmler in Mitau. Ganz links: Leg.-Untersturmführer Rolf Wirum.

From the left: unknown, Gottlob Berger, Heinrich Himmler, behind Himmler unknown, *SS-Hauptsturmführer* Olaf Lindvig, Karl Holter, *SS-Hauptsturmführer* Erich Dahm, *Leg.-Sturmbannführer* Finn Finson and unknown.

Von links: ein Unbekannter, Gottlob Berger, Heinrich Himmler, ein Unbekannter hinter Himmler, SS.-Hauptsturmführer Olaf Lindvig, Karl Holter, SS-Hauptsturmführer Erich Dahm, Leg.-Sturmbannführer Finn Finson und ein Unbekannter.

Himmler inspects the Legion.

Himmler inspiziert die SS-Frw.-Legion Norwegen.

Himmler greeting the German advisors to the Legion.

Himmler begrüßt die deutschen Berater der SS-Frw.-Legion Norwegen.

From the right: *SS-Standarten-Oberjunker* Kristoffer Dahl, *SS-Standarten-Oberjunker* Olaf Wahlmann and *Leg.-Obersturmführer* Kåre Meinert Opsahl.

Von rechts: die SS-Standarten-Oberjunker Kristoffer Dahl und Olaf Wahlmann, dann Leg.-Obersturmführer Kåre Meinert Opsahl.

Himmler and Berger inspecting the Legion.

Himmler und Berger während einer Besichtigung der SS-Frw.-Legion Norwegen.

Die SS-Freiwilligen-Legion Norwegen – Heimkehr nach Norwegen | The *Norwegian Legion* – back in Norway

Legionærer vender heim.

En reportasje fra 330 norske legionærers heimkomst etter endt innsats.

Legionäre bei ihrer Rückkehr.

Ein Bericht von der Heimkehr 330 norwegischer Legionäre nach beendetem Einsatz.

Foto: Bjørn Kihle (3) - NTB. (3).

Ø. til venstre: De første skritt på heimlandets jord.
Ø. til høyre: Endelig er pappa der.
O. til venstre: Legionærene defilerer for Føreren.
O. til høyre: Tilh.: for Føreren sees Obersturmbannführer Neumann.
U. til venstre: Føreren hilser de tapre frontkjempere.
U. til høyre: Fra mottagelsesfesten for legionærene. Tilv. for Føreren sees Sturmbannführer Qvist, kommandør for Den norske Legion.

Oben links: Der erste Schritt auf heimatlichem Boden.
Oben rechts: Endlich ist Pappa wieder da.
Mitte links: Die Legionäre marschieren am Fører vorbei.
Mitte rechts: Rechts vom Fører sieht man Obersturmbannführer Neumann.
Unten links: Der Fører begrüsst die tapferen Frontkämpfer.
Unten rechts: Vom Empfangsabend für die Legionäre. Rechts vom Fører ist Sturmbannführer Qvist, Kommandeur der norwegischen Legion, zu sehen.

Munin.

Munin
Føreren hilser sårede frontkjempere.
Der Fører begrüsst verwundete Frontkämpfer.
NR. 6 • 2. ÅRG.
JUNI 1943
PRIS 60 ØRE

Munin.

The Legion returns to Norway. *Leg.-Unterscharführer* Albert Tuxen Todnem, right, and *Leg.-Unterscharführer* Per Meidell.

Heimkehr nach Norwegen. Von rechts: Leg.-Unterscharführer Albert Tuxen Todnem und Leg.-Unterscharführer Per Meidell.

Banquet dinner for the *Norwegian Legion* in Oslo.

Festessen für die Legion in Oslo.

At the banquet, with Arthur Qvist in the middle.

Beim Festessen. In der Mitte Arthur Qvist.

At the banquet in Oslo.

Beim Festessen in Oslo.

At the banquet are, from the left, *Leg.-Hauptsturmführer* Frode Halle, *Leg.-Untersturmführer* Sophus Kahrs, *Leg.-Hauptscharführer* Arne Nilsen and *Leg.-Hauptscharführer* Bjarne Larsen.

Beim Festessen. Von links: Leg.-Hauptsturmführer Frode Halle, Leg.-Untersturmführer Sophus Kahrs, Leg.-Hauptscharführer Arne Nilsen und Leg.-Hauptscharführer Bjarne Larsen.

Legionaries attending one of several events organised in connection with the Legion's return. On the left is *Leg.-Untersturmführer* Knut Vestad, and behind him is *Leg.-Scharführer* Bjørn Noreger.

Die Legionäre bei einer Veranstaltung nach der Heimkehr nach Norwegen. Erster von links: Leg.-Untersturmführer Knut Vestad, hinter ihm Leg.-Scharführer Bjørn Noreger.

Legionaries in Stavanger after their return to Norway. From the right: three unknowns, Knud Rønneberg and Wilhelm Johnsen.

Heimgekehrte Legionäre in Stavanger. Von rechts: drei Unbekannte, Knud Rønneberg und Wilhelm Johnsen.

Die Woche, a German magazine with a drawing by Norwegian war reporter Finn Wigforss.

Die Woche eine Zeitschrift mit einer Zeichnung von den norwegischen Kriegsreporter Finn Wigforss.

(From left to right) Close Combat Clasp in Bronze. | Nahkampfspange in Bronze paar Norweger Wiking und Regiment Norge erhielt diese Auszeichnung.
Norwegian flag used by the *Den Norske Legion* during training in Germany. | Wurde Norwegen Flagge von der Den Norske Legion während der Ausbildung in Deutschland.
Edelweiss cap badge worn by Norwegians in *6 SS Div Nord.* | Edelweiß Hut Abzeichen wurde von Norweger in 6 SS Div Nord verwendet.

(From left to right) Infantry Assault Badge in Bronze. | Infanteriesturmabzeichen in Bronze einige Norweger in Wiking und die Legion erhielt diese Auszeichnung.
Assault Badge. | Sturmabzeichen mehrere Norweger Wiking und Regiment Norge erhielt diese Auszeichnung.
Iron Cross 1st Class – 30 Norwegians received this award. | Eisernes Kreuz 1. Klasse 30 Norweger erhielt diese Auszeichnung.
Collar patch used by volunteers *Regiment Norge.* | Kragenspiegel von Freiwilligen verwendet Regiment Norge.

(From left to right) Tank Assault Badge in Silver. | Panzerkampfabzeichen in Silber einige Norweger Wiking und Regiment Norge erhielt diese Auszeichnung.
Infantry Assault Badge in Silver. | Infanteriesturmabzeichen in Silber Norweger Wiking und die Legion erhielt diese Auszeichnung.
Tank Assault Badge in Bronze. | Panzerkampfabzeichen in Bronze einige Norweger Wiking und Regiment Norge erhielt diese Auszeichnung.
Armshield worn by volunteers from *Regiment Norge.* | Schild Flagge von Freiwilligen verwendet Regiment Norge.

(From left to right) Wound Badge in Silver. | Verwundetenabzeichen in Silber einige Norweger erhielt diese Auszeichnung.
Front Fighters Badge, an award given to Norwegian volunteers who had fought on the Eastern Front. | Frontkämpfer-Abzeichen eine norwegische Auszeichnung norwegischen Freiwilligen gegeben, die an der Ostfront gekämpft hatte.
Wound Badge in Black. | Verwundetenabzeichen in Schwarz einigen Norweger erhielt diese Auszeichnung.
Edelweiss arm badge worn by Norwegians in *6 SS Div North.* | Edelweiß Arm Abzeichen wurde von Norweger in 6 SS Div Nord verwendet.

Anti-aircraft Badge.

Flak-Abzeichen einige Norweger in Wiking erhielt diese Auszeichnung.

Wound Badge in Gold.

Verwundetenabzeichen in Gold-paar Norweger erhielt diese Auszeichnung.

Police insignia given to Norwegians in *1, 2* and *3 Police Kompani*.

Polizei Abzeichen auf Norweger gegeben in 1, 2 und 3 Police Kompani.

Norwegian National Samling Badge worn on uniforms of the Norwegian volunteers.

Verwendet Norwegischen National Samling-Abzeichen auf Uniformen für die norwegischen Freiwilligen.

Eastern Front Medal.

Winterschlacht im Osten norwegischen Freiwilligen in Wiking und die Legion diese Gote.

Iron Cross 2st Class – approximately 470 Norwegians received this award.

Eisernes Kreuz 2st Klasse ca. 470 Norweger erhielt diese Auszeichnung.

Wiking cuffband worn by Norwegians in *Wiking*.
Wiking Ärmelband von Norwegern in Wiking verwendet.

Den Norske Legion cuffband worn by the Army during training.
Den Norske Legion Ärmelband von Den Norske Legion während des Trainings verwendet.

Frw Legion Norwegen cuffband worn by the *Legion Norwegen* at the front.
Frw Legion Norwegen Ärmelband von der norwegischen Legion an der Front eingesetzt.

Badge that was used by Norwegians in the *Legion Norwegen*.

Arm-Abzeichen, die durch die Norweger in der norwegischen Legion verwendet wurde,.

Enlistment Poster for *Wiking*.

Anwerbung Plakat für Wiking.

Enlistment Poster for *SS-Schijäger-Bataillon 'Norge'*.

Anwerbung Plakat für SS-Schijäger-Bataillon 'Norge'.

Enlistment Poster for *Wiking* and *Legion Norwegen*.

Anwerbung Plakat für Wiking und die norwegische Legion.

Enlistment Poster for *Regiment Norge*.

Anwerbung Plakat für Regiment Norge.

Enlistment Poster for *SS-Schijäger-Bataillon 'Norge'*.

Anwerbung Plakat für SS-Schijäger-Bataillon 'Norge'.

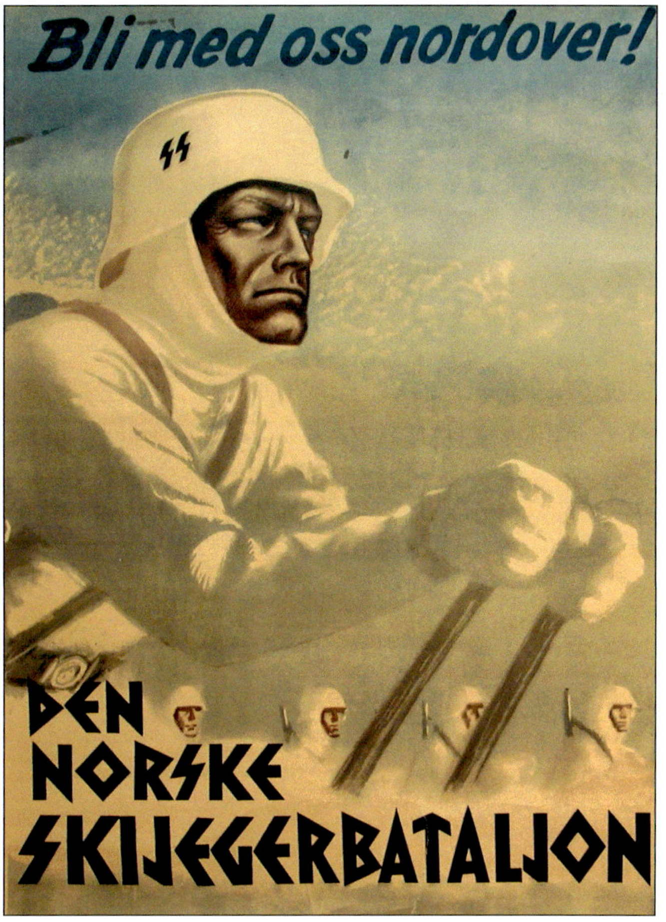

Enlistment Poster for *SS-Schijäger-Bataillon 'Norge'*.

Anwerbung Plakat für SS-Schijäger-Bataillon 'Norge'.

Enlistment Poster for *Legion Norwegen*.

Anwerbung Plakat für norwegische Legion.

Enlistment Poster for *SS-Schijäger-Bataillon 'Norge'*.

Anwerbung Plakat für SS-Schijäger-Bataillon 'Norge'.

Enlistment Poster for *Wiking*.

Anwerbung Plakat für Wiking.

Enlistment Poster for *Legion Norwegen*.

Anwerbung Plakat für norwegische Legion.

Enlistment Poster for *Legion Norwegen*.

Anwerbung Plakat für norwegische Legion.

Enlistment Poster for *Legion Norwegen*.

Anwerbung Plakat für norwegische Legion.

Poster for supporting the Front Fighter office.

Plakat für die Frontkämpfer Büro unterstützen.

1. SS-und Polizeikompanie

The *1. SS-und Polizeikompanie* (*1. Police Company*) was activated in the summer of 1942, made up of volunteers from the police force under the leadership of Jonas Lie. On 1 September 1942, all the volunteers were given a health check at Majorstua school in Oslo, before being sent on to Holmestrand, where they were handed uniforms and equipment. At Holmestrand, the recruits received some basic training in marching and close order. On 4 September 1942, the soldiers were sworn in by Rediess and taken to Skaugum by truck two days later. After parading for Terboven, they were served food and beverages before parading once again for Quisling at Palace Square in Oslo. On 7 September, they left Oslo by boat and arrived in Tallinn on the 12th, spending the night in a barracks until the 14th. The same day, they marched through Tallinn and held a parade for the *Höherer SS-und Polizeiführer* (Higher SS and Police Leader) Möller. At 1200, the train took them east through Narva, arriving at Krasnogvardeysk on September 15 before the journey continued on to Krasnoye Selo.

From here they marched to Duderhof West for further training. Unlike other companies, the unit had not been trained in Germany, but would now receive hands-on training right behind the front from 16 September to 10 October 1942. On 8 October, the company was sent to the frontmost lines of the Leningrad Front, where they took over the positions of *1. Company* of the *Norwegian Legion*. The *1. Police Company* was led by *SS-Hauptsturmführer* Jonas Lie and consisted of three platoons under the leadership of platoon leaders Paul Jørgenvåg, Peder Dahlen and Harald Svenke. When Jonas Lie some time later became deputy commander of the *Norwegian Legion*, *SS-Untersturmführer* Paul Jørgenvåg assumed leadership of the company, with Rasmus Hetland as deputy platoon leader.

From 8 October 1942 until 22 February1943, the company served on the front outside Leningrad. During all this time, they were able to hold their positions and experienced few losses. After holing up in Krasnoye Selo until February 27 1942, the company was sent to Riga by train and from there to Mitau, where they remained until their return to Norway.

The company arrived in Norway on 5 March 1943 and paraded up to Oslo's Palace Square in front of Quisling on the following day. On 7 March, the company paraded for Quisling once again and 100 of its soldiers received the Police Badge of Honour. The men were discharged the same day.

1. SS-und Polizeikompanie

Die 1. SS-und Polizeikompanie wurde im Sommer 1942 aufgestellt und bestand aus Freiwilligen der norwegischen Polizei unter Führung von Jonas Lie. Am 01.09.42 wurden alle Freiwilligen zur ärztlichen Untersuchung an der Majorstua Schule in Oslo geschickt, um danach nach Holmestrand verlegt zu werden, wo Uniformen und Ausrüstung ausgeliefert wurden. In Holmestrand standen Marschieren und Exerzieren auf der Tagesordnung. Am 04.09.42 wurden die Soldaten von Redieß vereidigt, und am 06.09. wurde die Kompanie mit LKWs von Holmestrand nach Skaugum verlegt. Hier defilierte die Kompanie vor Terboven und wurde zum Essen und Trinken eingeladen, bevor sie vor Quisling auf dem Schlossplatz in Oslo noch einmal aufmarschierte. Am 07.09.42 reiste die Kompanie auf dem Seeweg nach Tallinn, wo sie am 12.09.42 ankam. Am 14.09.42 marschierte die Kompanie vor dem Höheren SS-und Polizeiführer Möller durch die Straßen Tallinns. Um 12:00 Uhr wurde die Kompanie mit dem Zug über Narwa nach Krasnogwardeisk geschickt, wo sie am nächsten Tag ankam und weiter nach Krasnoje Selo reiste.

Von hier aus marschierte die Kompanie zur weiteren Ausbildung nach Duderhof West. Im Gegensatz zu anderen Einheiten war die Kompanie nicht in Deutschland ausgebildet worden, erhielt jetzt aber ihre Ausbildung gleich an der Front vom 16.09. bis zum 07.10.42. Am 08.10.42 wurde die Kompanie an die vordersten Linien der Leningrader Front geschickt, und übernahm die Stellungen der 1. Kompanie der SS-Frw.-Legion Norwegen. Die 1. SS-und Polizeikompanie wurde von SS-Hauptsturmführer Jonas Lie geführt und bestand aus drei Zügen unter der Leitung der Zugführer Leg.-Untersturmführer Paul Jørgenvåg, Leg.-Hauptscharführer Peder Dahlen und Leg.-Untersturmführer Harald Svenke. Als Jonas Lie einige Zeit später zum stellvertretenden Legionskommandeur ernannt wurde, übernahm Leg.-Untersturmführer Paul Jørgenvåg die Führung der Kompanie; stellvertretender Zugführer wurde Leg.-Oberscharführer Rasmus Hetland.

Vom 08.10.42 bis zum 22.02.43 lag die Kompanie in ihren Stellungen an der Leningrader Front. Nach einer Ruhepause in Krasnoje Selo bis zum 27.02.43 wurden die Mannschaften mit dem Zug nach Riga geschickt, und von dort aus weiter nach Mitau. Hier blieb die Kompanie bis zur Rückkehr nach Norwegen.

Die Kompanie kam am 05.04.43 in Norwegen an, und defilierte am nächsten Tag vor Quisling auf dem Schlossplatz in Oslo. Am Tag darauf marschierte die Kompanie abermals vor Quisling, wobei 100 Soldaten mit dem Ehrenzeichen der Polizei ausgezeichnet und daraufhin entlassen wurden.

1. SS-und Polizeikompanie – Abreise aus Norwegen | *1. SS-und Polizeikompanie* – departure from Norway

Volunteers from the Norwegian police force who signed up for *1. Police Company*. From the left: four unknowns, Ferdinand Bøe-Simonsen, Johan Lerstein, unknown, Reidar Laugsand and Sigfred Egeland.

Freiwillige aus den Reihen der norwegischen Polizei haben sich zur 1. SS-und Polizeikompanie gemeldet. Von links: vier Unbekannte, Ferdinand Bøe-Simonsen, Johan Lerstein, ein Unbekannter, Reidar Laugsand und Sigfred Egeland.

Volunteers of *1. Police Company* in Holmestrand. Second from the left in the first row is Per Andersen. Standing behind him is training officer Heinrich Petersen.

Freiwillige der 1. SS-und Polizeikompanie in Holmestrand. Erste Reihe von links: Nr. 2. Per Andersen, hinter ihm stehend Heinrich Petersen, der Ausbildungsleiter in Holmestrand.

Marching exercise in Holmestrand.

Marschübung in Holmestrand.

Front row from the left: *Leg.-Unterscharführer* Ole Kjos and *Leg.-Unterscharführer* Ferdinand Bøe-Simonsen. Second row from the left: unknown, Ole Olsen and Trond Kvaale.

Erste Reihe von links: Leg.-Unterscharführer Ole Kjos, Leg.-Unterscharführer Ferdinand Bøe-Simonsen. Zweite Reihe von links: ein Unbekannter, Ole Olsen und Trond Kvaale.

A line-up with all their equipment.

Aufstellung mit kompletter Ausrüstung.

Front row from the left: *Leg.-Unterscharführer* Ole Kjos and *Leg.-Unterscharführer* Ferdinand Bøe-Simonsen. Second row from the left: unknown, Ole Olsen and Trond Kvaale.

Erste Reihe von links: Leg.-Unterscharführer Ole Kjos und Leg.-Unterscharführer Ferdinand Bøe-Simonsen. Zweite Reihe von links: ein Unbekannter, Ole Olsen und Trond Kvaale.

Marching exercise in Holmestrand.

Marschübung in Holmestrand.

The company visits *Reichskommissar* Terboven at Skaugum before leaving for the front. Jonas Lie greets Terboven. In the background are Heinrich Petersen and the *Höherer SS-und Polizeiführer Norwegen, SS-Obergruppenführer* Wilhelm Rediess. The latter was leader of the German police force in Norway during the war.

Die Kompanie besucht Reichskommissar Terboven in Skaugum vor der Abreise zur Front. Jonas Lie und Terboven begrüßen sich. Im Hintergrund Heinrich Petersen und der Höhere SS-und Polizeiführer Norwegen, SS-Obergruppenführer Wilhelm Redieß. Letzterer war oberster Befehlshaber der deutschen Polizei in Norwegen während des Krieges.

Wilhelm Rediess in conversation with the volunteers.

Wilhelm Redieß im Gespräch mit den Freiwilligen.

The volunteers are served beer at Skaugum.

Den Freiwilligen wird in Skaugum Bier ausgeschenkt.

Munin
DET NYE NORGE I BILDER
NR. I • I. ÅRG.
SEPTEMBER 1942
PRIS 50 ØRE

Munin.

Die 1. SS-und Polizeikompanie an der Front | The *1. SS-und Polizeikompanie* at the front

Jonas Lie just behind the front. Here the company received a few days of training before being sent to the first front lines.

Jonas Lie hinter der Front. Hier wurde die Kompanie einige Tage lang ausgebildet, bevor sie in die vordersten Linien geschickt wurde.

Jonas Lie arrives at the front, where he acted as company commander of the *1. Police Company* before becoming deputy Legion commander.

Jonas Lie an der Front, wo er als Kompanieführer eingesetzt wurde. Später wurde er stellvertretender Legionskommandeur.

Three police soldiers in the trenches, with Erling Børstad in the centre.

Drei Ordnungspolizisten im Schützengraben. In der Mitte Erling Børstad.

A wounded soldier is brought to the medical bunker.

Ein verwundeter Soldat wird in den Sani-Bunker gebracht.

General and commander of the 2. *SS-Infanterie-Brigade (mot.), SS-Brigadeführer* Friedrich Jeckeln, visits *1. Police Company.*

General und Kommandeur der 2. SS-Infanterie-Brigade (mot.) SS-Brigadeführer Friedrich Jeckeln zu Besuch bei der 1. SS-und Polizeikompanie.

Leg.-Unterscharführer Alexsander Lange at the front.

Leg.-Unterscharführer Alexsander Lange an der Front.

MG exercise at the front.

MG-Übung an der Front.

Leg.-Untersturmführer Paul Jørgenvåg, here as a Norwegian second lieutenant. He assumed leadership of *1. Police Company* when Lie became deputy commander of the Legion.

Leg.-Untersturmführer Paul Jørgenvåg, hier als norwegischer Leutnant. Er übernahm die Führung der Kompanie als Lie zum stellvertretenden Legionskommandeur befördert wurde.

Per Nesbø was a policeman by profession before volunteering for *1. Police Company*. He is the father of the well-known author Jo Nesbø.

Per Nesbø war von Beruf Polizist, bevor er sich als Freiwilliger zur 1. SS-und Polizeikompanie meldete. Er ist der Vater des bekannten Schriftstellers Jo Nesbø.

Charging MG belts inside a bunker. In the middle is Jan Vinje.

Beim Laden von MG-Gurten in einem Bunker. In der Mitte Jan Vinje.

Jan Vinje in the first front line at Leningrad.

Jan Vinje an der vordersten Front vor Leningrad.

Everything is ready to fend off an attack from the trenches with grenades and sniper rifles.

Alles ist bereit, um aus dem Schützengraben einen Angriff mit Granaten und Scharfschützengewehren zurückzuschlagen.

The *1. Police Company*'s banner behind the front in Krasnoye Selo.

Die Fahne der 1. SS-und Polizeikompanie hinter der Front bei Krasnoje Selo.

Simen Laugsand, right, and an unknown MG gunner.

Von rechts: Simen Laugsand und ein unbekannter MG-Schütze.

Company commander Jonas Lie during a funeral ceremony in Krasnoye Selo.

Kompanieführer Jonas Lie bei einer Beerdigung in Krasnoje Selo.

Two brothers at the front, *Leg.-Unterscharführer* Reidar, left, and Simen Laugsand.

Zwei Brüder an der Front. Von links: Leg.-Unterscharführer Reidar und Simen Laugsand.

Leg.-Unterscharführer Reidar Laugsand, right, in the cold trenches.

Zur Rechten: Leg.-Unterscharführer Reidar Laugsand im kalten Schützengraben.

Two police soldiers on duty in the trenches.

Zwei Polizisten stehen Wache im Schützengraben.

From the left: Bjarne Rosland, Henrik Preus Olsen, unknown and Per Marschhauser.

Von links: Bjarne Rosland, Henrik Preus Olsen, ein Unbekannter und Per Marschhauser.

General Fritz von Scholz during the award ceremony for police soldiers. On the right is Jonas Lie.

Von links: General Fritz von Scholz während der Verleihung von Auszeichnungen an Polizisten. Rechts Jonas Lie.

From the left: Jonas Lie, Fritz von Scholz and Paul Jørgenvåg.

Von links: Jonas Lie, Fritz von Scholz und Paul Jørgenvåg.

Standing and facing the camera, from the left: Ole Olsen, two unknowns, Henrik Preus Olsen and *Leg.-Unterscharführer* Ferdinand Bøe-Simonsen.

Von links, stehend mit dem Geschicht zur Kamera: Ole Olsen, zwei Unbekannte, Henrik Preus Olsen und Leg.-Unterscharführer Ferdinand Bøe-Simonsen.

1. SS-und Polizeikompanie – Heimkehr | *1. SS-und Polizeikompanie* – back in Norway

The return journey to Norway by boat. In the centre is *Leg.-Untersturmführer* Paul Jørgenvåg.

Heimkehr mit dem Schiff nach Norwegen. In der Mitte: Leg.-Untersturmführer Paul Jørgenvåg.

The Police Company marches through the streets of Oslo. First row from the left: *SS-Obersturmführer* Hans Georg Holter, *SS-Sturmbannführer* Jonas Lie and *SS-Obersturmführer* Tor Marstrander.

Die Polizeikompanie marschiert durch die Straßen Oslos. Erste Reihe von links: SS-Obersturmführer Hans Georg Holter, SS-Sturmbannführer Jonas Lie und SS-Obersturmführer Tor Marstrander.

1. Police Company line-up at Palace Square in Oslo.

Die 1. SS-und Polizeikompanie auf dem Schlossplatz in Oslo.

SS-Oberscharführer Rasmus Hetland with the Police Company's guidon.

SS-Oberscharführer Rasmus Hetland mit der Standarte der Kompanie.

From the left: *SS-Untersturmführer* Paul Jørgenvåg, *SS-Unterscharführer* Erling Børstad, *SS-Oberscharführer* Rasmus Hetland and *SS-Unterscharführer* Carl Stephansen.

Von links: SS-Untersturmführer Paul Jørgenvåg, SS-Unterscharführer Erling Børstad, SS-Oberscharführer Rasmus Hetland und SS-Unterscharführer Carl Stephansen.

SS-Sturmbannführer Jonas Lie in front of his company.

SS-Sturmbannführer Jonas Lie vor seiner Kompanie.

SS-Sturmbannführer Jonas Lie greeting Wilhelm Rediess.

SS-Sturmbannführer Jonas Lie und Wilhelm Redieß begrüßen einander.

HEIM -- etter endt tjeneste.

Norges hovedstad hilste sine tapre soldater på en verdig måte. De heimvendte, blandt hvem det også fantes et kompani permitterte legionærer, ble på sin marsj gjennom byen hyldet på det hjerteligste. Norske gjenter smykket de frivillige med årets første blomster.

Wieder zu Hause – nach beendigtem Dienste.

Norwegens Hauptstadt begrüsste ihre tapferen Soldaten auf eine würdige Weise. Die Heimkehrer, unter denen sich auch eine Kompanie beurlaubter Legionäre befand, wurden auf ihrem Marsche durch die Stadt auf das herzlichste empfangen. Norwegische Mädchen schmückten die Freiwilligen mit den ersten Blumen des Jahres.

Munin.

Minister SS-Sturmbannführer Jonas Lie melder av styrken for Føreren.

Minister SS-Sturmbannführer Jonas Lie meldet die vor dem Förer Angetretenen.

Før det I. Politikompani var kommet heim fra Østfronten etter endt tjeneste, lå det 2. Politikompani allerede i treningsleir, for siden å bli satt inn i kampen mot bolsjevismen.

Bevor die 1. Polizeikompanie von der Ostfront nach einem beendeten Dienste heimgekommen war, lag die 2. Polizeikompanie schon im Ausbildungslager, um zur gegebenen Zeit im Kampfe gegen den Bolschewismus eingesetzt zu werden.

Foto: Haug Syvertsen (2), Bjørn Kihle (2), NTB (1).

Det 2. Politikompani tok den 29. mars avskjed med Føreren og ble da overrakt sin fane. Høytideligheten fant sted på Slottsplassen, hvor lederen av det 2. Politikompani, kaptein Hoel, ble overrakt fanen.

Die 2. Polizeikompanie nahm an 29. März Abschied vom Fører, und erhielt dabei ihre Fahne überreicht. Die Feierlichkeit fand auf dem Schlossplatz statt, wo dem Führer der 2. Polizeikompanie, Hauptmann Hoel die Fahne übergeben wurde.

Munin.

From the left: *SS-Sturmbannführer* Jonas Lie, *SS-Obersturmführer* Hans Georg Holter and Minister of Justice Sverre Riisnæs.

Von links: SS-Sturmbannführer Jonas Lie, SS-Obersturmführer Hans Georg Holter und Justizminister Sverre Riisnæs.

From the left: *SS-Obersturmführer* Hans Georg Holter, *SS-Untersturmführer* Paul Jørgenvåg and an unknown officer.

Von links: SS-Obersturmführer Hans Georg Holter, SS-Untersturmführer Paul Jørgenvåg und ein unbekannter Offizier.

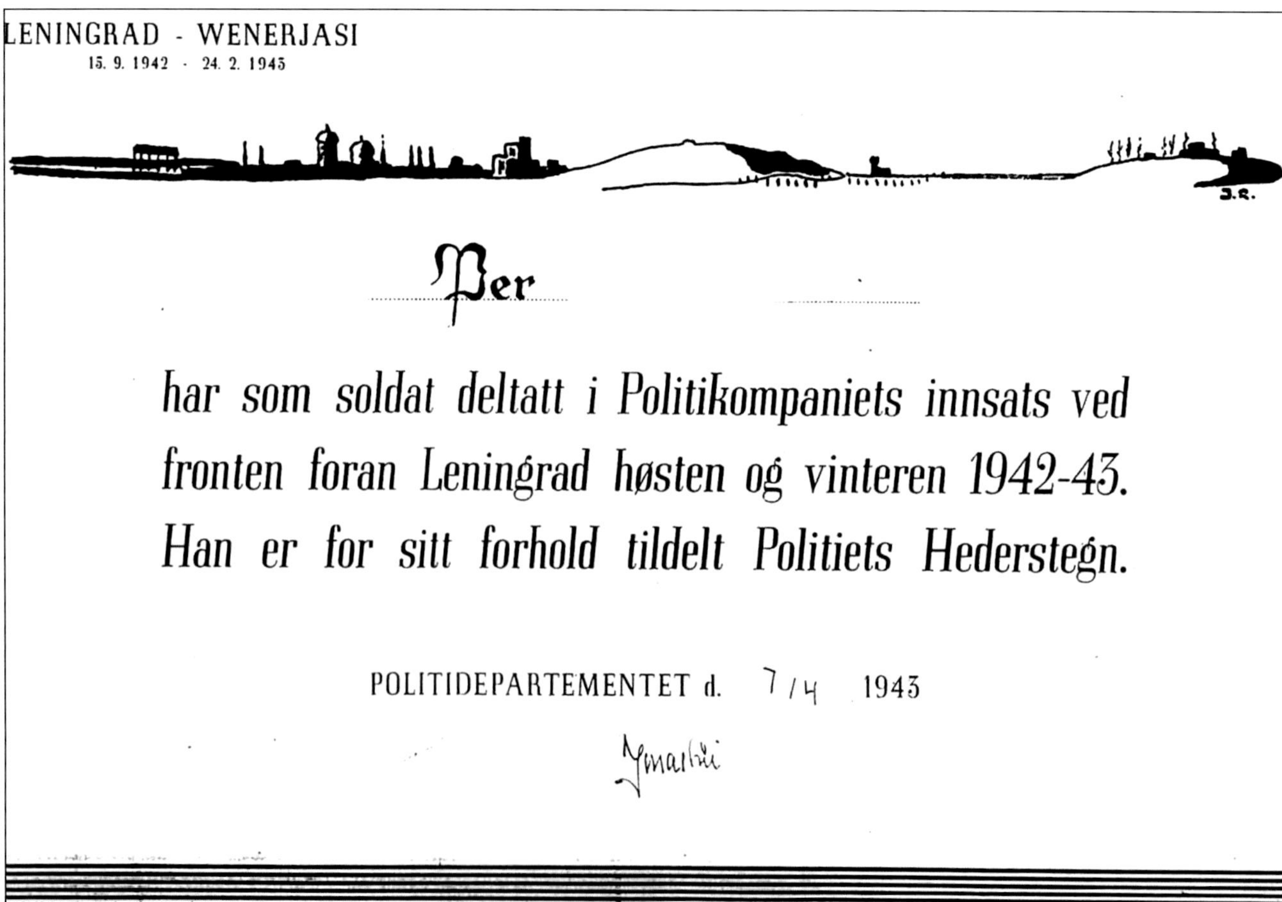

LENINGRAD - WENERJASI
15. 9. 1942 - 24. 2. 1943

Per

har som soldat deltatt i Politikompaniets innsats ved fronten foran Leningrad høsten og vinteren 1942-43. Han er for sitt forhold tildelt Politiets Hederstegn.

POLITIDEPARTEMENTET d. 7/4 1943

Awarding the Police Badge of Honour. One hundred members of the company received this distinction.

Verleihung des Ehrenzeichens der Polizei. 100 Angehörige der Kompanie erhielten diese Auszeichnung.

Per Marschhauser, left, and Kåre Aspås after having been awarded the Police Badge of Honour.

Von links: Per Marschhauser und Kåre Aspås nach der Verleihung des Ehrenzeichens der Polizei.

3

SS-Schikompanie "Norwegen"

Die SS-Schikompanie "Norwegen" wurde im Spätsommer und Herbst 1942 unter Führung von Gust Jonassen aufgestellt. Jonassen war Sportleiter des nationalsozialistischen norwegischen Jugendverbands *Nasjonal Samlings Ungdomsfylking* (NSUF). Die NSUF sah es als ihre wichtigste Aufgabe an, den Verteidigungswillen der Jugend zu fördern. Die Schikompanie war als selbstständige norwegische Einheit geplant, und Rekruten wurden weitgehend aus den Reihen der NSUF angeworben. Die Anwerbung richtete sich vor allem an die sportliche Jugend, insbesondere die, die gute Skiläufer waren. Ungefähr 120 Freiwillige meldeten sich. Die deutschen militärischen Behörden hatten ihr Einverständnis gegeben, die Kompanie kurz nach der militärischen Ausbildung in Finnland einzusetzen. Während sich die Kompanie im Ausbildungslager Sennheim befand, wurde Gust Jonassen zur SS-Junkerschule Tölz kommandiert, um an einem Lehrgang teilzunehmen. Nur die Ausbilder der Kompanie waren Deutsche. Eine der Bedingungen für den Einsatz der norwegischen Einheit war ein hohes skitechnisches Können. Die Kompanie sollte als Divisionseinheit eingesetzt werden und Sonderaufträge ausführen, die hohe Forderungen an gute Skikenntnisse stellten.

Die erste Schulung erfolgte im SS-Ausbildungslager Sennheim. Hier gewannen die norwegischen Freiwilligen, unter ihnen viele gute Boxer und Fußballspieler, sämtliche Sportwettkämpfe. Nach der Ausbildung in Sennheim wurden die Rekruten zum SS-Polizei-Lehr-Bataillon Hellerau in Dresden versetzt. Da die Skiausbildung innerhalb der Waffen-SS ein eigenes, der Polizei unterstelltes Fach war, mussten die Rekruten die Uniform der deutschen Polizei tragen. Die Schikompanie verließ Hellerau am 28. Februar 1943, und die Skiausbildung setzte in Turku, Finnland, fort, unter anderem mit Schießübungen, Anwendung von Tarnausrüstung, usw. Im April 1943 wurde die Kompanie nach Kiestinki geschickt, und von dort aus weiter an die Front. Die Schikompanie wurde nun der 6. SS-Gebirgs-Division "Nord" unterstellt, und schloss sich den Stellungen der Division an der nördlichen Flanke an.

Die Front war keine zusammenhängende Linie. Die Deutschen hatten in einem gewissen Abstand voneinander Stützpunkte errichtet, die als Ausgangspunkt für Fernaufklärungsaufträge dienten. Die Aufgabe der Skikompanie bestand darin, die Verbindung mit anderen Stützpunkten aufrechtzuerhalten, auf russische Truppen zu achten, und die im Niemandsland befindlichen Stützpunkte zu sichern. Von diesen weit vor der Front liegenden Stützpunkten aus unternahm man Aufklärungsaufträge ins Niemandsland, um von dort aus weiter in die russischen Stellungen einzudringen. Die Größe der Jagdkommandos betrug etwa 20–30 Mann, und bei längeren Kommandounternehmen wurde oft die gesamte Kompanie eingesetzt. Die Jagdkommandos benutzten hauptsächlich leichte Waffen, aber auch kleinere Kommandogruppen trugen oft ein MG bei sich. Die Benutzung von Gewehrgranaten war weit verbreitet, und die scharfe Detonation der Waffe konnte im Wald mit Granatwerfern verwechselt werden. Bei einem dieser Jagdkommandos wurde der Kompanieführer Gust Jonassen getötet als er seine Männer versehentlich in das eigene Minenfeld führte. Nach Jonassens Tod übernahm SS-Obersturmführer Otto Holmen die Führung der Kompanie.

Der Fronteinsatz hielt das ganze Frühjahr 1943 an. Im Juni desselben Jahres wurden die Männer beurlaubt und nach Norwegen geschickt, wo die Kompanie damit beauftragt wurde, neue Mannschaften für das SS-Schijäger-Bataillon "Norge" zu gewinnen. Daher reisten sie umher und nahmen an verschiedenen Sportveranstaltungen teil um neue Freiwillige anzuwerben. Einzelne Mitglieder der Kompanie unternahmen Werbereisen im ganzen Land, wobei in einigen dokumentierten Fällen bei der Anwerbung eher von Zwang als von Freiwilligkeit die Rede war. 1943 nahm die Schikompanie am "Tag der SS" teil, wo sie unter anderem die Germanische SS bei einem Fußballspiel 3:1 besiegte. Als das SS-Schijäger-Bataillon aufgestellt wurde, kehrte die Kompanie zurück an die Front, diesmal aber als Grundstock des Bataillons. Die Mannschaften der Kompanie wurden über das ganze Bataillon verteilt. Einige Tage vor dem Kampf um die Stützpunkte Kaprolat und Hasselmann reisten die ursprünglichen Mitglieder der Kompanie zurück nach Norwegen und wurden aus der Waffen-SS entlassen.

3

SS-Schikompanie 'Norwegen'

The *SS-Schikompanie 'Norwegen'* (The Norwegian Ski Company) was activated in the late summer and autumn of 1942 under the leadership of Gust Jonassen. Jonassen was sports leader of the NS youth organisation *Nasjonal Samlings Ungdomsfylking* (NSUF). The NSUF considered its most important task to be the revitalisation of young people's readiness to defend themselves. The Ski Company was to be a separate all-Norwegian unit, and recruitment took largely place within the NSUF's own ranks. It was aimed at young people with a passion for sports, and particularly those with good skiing abilities. Some 120 volunteers enlisted for the company. The German military authorities agreed to deploy the company in Finland immediately following the men's completion of their physical and military training. While the company was stationed at Sennheim training camp, Gust Jonassen was a student at the *SS-Junkerschule* in Bad Tölz before taking over as company commander. Only the instructors were German. One of the conditions for Norwegian participation was the ability to demonstrate superior skiing skills. The company was to be inserted as a divisional unit and carry out special missions requiring good skiers.

The initial training took place at Sennheim training camp in Germany. Here the Norwegian volunteers, among them several capable boxers and football players, won nearly all athletic contests. After Sennheim, the recruits were transferred to the *SS-Polizei-Lehr-Bataillon* (SS police training battalion) at Hellerau, Dresden. Ski training was part of the curriculum of the *Waffen-SS*, supervised by the German police. Therefore, recruits had to wear German police uniforms during their stay at Hellerau. The Ski Company left Hellerau on 28 February 1943. Ski training continued in Turku, Finland, with shooting exercises, camouflage lessons and more. In April 1943, the company was sent to Kiestinki on its way to the front. The Ski Company was now attached to the *SS-Aufklärungs-Abteilung 6* (reconnaissance detachment No. 6) of the *6. SS-Gebirgs-Division 'Nord'*, and assumed its positions on the division's northern wing.

The front was not a continuous line. The Germans had established strongpoints at regular distances. These strongpoints served as a basis for reconnaissance patrols, and the Ski Company, among others, was charged with maintaining communications between the various strongpoints, keeping tabs on Russian patrols and making sure that forward strongpoints – more or less in No Man's Land – were held. From these forward supports, patrols entered No Man's Land to continue their advance towards Russian positions. The size of the commandos varied, but a unit of 20–30 men was common. Often, for longer trips, entire companies were used as command units. The weapons of these *Jagdkommandos* – special operations units or fighting commandos – consisted primarily of light automatic firearms, but even a small command unit frequently brought along at least one machine gun. The use of rifle grenades was widespread, and the sharp blasting sound they made in a forest grove could be confused with mortar fire. During one such patrol, company commander Gust Jonassen was killed when he accidentally led his men into their own minefield. After Jonassen's death, *SS-Obersturmführer* Otto Holmen took over leadership of the Ski Company.

Service on the front continued throughout the spring of 1943. In June 1943, the Ski Company was granted leave of absence and sent back to Norway. After its return, the company was charged with the recruitment of personnel for the *SS-Schijäger-Bataillon 'Norge'*. They travelled from place to place, participating in various sports events and enlisting volunteers. Some of the company's members went on recruiting trips around the country, and documents show that recruitment in certain cases had more to do with coercion rather than voluntary assent. The Ski Company also attended 'SS Day' in 1943, where among other things it won 3–1 in a football match against the Germanic *SS 'Norge'*. When the *SS-Schijäger-Bataillon 'Norge'* was activated, the company returned to the front, but now as the bedrock of the battalion. The original members of the Ski Company were distributed throughout the entire battalion. A few days before the battle for the strongpoints at Kaprolat and Hasselmann, the original members of the Ski Company returned home to Norway, where they were discharged.

SS-Schikompanie "Norwegen" – Abreise aus Norwegen | *SS-Schikompanie 'Norwegen'* – departure from Norway

The *SS-Schikompanie 'Norwegen'* marches through Oslo before leaving for training in Germany.

Die SS-Schikompanie "Norwegen" marschiert durch die Straßen Oslos kurz vor der Abreise zur Weiterausbildung in Deutschland.

The first volunteers of the Ski Company pose for a group photo prior to the departure from Norway.

Die ersten Freiwilligen der Schikompanie stellen sich vor der Abreise aus Norwegen für ein Gruppenbild auf.

SS-Schikompanie "Norwegen" – Ausbildung in Sennheim | *SS-Schikompanie 'Norwegen'* – training in Sennheim

Sports exercise in Sennheim. First row from the left: Karl Aagaard Østvig, Per Vinje, Kåre Westby, Kjell Marthinsen and Hans Nordengen. Second row from the left: Ivar Thorsen, Egil Kyllo, Helge Staff, Thomas Henriksen and Leif Nordgård.

Sportliches Training in Sennheim. Erste Reihe von links: Karl Aagaard Østvig, Per Vinje, Kåre Westby, Kjell Marthinsen und Hans Nordengen. Zweite Reihe von links: Ivar Thorsen, Egil Kyllo, Helge Staff, Thomas Henriksen und Leif Nordgård.

A break during the training in Sennheim.

Eine Ruhepause während der Ausbildung in Sennheim.

Marching to Hartmannsweilerkopf near Sennheim.

Marsch zum Hartmannsweilerkopf in der Nähe von Sennheim.

Departure from Sennheim. This is one of the last photographs taken before the men received their police uniforms in Dresden.

Abreise von Sennheim. Eines der letzten Fotos vor der Auslieferung von Uniformen der Ordnungspolizei in Dresden.

SS-Schikompanie "Norwegen" – Ausbildung in Dresden | *SS-Schikompanie 'Norwegen'* – training in Dresden

The Ski Company arrives in Dresden.

Die Schikompanie nach der Ankunft in Dresden.

From the left: Hans Nordengen, unknown and Øivind Ringen wearing new police uniforms.

Von links: Hans Nordengen, ein Unbekannter und Øivind Ringen mit neuen Polizeiuniformen.

Line-up together with a German instructor.

Aufstellung zusammen mit einem deutschen Ausbilder.

Field training in Dresden.

Feldübung in Dresden.

Volunteers from the Ski Company during a skiing competition in Seefeld. Since all the Norwegians were good skiers, they performed well in these competitions. From the left: Kristian Busterud, Ove Eriksen, Helge Staff, Hans Nordengen, Rolf Jacobsen, Aleksander Herseth and Magne Rødvik.

Freiwillige der Schikompanie nehmen an einem Skiwettbewerb in Seefeld teil. Da sämtliche Norweger gute Skiläufer waren, erzielten sie äußerst gute Resultate bei diesen Wettbewerben. Von links: Kristian Busterud, Ove Eriksen, Helge Staff, Hans Nordengen, Rolf Jacobsen, Aleksander Herseth und Magne Rødvik.

Christmas celebration for the Ski Company in Dresden, with gifts and guests from Norway.

Weihnachtsfeier der Schikompanie in Dresden mit Geschenken und Gästen aus Norwegen.

From the left: Egil Habberstad, Rolf Gregersen, Kjell Marthinsen and Håkon Windingstad.

Von links: Egil Habberstad, Rolf Gregersen, Kjell Marthinsen und Håkon Windingstad.

SS-Schikompanie "Norwegen" an der Front | *SS-Schikompanie 'Norwegen'* at the front

SS-Obersturmführer Gust Jonassen, left, greeting General Matthias Kleinheisterkamp, commander of the *6. SS-Gebirgs-Division 'Nord'*, to which the *SS-Schikompanie 'Norwegen'* was attached.

Von links: SS-Obersturmführer Gust Jonassen begrüßt General Matthias Kleinheisterkamp, Divisionskommandeur der 6. SS-Gebirgs-Division "Nord", der die Schikompanie unterstellt war.

Company commander *SS-Obersturmführer* Gust Jonassen, left, and platoon leader Helge Staff.

Von links: Kompanieführer SS-Obersturmführer Gust Jonassen und Zugführer Helge Staff.

Preparing skis in front of the bunker referred to as 'Oslo'.

Vorbereitung von Skiern außerhalb des Bunkers der "Oslo" genannt wurde.

Four Schijäger ready for patrol.

Vier Schijäger parat für den Auftrag.

On patrol along corduroy, or log roads before reaching more rugged terrain.

Eine Patrouille auf Bohlenwegen, die in die unwegsame Landschaft führen.

Jan Strømsnes on patrol, wearing a camouflage helmet cover over his skiing cap.

Jan Strømsnes bei einem Auftrag mit Tarnüberzug über der Skimütze.

From the left: war correspondent Osvald Olsen, platoon leader Helge Staff, war correspondent Ulf Tur and deputy company commander Otto Holmen.

Von links: Kriegsberichter Osvald Olsen, Zugführer Helge Staff, Kriegsberichter Ulf Tur und stellvertretender Kompanieführer Otto Holmen.

Platoon leader Helge Staff on patrol.

Zugführer Helge Staff bei einer Aufklärungsfahrt.

The German company sergeant in conversation with visiting war correspondent Ulf Tur.

Der deutsche Kompaniefeldwebel im Gespräch mit Kriegsberichter Ulf Tur, der zu Besuch bei der Kompanie war.

Company commander *SS-Obersturmführer* Gust Jonassen during a lunch break at the front.

Kompanieführer SS-Obersturmführer Gust Jonassen während einer Essenspause an der Front.

The company is filmed by war correspondents during a patrol.

Die Kompanie wird von Kriegsberichtern während eines Aufklärungsauftrags gefilmt.

Company commander *SS-Obersturmführer* Gust Jonassen was killed during the return march when the company strayed into its own minefield. The picture shows his grave in the division's graveyard at Mayweg.

Kompanieführer SS-Obersturmführer Gust Jonassen wurde im eigenen Minenfeld getötet. Hier sein Grab auf dem Friedhof der Division am Mayweg.

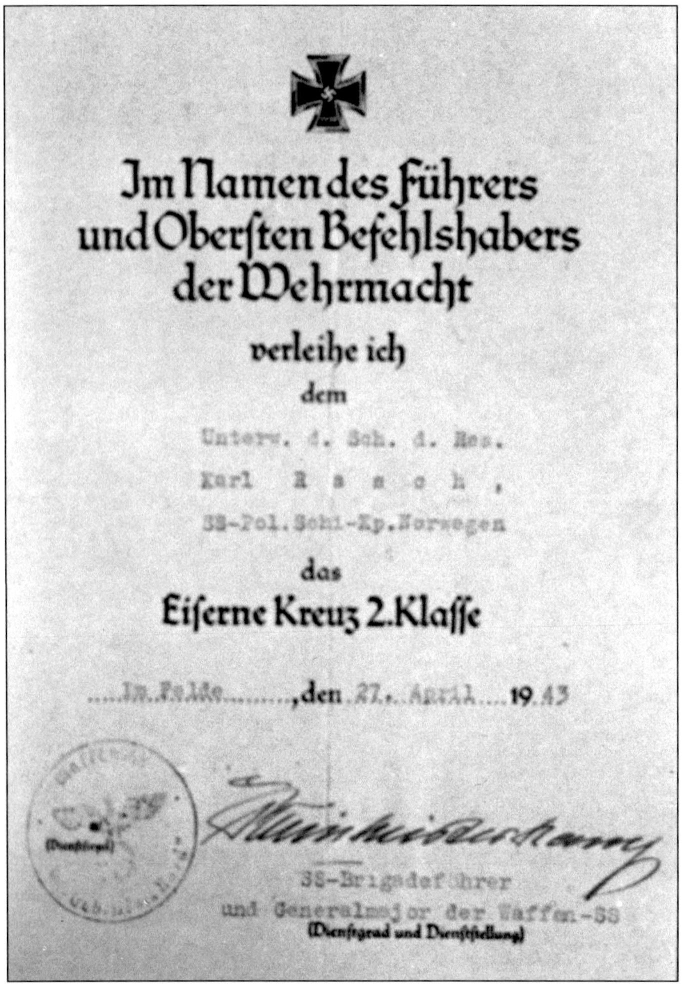

Im Namen des Führers
und Obersten Befehlshabers
der Wehrmacht

verleihe ich
dem

Unterw. d. Sch. d. Res.
Karl R a s c h ,
SS-Pol. Schi-Kp. Norwegen

das
Eiserne Kreuz 2. Klasse

....Im Felde........, den 27. April....19 43

(Dienstsiegel)

SS-Brigadeführer
und Generalmajor der Waffen-SS
(Dienstgrad und Dienststellung)

Karl Rasch-Haugen received the Iron Cross 2nd Class for his efforts in Karelia. After the war he joined the *1. Company* of the French Foreign Legion, *13. DBLE*, and fought in Indochina, where he was seriously wounded in February 1947. Here he was awarded the French War Cross.

Karl Rasch-Haugen wurde für seinen Einsatz in Karelien mit dem Eisernen Kreuz 2. Klasse ausgezeichnet. Nach dem Krieg schloss er sich als Kriegsgefangener der 1. Kompanie, 13. DBLE, der Französischen Fremdenlegion an und kämpfte in Indochina, wo er im Februar 1947 schwer verwundet wurde. Er wurde mit dem französichen Kriegskreuz ausgezeichnet.

When Gust Jonassen was killed, *SS-Obersturmführer* Otto Holmen took over the company and continued as company commander for the remainder of the time at the front.

Als Gust Jonassen fiel, übernahm SS-Obersturmführer Otto Holmen die Führung der Kompanie für die restliche Zeit an der Front.

A group lining up for the photographer.

Eine Gruppe hat sich für den Fotografen aufgestellt.

Kneeling in front is an unknown front line fighter. Front row from the left: Aleksander Herseth, Egil Kyllo and Martin Løvlien. Second row from the left: Olaf Weberg, Marius Sagbakken, Ove Eriksen and Asbjørn Narmo.

Vorne kniend ein unbekannter Frontkämpfer. Erste Reihe von links: Aleksander Herseth, Egil Kyllo und Martin Løvlien. Zweite Reihe von links: Olaf Weberg, Marius Sagbakken, Ove Eriksen und Asbjørn Narmo.

From the left: Syver Stormoen, Kåre Ringen, Øivind Ringen, Magne Rødvik, Karl Rasch-Haugen, Hans Nordengen and Øystein Kristensen.

Von links: Syver Stormone, Kåre Ringen, Øivind Ringen, Magne Rødvik, Karl Rasch-Haugen, Hans Nordengen und Øystein Kristensen.

Company supplies were transported to forward positions by horse.

Verpflegung für die Kompanie wurde mit Pferden an die Stellungen gebracht.

Platoon leader Rolf Jacobsen had a background as an officer in the Norwegian Army.

Zugführer Rolf Jacobsen war Offizier beim früheren norwegischen Heer gewesen.

Kåre Ringen had three brothers who were front line fighters as well, and four relatives who had volunteered. At one point, seven of them were together in the same unit in Karelia.

Kåre Ringen hatte drei Brüder, die auch Frontkämpfer waren, und vier weitere Verwandte, die sich freiwillig gemeldet hatten. Eine Zeit lang waren sieben von ihnen in der gleichen Abteilung in Karelien.

Rolf W. Johannesen in front of one of the company's makeshift positions.

Rolf W. Joahnnesen vor einer der gezimmerten Stellungen der Kompanie.

General Matthias Kleinheisterkamp was commander of the *6. SS-Division 'Nord'*. He is pictured on his birthday while the Ski Company sings for him.

General Matthias Kleinheisterkamp war Kommandeur der 6. SS-Division "Nord". Hier eine Aufnahme von seinem Geburtstag mit Gesang der Schikompanie.

Minister Axel Stang, left, and Minister Jonas Lie visiting the company in Karelia.

Von links: Minister Axel Stang und Minister Jonas Lie zu Besuch be der Kompanie in Karelien.

From the left: Wilhelm Rediess, Matthias Kleinheisterkamp, Axel Stang and Jonas Lie inspecting the company.

Von links: Wilhelm Redieß, Matthias Kleinheisterkamp, Axel Stang und Jonas Lie bei der Besichtigung der Kompanie.

Wilhelm Rediess, left, and Matthias Kleinheisterkamp in conversation.

Von links: Wilhelm Redieß und Matthias Kleinheisterkamp im Gespräch.

Minister Jonas Lie addresses the volunteers.

Minister Jonas Lie hält eine Rede an die Freiwilligen.

The volunteers made Karelian walking canes during quiet moments at the front.

Wenn es ruhig an der Front war, fertigten die Freiwilligen Karelische Wanderstöcke an.

On patrol in the spring of 1943.

Aufklärungsauftrag, Frühjahr 1943.

The company also used assault boats to navigate the many small lakes in the area.

Die Kompanie benutzte auch Sturmboote, um die vielen kleinen Seen im Gebiet zu überqueren.

Before returning to Norway, the company bids farewell to its fallen comrades at the division's graveyard at Mayweg.

Vor dem Abmarsch nach Norwegen nimmt die Kompanie Abschied von ihren Gefallenen am Friedhof Mayweg.

Company commander *SS-Obersturmführer* Otto Holmen led the funeral ceremony.

Kompanieführer SS-Obersturmführer Otto Holmen bei der Trauerfeier.

Train ride back to Norway.

Zugfahrt zurück nach Norwegen.

Company commander *SS-Obersturmführer* Otto Holmen, left, during the journey home to Norway.

Links: Kompanieführer SS-Obersturmführer Otto Holmen während der Heimfahrt nach Norwegen.

SS-Schikompanie "Norwegen" – Heimkehr | *SS-Schikompanie 'Norwegen'* – back in Norway

The company returned to Oslo and was issued SS uniforms once again. From the left: *SS-Oberscharführer* Helge Staff, *SS-Unterscharführer* Karl Rasch-Haugen, unknown and *SS-Unterscharführer* Magne Rødvik. All three who are named later attended the officer school in Bad Tölz, but only Staff completed his studies.

Die Kompanie ist zurück in Oslo, wo erneut Waffen-SS-Uniformen ausgehändigt werden. Von links: SS-Oberscharführer Helge Staff, SS-Unterscharführer Karl Rasch-Haugen, ein Unbekannter und SS-Unterscharführer Magne Rødvik. Die drei letztgenannten wurden an die SS-Junkerschule in Bad Tölz kommandiert, aber nur Staff schloss den Lehrgang ab.

SS-Unterscharführer Odd Nordmann from Hedmark County in Norway. Most of the pictures of the company were taken by him.

SS-Unterscharführer Odd Nordmann aus der norwegischen Provinz Hedmark zurück in der Heimat. Die meisten Fotos der Kompanie wurden von ihm aufgenommen.

SS-Oberscharführer Rolf Jacobsen while the company files past Quisling at Palace Square in Oslo.

SS-Oberscharführer Rolf Jacobsen beim Defilieren der Kompanie vor Quisling auf dem Schlossplatz in Oslo.

På vakt mot øst — Auf der Wacht gegen Osten

Fra FINNLAND til NORGE

Det norske skiløperkompani heime på permisjon

Von Finnland nach Norwegen.

Die norwegische Schiläuferkompanie erhielt Heimaturlaub

Under: Føreren inspiserer de frivillige
Unten: Der Förer besichtigt die Freiwilligen

Nederst tilv.: Forbimarsj for Føreren
Unterst: Vorbeimarsch vor dem Förer

Foto: NTB. (3) ϟϟ-PK. (3)

Over: En soldats første plikt er å holde sine våpen i orden

Oben: Erste Pflicht eines jeden Soldaten ist es, seine Waffen in Ordnung zu halten

Tilh.: Sjefen for det norske skikompani, ϟϟ-Obersturmführer Gust Jonassen som fant heltedøden i Lapplands skoger
Rechts: Der Chef der norwegischen Schiläuferkampanie, ϟϟ-Obersturmführer Gust Jonassen, der in Lapplands Wäldern den Heldentod fand

Under: Fra festen for frontkjemperne. Fra venstre sees: Minister Axel Stang, NS-Fører, ϟϟ-Obersturmbannführer Neumann og minister Jonas Lie

Unten: Vom Festabend für die Frontkämpfer. Links sieht man neben dem NS-Förer Axel Stang, rechts ϟϟ-Obersturmbannführer Neumann und Minister Jonas Lie

Munin.

During 'SS day' in 1943, the Ski Company played football against the *Germanische SS Norwegen*, winning 2–1. Afterwards, the company's members travelled around Norway to recruit new volunteers for what later would become the *Schijäger Battalion*.

Am "Tag der SS" spielte die Schikompanie Fußball gegen die Germanische SS Norwegen, und gewann 2:1. Danach reisten die Angehörigen der Kompanie durch ganz Norwegen, um neue Soldaten anzuwerben.

4

2. SS-und Polizeikompanie

Die Kompanie, insgesamt etwa 160 Mann, wurde Februar/März 1943 aufgestellt. Die Ausbildung begann in Holmestrand, setzte in Sennheim fort, und wurde in Grafenwöhr-Auerbach in Bayern abgeschlossen. Deutschen Quellen zufolge war die Kompanie nur für leichte Waffen ausgebildet. Anfangs leitete SS-Hauptsturmführer Reidar Egil Hoel die Kompanie mit den SS-Obersturmführern Erling Waksvik und Othar Lislegaard, und SS-Untersturmführer Eystein Bech als Zugführer. Hoel und Lislegaard wurden zur Division "Nordland" versetzt. Hoel kam als Kompanieführer zur16. Kompanie, der Pionierkompanie des SS-Pz.Gren.Rgts. 23 "Norge", und Lislegaard wurde zum SS-Pz.Artillerie-Regiment 11 der Division "Nordland" versetzt. Während der Ausbildung in Auerbach versuchten die Deutschen, die Kompanie in das SS-Pz.Gren.Rgt 23 "Norge" einzugliedern, doch auf politischen Druck aus Norwegen hin genehmigte General Steiner, die Kompanie im Herbst 1943 nach Finnland verlegen zu lassen. Kompanieführer war jetzt SS-Hauptsturmführer Erling Waksvik. In Kiestinki wurde die 2. SS-und Polizeikompanie, wie früher schon die Schikompanie, dem III. Bataillon des SS-Gebirgs-Jäger-Regiments 11 "Reinhardt Heydrich", 6. SS-Geb.Div. "Nord", unterstellt, und später der SS-Geb.Aufklärungs-Abteilung 6. Der Stamm der Kompanie bestand aus norwegischen Unteroffizieren – Veteranen der Division "Wiking" – und einzelnen Angehörigen der norwegischen Polizei. Die meisten der Soldaten kamen aus den Reihen der norwegischen Polizei. Mehrere Leiter der norwegischen *Hirden* hatten sich als Freiwillige gemeldet, darunter auch hohe Parteimitglieder wie Gauleiter Anders Brokstad aus Møre im nördlichen Teil West-Norwegens, Regimentsführer der *Hirden* Bjørn Falchenberg, und Regimentsführer Arne Waage. Auch Justizminister Sverre Riisnæs und Karl Marthinsen, Leiter der norwegischen Staatspolizei und der *Hirden*, hatten sich als freiwillige SS-Schützen gemeldet. Die zwei letzteren waren von Ministerpräsident Vidkun Quisling beurlaubt worden, um als Freiwillige an der Front in Finnland kämpfen zu können. Doch kurze Zeit nach der Ankunft in Finnland, mit Weihnachtspäckchen für die Kompanie, wurden beide am 22. Dezember 1943 auf Grund von Unruhen bei der norwegischen Polizei wieder zurück nach Norwegen berufen.

Die Kompanie wurde auf dem Seeweg von Stettin nach Turku in Finnland befördert. Auf dem Weg zur Front per LKW erlitt die Kompanie die ersten Verluste. Als einer der LKWs von russischen Flugzeugen bombardiert wurde, verlor ein Soldat das Leben. Ein weiterer wurde schwer verwundet und starb später an seinen Verletzungen. In Kiestinki wurde die Kompanie dem III. Bataillon des SS-Geb.Jäger.Rgts. 11 "Reinhard Heydrich" unterstellt, wobei ein deutscher SS-Hauptsturmführer als Berater diente. Später wurde die 2. SS-und Polizeikompanie dem Leiter der SS-Aufklärungs-Abteilung 6 der Division, SS-Sturmbannführer Richard Benner, unterstellt.

Die beiden Kompanieführer Waksvik und Reppen hatten bei den norwegischen Soldaten einen äußerst schlechten Ruf. Waksvik war selten an der Front. Er war oft krank und befand sich meistens hinter der Front beim Stab der 6. SS-Geb.Div. "Nord". Während seiner Zeit als Kompanieführer hatte er den Soldaten viel versprochen, aber nur wenig gehalten – im Grunde war es SS-Oberscharführer Thoralf Gjølberg, der die Kompanie führte.

Während die Kompanie sich in ihrer Stellung bei Schasjajek befand, wurden mehrere Kompaniemitglieder zu anderen Abteilungen der Division als Ski-Ausbilder versetzt.

Im Winter 1943/44 und Frühjahr 1944 war die Kompanie an der Front eingesetzt, und löste Anfang 1944 zwei deutsche Kompanien an den Stützpunkten Schapkosero und Mendewara ab. Ein Zug der 2. SS-und Polizeikompanie unter Führung von SS-Untersturmführer Eystein Bech traf im Februar 1944 am Stützpunkt Schapkosero ein. Schapkosero lag 10 Kilometer hinter der linken Flanke des Divisionsabschnitts. Ein weiterer Zug unter der Leitung von SS-Oberscharführer Thoralf Gjølberg wurde weiter nördlich am Stützpunkt Mendewara, dem höchsten Hügel im näheren Umfeld, eingesetzt. An beiden Stützpunkten waren Bunker und einfache Abwehrstellungen gebaut worden. Auf Grund der isolierten Lage dieser Stellungen mussten die Männer einen harten Winter mit vielen Jagdkommandos durchleben.

Am 7. März 1944 griffen die Russen den norwegische Stützpunkt Schapkosero mit einem verstärkten Bataillon von insgesamt 1200 Mann an. Die Norweger hatten lediglich 52 Mann, einschließlich einer Handvoll deutscher MG-Schützen, und standen folglich einer mehr als zwanzigfachen Übermacht gegenüber. SS-Untersturmführer Eystein Bech wurde von Granatsplittern und einer MG-Garbe in den Bauch getroffen, als er auf der Bunkerdecke

4

2. SS-und Polizeikompanie

The *2. Police Company*, consisting of some 160 men, was activated in February/March 1943. Training began in Holmestrand, continuing on to Sennheim and finally Grafenwöhr-Auerbach in Bavaria. According to German sources, the company only carried light weapons. Initially, *SS-Hauptsturmführer* Reidar Egil Hoel commanded the company, with *SS-Obersturmführer* Othar Lislegaard, *SS-Obersturmführer* Erling Waksvik and *SS-Untersturmführer* Eystein Bech as platoon leaders. Hoel and Lislegaard were transferred to *Division 'Nordland'*. Hoel joined the *23. SS-Panzergrenadier-Regiment 'Norge'* as commander of *16. Company*, the Regiment's reconnaissance unit. Lislegaard joined *Artillerie-Regiment 11*, the artillery unit of *Division 'Nordland'*. During the training period, attempts were made to transfer the entire company to *Regiment 'Norge'*. After considerable political pressure from Norway, General Felix Steiner agreed to move the company to Finland in the autumn of 1943. *SS-Hauptsturmführer* Erling Waksvik became the new company commander. In Kiestinki, the *2. Police Company* – like the Ski Company – was first attached to the *3. Battalion* of the *SS-Gebirgs-Jäger-Regiment 11 'Reinhard Heydrich'*, *6. SS-Gebirgs-Division 'Nord'*, and later to the division's *SS-Aufklärungs-Abteilung 6* (reconnaissance battalion No. 6). The core of the company's NCOs was composed of Norwegian veterans from *Division 'Wiking'* and a few police officers, while most of the soldiers came from the police. Some leaders from the Norwegian *Hirden* joined as volunteers, including senior party members such as *fylkesleder* (local county leader) Anders Brokstad from the *Møre NS*, and regiment leaders Bjørn Falchenberg and Arne Waage. Minister of Justice Sverre Riisnæs and Karl Marthinsen, commander of the State Police and the *Hirden*, also volunteered as common soldiers. The latter two had been granted leave of absence by Minister-President Vidkun Quisling in order to fight in Finland. However, shortly after their arrival in Finland on 22 December 1943 with Christmas presents for the company, they were called home to Norway due to unrest among the police._

The company was shipped from Szczecin (Stettin) to Turku in Finland. While travelling to the front in trucks, the company suffered its first losses. When one of the trucks was bombed, a soldier was killed while another died of his injuries some time later. Upon their arrival in Kiestinki, the company was attached to the *3. Battalion* of the *SS-Gebirgs-Jäger-Regiment 11 'Reinhard Heydrich'*, where a German *SS-Haupsturmführer* acted as advisor (Berater) in order to assist the company in Finland. Following this, the *2. Police* Company was placed under the command of *SS-Sturmbannführer* Richard Benner, leader of the division's *SS-Aufklärungs-Abteilung 6* (reconnaissance battalion No. 6).

Company commanders Waksvik and Reppen were thoroughly disliked by the soldiers of the company. Waksvik practically never made it to the front, being mostly sick and remaining at staff HQ of *6./Nord*. During his time as company commander, Reppen had made major promises but accomplished little of what he had assured the soldiers, and it was *SS-Oberscharführer* Thoralf Gjølberg who essentially commanded the company.

While the unit was stationed at Schasajek, several of the men were transferred to other divisional units as skiing instructors._

In the winter of 1943/44 and spring of 1944, the *2. Police Company* was stationed at the front. At the beginning of 1944, the company was ordered to replace two German units that were holding the strongpoints Shapkozero and Gora Mende-Vara. A platoon from the Police Company, commanded by *SS-Untersturmführer* Eystein Bech, arrived at Shapkozero in February 1944. Shapkozero was a stronghold some 10 kilometres (six miles) behind the division's left wing. Another platoon, under the command of *SS-Oberscharführer* Thoralf Gjølberg, was sent further north to strongpoint Gora Mende-Vara, the highest of the low hills for miles around. Both strongpoints had bunkers and simple defences. Because of their exposed and isolated position, the men went through a rough winter with many fighting commandos.

On 7 March 1944, the Russians attacked the Norwegian strongpoint Shapkozero with a reinforced battalion of approximately 1,200 men. The Norwegian unit consisted of 52 men, including a number of German machine-gunners, and faced a force more than 20 times their own size. *SS-Untersturmführer* Eystein Bech was struck by a piece of shrapnel and hit in the stomach by a machine-gun burst. Standing on top of the combat bunker and shooting from the hip with a machine gun, he was hit in the stomach and side. Bech suffered a painful death at

stand und ein MG aus der Hüfte schoss. Er starb einen qualvollen Tod. Nach dem Angriff kommandierte SS-Hauptsturmführer Asbjørn Reppen eine Zeit lang die Kompanie, bis Waksvik abermals die Führung im Anschluss an die Rückkehr nach Norwegen übernahm.

Als der Vertrag der Freiwilligen ausgelaufen war, wurde die 2. SS-und Polizeikompanie Ende April 1944 aus der Front zurückgezogen. Die Heimkehr wurde am 17. Mai 1944 auf dem Schlossplatz in Oslo mit einer Parade gefeiert. Hier hielt Ministerpräsident Quisling eine Dankesrede an die Kompanie. Noch am selben Tag wurden etwa 100 Mann der Kompanie von Minister Jonas Lie mit dem Ehrenzeichen der Polizei ausgezeichnet, und daraufhin aus der Waffen-SS entlassen. Die meisten kehrten zurück zu ihrem Arbeitsplatz bei der Polizei.

Shapkozero. Following the attack, *SS-Hauptsturmführer* Asbjørn Reppen took over the company until Waksvik once again assumed command upon their return to Norway.

Once the volunteers' contract period had expired, the *2. Norwegian Volunteer Police Company* was called back from the front at the end of April 1944. On 17 May 1944, their homecoming was celebrated with a parade on Palace Square in Oslo, and Minister-President Quisling gave a speech to thank members of the company for their effort. Later that day, about 100 men were awarded the Police Badge of Honour by Minister Jonas Lie before being discharged. Most of the company's soldiers later returned to their positions in the police force.

2. SS-und Polizeikompanie – Abmarsch aus Norwegen | *2. SS-und Polizeikompanie* – departure from Norway

The *2. Police Company* during training in Holmestrand, shortly before leaving for Sennheim.

Die 2. SS-und Polizeikompanie bei der Ausbildung in Holmestrand, kurz vor dem Abmarsch nach Sennheim.

The *2. Police Company* marching before its departure from Norway. At the head is company commander Erling Waksvik, followed by Thoralf Gjølberg with the company's guidon.

Die 2. SS-und Polieikompanie marschiert vor der Abfahrt aus Norwegen. Vorne der Kompanieführer Erling Waksvik, gefolgt von Thoralf Gjølberg mit der Standarte der Kompanie.

2. SS-und Polizeikompanie – Ausbildung in Sennheim | *2. SS-und Polizeikompanie* – training in Sennheim

Three volunteers in Sennheim. In the middle is *SS-Unterscharführer* Thoralf Gjølberg, a veteran of *Division 'Wiking'*.

Drei Freiwillige in Sennheim. In der Mitte SS-Unterscharführer Thoralf Gjølberg, ein Veteran der Division "Wiking".

The company filing out in Sennheim.

Die Kompanie beim Ausmarsch in Sennheim.

Camouflage training in Sennheim.

Tarnübung in Sennheim.

Obstacle course in Sennheim. The *2. Police Company* won most of the competitions.

Hindernisstrecke in Sennheim. Die 2. SS-und Polizeikompanie gewann die meisten Wettbewerbe.

Soldiers on an outing during one of their few days of leave. They often used the opportunity to visit a place that sold beer.

Soldaten bei einem ihrer wenigen dienstfreien Ausflüge. Oft nutzten sie die Gelegenheit, um sich Bier zu kaufen.

Front row from the left: Jørgen Johannessen, Gunnar Verpe and Gunnar Haug. Second row from the left: Magne Martinsen, Kåre Berger and Odd Blom Sandvik. All but Magne Martinsen were veterans of *Division 'Wiking'* and became NCOs in the company.

Erste Reihe von links: Jørgen Johannessen, Gunnar Verpe und Gunnar Haug. Zweite Reihe von links: Magne Martinsen, Kåre Berger und Odd Blom Sandvik. Außer Magne Martinsen waren alle Veteranen der Division "Wiking", und wurden zu Unteroffizieren der Kompanie befördert.

Gunnar Haug runs an obstacle course in Sennheim.

Gunnar Haug auf der Hindernisstrecke in Sennheim.

Odd Blom Sandvik at former First World War emplacements near Sennheim.

Odd Blom Sandvik in alten Stellungen aus dem 1. Weltkrieg in der Nähe von Sennheim.

2. SS-und Polizeikompanie – Ausbildung in Grafenwöhr | *2. SS-und Polizeikompanie* – training in Grafenwöhr

Eystein Bech in front of the *2. Police Company* in Grafenwöhr. Here, attempts were made to absorb the company into *Regiment 'Norge'*, but after many complaints, the company was permitted to leave for Finland.

Eystein Bech vor der 2. SS-und Polizeikompanie in Grafenwöhr. Hier bemühte man sich, die Kompanie dem Regiment "Norge" anzuschließen, aber da dies viel Unzufriedenheit hervorrief, kam die Kompanie an die Front in Finnland.

Tjostolf Moland in Grafenwöhr. He was one of the few to receive the Iron Cross 2nd Class for his efforts in the company.

Tjostolf Moland in Grafenwöhr. Er war einer der wenigen, die das Eiserne Kreuz 2. Klasse für ihren Einsatz in der Kompanie erhielten.

Ove Semb was one of three company medics. He had almost completed his training as a doctor when he joined the *2. Police Company*.

Ove Semb war einer von drei Kompanie-Sanitätern. Er war nahezu fertig mit seiner Ausbildung als Arzt, als er sich zur 2. SS-und Poliziekompanie meldete.

Physician Ørnulf Engen died while treating wounded soldiers, when Russian troops stormed the bunker and shot him.

Der Arzt Ørnulf Engen behandelte die Verwundeten, als er von russischen Soldaten im Bunker erschossen wurde.

The company ready for the departure for Karelia.

Die Kompanie ist klar zum Abmarsch nach Karelien.

2. SS-und Polizeikompanie an der Front | *2. SS-und Polizeikompanie* at the front

Floats were used for transportation across the many lakes. Due to Russian aircraft in the area, this was an extremely dangerous mode of transport.

Ein Teil des Transports ging per Boot über die Seen, eine äußerst gefährliche Situation aufgrund von russichen Flugzeugen.

While transporting supplies to the front by truck, the company was attacked by Russian planes. Two soldiers were killed and several wounded. Platoon leader *SS-Untersturmführer* Eystein Bech performed the funeral.

Beim LKW-Transport an die Front wurde die Kompanie von zwei russischen Flugzeugen angegriffen. Zwei Mann wurden getötet und mehrere verwundet. Der Zugführer SS-Untersturmführer Eystein Bech führte die Beerdigung am Friedhof.

Platoon leader *SS-Oberscharführer* Thoralf Gjølberg gives instructions before a scout squad begins to move towards the Russian positions.

Zugführer SS-Oberscharführer Thoralf Gjølberg gibt Anweisungen bevor ein Spähtrupp auf russische Stellungen marschiert.

A scout squad during a smoke break in the Karelian forests.

Ein Spähtrupp bei der Raucherpause in den karelischen Wäldern.

Platoon leader *SS-Oberscharführer* Thoralf Gjølberg in front of his men during a reconnaissance patrol. He is carrying a captured Russian machine gun of type PPSh.

Zugführer SS-Oberscharführer Thoralf Gjølberg mit seinen Männern bei einem Spähtrupp. Bei sich hat er eine erbeutete russische Maschinenpistole vom Typ PPSch.

Platoon leader Thoralf Gjølberg, right, and section leader *SS-Unterscharführer* Odd Blom Sandvik. Both were veterans of *Division 'Wiking'*.

Von rechts: Zugführer Thoralf Gjølberg und Gruppenführer SS-Unterscharführer Odd Blom Sandvik. Beide waren Veteranen der Division "Wiking".

In a bunker door near Kiestinki. Seated to the left is Karl Tangen.

An einer Bunkertür in der Nähe von Kiestinki. Links sitzend: Karl Tangen.

Inside one of the company's bunkers. In the first row is *SS-Unterscharführer* Gunnar Haug, left, and Per Båtenes. In the second row is *SS-Unterscharführer* Jørgen Johannessen, left, and *SS-Unterscharführer* Kåre Berger.

In einem Bunker der Kompanie. Erste Reihe von links: SS-Unterscharführer Gunnar Haug und Per Båtenes. Zweite Reihe von links: SS-Unterscharführer Jørgen Johannessen und SS-Unterscharführer Kåre Berger.

Platoon leader *SS-Untersturmführer* Eystein Bech.

Zugführer SS-Untersturmführer Eystein Bech.

Section leader *SS-Unterscharführer* Jørgen Johannessen, a veteran of *Division 'Wiking'*, outside his bunker.

Gruppenführer SS-Unterscharführer Jørgen Johannessen, ein Veteran der Division "Wiking", vor seinem Bunker.

A team outside their bunker. Fifth from the left is section leader Gunnar Haug.

Ein Gruppe vor ihrem Bunker. Nr. 5 von links: Gruppenführer Gunnar Haug.

SS-Untersturmführer Paul Nielsen and *SS-Sturmmann* Gunnar Andersen in Kiestinki.

SS-Untersturmführer Paul Nielsen und SS-Sturmmann Gunnar Andersen in Kiestinki.

SS-Sturmmann Gunnar Andersen in front of the *Soldatenheim,* a meeting place for soldiers, in Kiestinki.

SS-Sturmmann Gunnar Andersen vor dem Soldatenheim in Kiestinki.

SS-Untersturmführer Roald Theting-Johannessen was one of the company's platoon leaders. Formerly a police officer, he had attended the officer school in Bad Tölz before serving at the front.

SS-Untersturmführer Roald Theting-Johannessen war Zugführer in der Kompanie. Er kam aus den Reihen der Polizei und hatte einen Lehrgang an der SS-Junkerschule Tölz durchgeführt, bevor er an die Front kam.

Kåre Bekkevold had signed up for the *Norwegian Legion* previously, but had been too young at the time. Later he managed join the *2. Police Company*.

Kåre Bekkevold hatte sich ursprünglich zur SS-Frw.-Legion Norwegen gemeldet, war aber noch zu jung. Später kam er mit der 2. SS-und Polizeikompanie an die Front.

Magne Martinsen, here in the uniform of Quisling's personal bodyguard unit *Førergarden*, was killed during a patrol when he was severely injured and bled to death on the trip back to his own lines.

Magne Martinsen in der Uniform der Wachmannschaft Quislings, *Førergarden*. Er wurde bei einem Spähtrupp verwundet und verblutete auf dem Weg zurück zu den eigenen Linien.

State-of-the-art MG-42s were handed out to the *2. Police Company* upon their arrival at the Karelian front.

Die 2. SS-und Polizeikompanie wurde an der karelischen Front mit dem neuen MG 42 ausgestattet.

The MG-34 was also frequently used in Karelia.

Das MG 34 war auch im ständigen Gebrauch an der Front.

An MG-34 being used as an anti-aircraft gun.

Ein MG 34 als Flak montiert.

Dead Russians after the attack on Shapkozero. Many Russians fell at this spot, but only one Norwegian, *SS-Untersturmführer* Eystein Bech.

Tote Russen nach dem Angriff auf Schapkosero. Viele Russen sind hier gefallen, aber nur ein Norweger, SS-Untersturmführer Eystein Bech.

Russian prisoners are escorted to the HQ of *6. SS-Gebirgs-Division 'Nord'*.

Russische Gefangene werden zum Stab der 6. SS-Gebirgs-Division "Nord" geführt.

Veterans of *Division 'Wiking'*,. *SS-Oberscharführer* Thoralf Gjølberg, left, and *SS-Unterscharführer* Kåre Berger. Berger received the Iron Cross 2nd Class after the Battle of Shapkozero.

Veteranen der Division "Wiking". Links SS-Oberscharführer Thoralf Gjølberg, rechts SS-Unterscharführer Kåre Berger. Berger wurde nach den Kämpfen um Schapkosero mit dem Eisernen Kreuz 2. Klasse ausgezeichnet.

SS-Oberscharführer Thoralf Gjølberg was awarded the War Merit Cross 2nd Class with Swords.

SS-Oberscharführer Thoralf Gjølberg wurde mit dem Kriegsverdienstkreuz 2. Klasse mit Schwertern ausgezeichnet.

Sturmmann Gunnar Andersen ready for a reconnaissance patrol.

SS-Sturmmann Gunnar Andersen klar für einen Spähtrupp.

A lookout post in Karelia.

Ein Beobachtungsposten in Karelien.

A police soldier scouting for the enemy in the Karelian forests.

Ein Polizist hält Ausschau nach dem Feind in den karelischen Wäldern.

Wulf Luttichau with a captured Russian machine gun.

Wulf Luttichau mit einer eroberten russischen Maschinenpistole.

From the left: Gunnar Andersen, *SS-Unterscharführer* Gunnar Haug and Gunnar Verpe.

Von links: Gunnar Andersen, SS-Unterscharführer Gunnar Haug und Gunnar Verpe.

Edvard Narum, left, and two unknown police soldiers.

Von links: Edvard Narum und zwei unbekannte Polizisten.

From the left: unknown, Edvard Narum, Martinius Sandbekk and unknown.

Von links: ein Unbekannter, Edvard Narum, Martinius Sandbekk und ein Unbekannter.

At the cemetery at Mayweg,. the *2. Police Company* bids farewell to its fallen comrades before returning home to Norway.

Friedhof Mayweg. Vor dem Abmarsch nach Norwegen nimmt die 2. SS-und Polizeikompanie Abschied von ihren gefallenen Kameraden.

SS-Hauptsturmführer Erling Waksvik, left, and *SS-Untersturmführer* Roald Theting-Johannessen.

Von links: SS-Hauptsturmführer Erling Waksvik und SS-Untersturmführer Roald Theting-Johannessen.

2. Police Company line-up.

Aufstellung der 2. SS-und Polizeikompanie.

Front row from the left: *SS-Unterscharführer* Jørgen Johannessen, Bjørn Falkenberg and Gunnar Verpe.

Erste Reihe von links: SS-Unterscharführer Jørgen Johannessen, Bjørn Falkenberg und Gunnar Verpe.

SS-Gruppenführer Lothar Debes thanks members of the company for their efforts.

SS-Gruppenführer Lothar Debes dankt der Kompanie für ihren Einsatz.

SS-Gruppenführer Lothar Debes in conversation with Norwegian officers. To the right is Erling Waksvik.

SS-Gruppenführer Lothar Debes im Gespräch mit norwegischen Offizieren. Rechts: Erling Waksvik.

SS-Oberscharführer Thoralf Gjølberg gives final orders before departure.

SS-Oberscharführer Thoralf Gjølberg gibt die letzten Befehle vor dem Abmarsch.

In Oulu, Finland. From the left: *SS-Unterscharführer* Johannes Gundersen, *SS-Unterscharführer* Gunnar Haug, Karl Tangen, Gunnar Verpe, Reidar Winnes, Wulf Luttichau, unknown and Hans Bråten.

In Oulu, Finnland. Von links: SS-Unterscharführer Johannes Gundersen, SS-Unterscharführer Gunnar Haug, Karl Tangen, Gunnar Verpe, Reidar Winnes, Wulf Luttichau, ein Unbekannter und Hans Bråten.

The train ride home. Karl Tangen, right, with an unknown comrade.

Die Zugfahrt zurück in die Heimat. Von links: ein Unbekannter und Karl Tangen.

2. SS-und Polizeikompanie – Heimkehr | *2. SS-und Polizeikompanie* – back in Norway

The company arrives in Oslo after several months at the front.

Nach mehreren Monaten an der Front rückt die Kompanie in Oslo ein.

From the left: Minister of Justice Sverre Riisnæs, Minister Jonas Lie, Erling Waksvik and Roald Theting-Johannessen.

Von links: Justizminister Sverre Riisnæs, Minister Jonas Lie, Erling Waksvik und Roald Theting-Johannessen.

In the centre is assistant physician and medic Breien.

In der Mitte der Hilfsarzt und Sanitäter Breien.

Police soldier Morten Skjærstad.

Der Polizist Morten Skjærstad.

Police soldier Karl Tangen.

Der Polizist Karl Tangen.

Jørgen Johannessen gets his men ready for the parade through the streets of Oslo.

Jørgen Johannessen bereitet die Mannschaft für die Parade durch die Straßen von Oslo vor.

The Police Company marches through the streets of Oslo. From the left: Oddvar Brynjulfsen, Reidar Kopstad, Johannes Gundersen, unknown, Otto Strøm, Hjalmar Steenstrup, Gunnar Andersen and Ivar Magne Tofte.

Die Polizeikompanie marschiert durch die Straßen Oslos. Von links: Oddvar Brynjulfsen, Reidar Kopstad, Johannes Gundersen, ein Unbekannter, Otto Strøm, Hjalmar Steenstrup, Gunnar Andersen und Ivar Magne Tofte.

Erling Waksvik, right, and Thoralf Gjølberg with the company's guidon.

Von rechts: Erling Waksvik und Thoralf Gjølberg mit der Kompanie-Standarte.

Front row from the left: Roald Theting-Johannessen, unknown and Johannes Gundersen.

Erste Reihe von links: Roald Theting-Johannessen, ein Unbekannter und Johannes Gundersen.

Front row from the left: Kåre Berger, Helge Nyfeld Wiik and Odd Blom Sandvik.

Erste Reihe von links: Kåre Berger, Helge Nyfeld Wiik und Odd Blom Sandvik.

NS-leader Quisling inspects the soldiers. From the right: Hans Bråten, Per H. Bråtenes, Odd Sondresen, Torjus Rike and Asbjørn Waksvik.

Ministerpräsident Quisling inspiziert die Soldaten. Von rechts: Hans Bråten, Per H. Bråtenes, Odd Sondresen, Torjus Rike und Asbjørn Waksvik.

The Police Badge of Honour was awarded by Jonas Lie, assisted by his adjutant Hans Haug. From the right: unknown, Gunnar Haug, Jørgen Johannessen, Kjartan Holø, unknown, Thoralf Gjølberg, Kåre Berger, Roald Theting-Johannessen, Asbjørn Waksvik and Othar Lislegaard.

Das Ehrenzeichen der Polizei wurde von Jonas Lie verliehen, assistiert von seinem Adjutant Hans Haug. Von rechts: ein Unbekannter, Gunnar Haug, Jørgen Johannessen, Kjartan Holø, ein Unbekannter, Thoralf Gjølberg, Kåre Berger, Roald Theting-Johannessen, Asbjørn Waksvik und Othar Lislegaard.

Company commander Erling Waksvik greets Quisling.

Kompanieführer Erling Waksvik begrüßt Quisling.

5

SS-Schijäger-Bataillon "Norge"

SS-Brigadeführer und Generalmajor der Waffen-SS, Mathias Kleinheisterkamp, Kommandeur der 6. SS-Gebirgs-Division "Nord", war äußerst zufrieden mit dem Einsatz der SS-Schikompanie und wünschte, die Kompanie zu einem Bataillon zu erweitern. Die Soldaten der Schikompanie, die im Sommer 1943 auf Heimaturlaub nach Norwegen gereist waren, warben daher neue Freiwillige für den Ausbau der Einheit zu einem etwa 800 Mann starken Bataillon an.

Die Anwerbung fand sowohl innerhalb der norwegischen faschistischen Partei *Nasjonal Samling* (NS) statt, unter anderem unter Jugendlichen aus der Hirdmarine, als auch durch lokale Rekrutierungskampagnen im ganzen Land. Die Offiziere waren junge Männer, die ihre Feuertaufe bei "Wiking" oder der SS-Frw.-Legion Norwegen bestanden hatten, und später eine Weiterausbildung an der SS-Junkerschule Tölz absolviert hatten. Die norwegischen Offiziere konnten zunächst drei Stellungen als Kompanieführer besetzen, der vierte war ein deutscher Offizier. Das weitere Führungspersonal bestand überwiegend aus Norwegern, aber auch einige deutsche Unterführer wurden in den verschiedenen Kompanien eingesetzt. Der Bataillonskommandeur SS-Sturmbannführer Richard Benner war Deutscher, und wurde später von SS-Obersturmbannführer Albrecht abgelöst. Im April 1944 übernahm der norwegische SS-Hauptsturmführer Frode Halle das Kommando des Bataillons. Mehr als einhundert Norweger des SS-Panzer-Grenadier-Regiments 23 "Norge" hatten sich um die Versetzung zum SS-Jäg.Schi.Btl. "Norge" beworben.

In vieler Hinsicht war das SS-Schijäger-Bataillon "Norge" eine erweiterte Ausgabe der Schikompanie mit den gleichen Aufträgen, aber in größerem Maßstab und Umfang. Die norwegischen Freiwilligen wurden an der südlichen Front – der sogenannten Louchi-Front – eingesetzt. Nach einem Winter mit vielen Spähtrupps ins Niemandsland und hinter die russischen Stellungen, begann die Front im Frühjahr 1944 dank größerer Aktivität auf der russischen Seite zum Leben zu erwachen.

Am 11. Oktober 1943 begaben sich die neuen Rekruten des SS-Jäger.Schi.Bataillons "Norge" zur ärztlichen Untersuchung in Oslo. Danach bekamen sie ihre Uniformen und wurden auf der Festung Akershus in Oslo stationiert. Am 18. Oktober verließen sie Oslo per Schiff und Zug zur Weiterausbildung in Sennheim. Am 20. Oktober kamen sie in Sennheim an und wurden nach neun Tagen weiter nach Hallein geschickt, wo die Grundausbildung stattfand.

Am 18. Dezember 1943 reiste das Bataillon endlich nach Finnland. Am 23. Dezember kamen die Männer in Danzig an und mussten hier die Weihnachtsfeiertage verbringen, da einige Angehörige des Bataillons erkrankt waren, und das gesamte Bataillon unter Quarantäne gestellt wurde.

Neujahr 1944 kam das Bataillon in Oulu, Finnland, an, und wurde weiter nach Kistinga geschickt, wo es zur Wiederbegegnung mit alten Kameraden der Schikompanie kam. In dieser Gegend lag das Bataillon und setzte die Weiterausbildung fort, bis die Einheit am 18. März 1944 zur Höhe 200 verlegt wurde. Von hier aus wurden viele Spähtrupps gegen den Feind durchgeführt, wobei mehrere Norweger bei diesen Unternehmen fielen. Am 18. April wurden die 1. und 2. Kompanie an die Hasselmann-Stellung verlegt, während die 3. Kompanie an die Kaprolat-Stellung kommandiert wurde. Hier lagen die drei Kompanien, bis sie von den Russen niedergekämpft wurden. Dabei fielen etwa 99 Norweger, und 40 wurden gefangengenommen.

Nach Kaprolat und Hasselmann

Nach den schweren Kämpfen an den Kaprolat- und Hasselmannhöhen genoss das SS-Schijäger-Bataillon "Norge" einen ruhigen Sommer. Die 2. Kompanie belegte einen Stützpunkt auf einer Insel im Pundom-See. Überdies gingen sie auf Partisanenjagd im Gebiet westlich der Straße von Kiestinki nach Jeletjosero. Der Rest des Bataillons beteiligte sich am Ausbau neuer Stellungen entlang des Flusses zwischen Toposero und Pjaosero, um die Frontlinie noch vor dem Winter auf diese Position zurückzuziehen.

Waffenruhe in Finnland, 4. September 1944

Das Waffenstillstandsabkommen zwischen Finnland und der Sowjetunion am 4. September 1944 bedeutete das Ende des Fortsetzungskrieges 1941–44. Eine der russischen Bedingungen war der Rückzug der 20. Gebirgsarmee,

5

SS-Schijäger-Bataillon 'Norge'

SS-Brigadeführer and Major General of the *Waffen-SS*, Matthias Kleinheisterkamp, commander of the *6. SS-Gebirgs-Division 'Nord'*, was extremely pleased with the efforts of the *SS-Schikompanie 'Norwegen'* and wished to expand the company into a battalion. Therefore, members of the *Schikompanie* on home leave in the summer of 1943 actively sought to recruit volunteers in order to expand the *Schikompanie* into a unit of nearly 800 men, the size of a battalion.

Recruitment took place both within the ranks of the Norwegian fascist party, including attempts to enlist young people from the *Unghirdmarinen*, as well as by launching regular local recruitment campaigns across the country. The officers were young people who had been blooded as members of *'Wiking'* or the *Norwegian Legion*, and continued their training at the *SS-Junkerschule Tölz*. Initially, the Norwegians were able to fill three company commander positions; the fourth was a German. The remaining officers were mostly Norwegian, but a few German officers were spread throughout the various companies. Early on, *SS-Sturmbannführer* Richard Benner from Germany headed the battalion, followed by *SS-Obersturmbannführer* Albrecht and finally, in April of 1944, *SS-Haupsturmführer* Frode Halle from Norway. Over 100 Norwegians who had trained in Croatia as members of the *23. SS-Panzergrenadier-Regiment 'Norge'* had also applied for transfer to the *SS-Schijäger-Bataillon 'Norge'*.

In many ways, the *Schijäger* Battalion was an enlarged version of the *Schikompanie*, with the same type of tasks but on a larger and more extended scale. The Norwegian volunteers were deployed on the second southernmost line of the battlefront, the so-called Louchi Front. After a winter with many patrols into No Man's Land and behind Russian lines, the front began to liven up in the spring of 1944, with signs of increasing activity on the Russian side.

On 11 October 1943, the new recruits of the *Schijäger* Battalion were called in for a medical check in Oslo, handed their uniforms and stationed at Akershus Fortress. Here they remained until 18 October, when they left by boat and train for Sennheim to undergo training. Arriving in Sennheim nine days later on 27 October, they were transferred to Hallein, where they received their basic military training.

On 18 December 1943, the men were finally able to leave for Finland. Arriving in Gdánsk on 23 December, they spent their Christmas there, since some of the men were taken ill and the entire battalion was quarantined.

At the very beginning of 1944, the battalion arrived in the Finnish city of Oulu, continuing on to Kistinga, where they met veterans of the *Schikompanie* and a number of officers who had arrived earlier. Here they remained and continued to train until 18 March 1944, when they were assigned to Hill 200 to carry out reconnaissance patrols against enemy positions. A number of Norwegians were killed during these operations. On 18 April 1944, *1.* and *2. Company* were relocated to Hasselmann Position, while *3. Company* was moved to Kaprolat. Here they remained until both positions were captured by the Russians, with an estimated 99 Norwegians killed and 40 captured.

After Kaprolat and Hasselmann

After the fiasco at Kaprolat and Hasselmann, the *Schijäger Battalion* enjoyed a quiet summer. The *2. Company* was dispatched to a stronghold on an island in Lake Pundom. In addition they hunted down partisans in the area west of the road leading from Kiestinki to Jeletjosero. The rest of the battalion was preparing to set up new emplacements along the river between Toposero and Pjaosero in order to pull back the front line to this position before the arrival of winter.

der sogenannten Lappland-Armee, samt aller unterstellten Einheiten aus finnischem Territorium bis zum 15. September 1944. Mit ihren drei Armeekorps bestand die 20. Gebirgsarmee aus 200 000 Mann. Innerhalb des vorgegebenen Zeitraums war es nicht möglich, eine so große Anzahl an Personen zu befördern. Verfolgt von russischen Streitkräften zog sich die Armee letztendlich mit Hilfe von finnischen Truppen aus Finnland zurück. Zum Rückzug durch Nord-Finnland über Kuusamo und Rovaniemi, eine Strecke von über 350 Kilometern, schloss sich das SS-Schijäger-Bataillon "Norge" der Lappland-Armee an. Danach legten sie 700 Kilometer auf dem Weg nach Skibotn und Narvik in Norwegen zurück. Vom ersten Tag an wurde das Bataillon "Norge" für Wach- und Sicherungsaufgaben benutzt. Um feindlichen Flugzeugen zu entgehen, bewegte sich die Division in der Nacht. Es kam auch zu kleineren Zusammenstößen zwischen dem Bataillon und finnischen Truppen. Von Narvik aus wurde das Bataillon nach Oslo geschickt, und kam dort Anfang Dezember 1944 an. Im Frühjahr 1945 wurde das Bataillon nach Mysen verlegt.

Truce with Finland, 4 September 1944

The armistice agreement with Finland on 4 September 1944 marked the end of the Continuation War 1941–44. One of the Soviet demands was to call for the removal of the 20. *Gebirgsarmee*, the German Lapland Army, including all attached units from Finland by 15 September 1944. With its three army corps, the *20. Gebirgsarmee* consisted of close to 200,000 men. The transfer of all these personnel turned out to take longer than the deadline agreed on. Pursued by Russian forces, the army finally pulled out of Finland with the help of Finnish forces. The *SS-Schijäger-Bataillon 'Norge'* followed the Lapland Army on its retreat through northern Finland, Kuusamo and Rovaniemi, a total distance of 350 km. Following that, it continued another 700 km to Skibotn and Narvik in Norway. From day one, the battalion was deployed for security and protection. In order to avoid enemy aircraft, the division moved at night. At times there were minor clashes with Finnish troops. From Narvik, the battalion was transported to Oslo, where the first units arrived in early December 1944. In spring of 1945, the battalion was transferred to Mysen.

SS-Schijäger-Bataillon "Norge" – Ausbildung | *SS-Schijäger-Bataillon 'Norge'* – training

Schijäger during training. Some were veterans of the old *Schikompanie*, while others had been recruited recently. The picture shows five young men from Hurdal in Akershus County, who were all related to one other. Harald Ringen had three additional brothers who had volunteered as front line fighters (not pictured here). From the left: the brothers Øyvind, Adolf and Oddvar Ringen, Harald Ringen and Hans Nordengen. Oddvar Ringen was killed at Hasselmann and Adolf died in Russian captivity.

Schijäger bei der Ausbildung. Einige waren Veteranen der alten Schikompanie, während andere neu angeworben waren. Das Bild zeigt fünf junge Männer aus Hurdal in der norwegischen Provinz Akershus. Alle waren miteinader verwandt. Harald Ringen hatte drei weitere Brüder, die als Frontkämpfer tätig waren (hier nicht abgebildet). Von links: die Brüder Øyvind, Adolf und Oddvar Ringen, Harald Ringen und Hans Nordengen. Oddvar fiel auf der Hasselmannhöhe, während Adolf in russischer Gefangenschaft starb.

Recruits and veterans. On the right is Ragnar Clausen, a veteran of the *Norwegian Legion*.

Rekruten und Veteranen. Rechts Ragnar Clausen, ein Veteran der SS-Frw.-Legion Norwegen.

Exercise with gas masks.

Übung mit Gasmasken.

In Holmestrand before leaving for training in Germany and Austria are *SS-Standarten-Oberjunker* Ole Selnes, left, and *SS-Obersturmführer* Otto Holmen.

In Holmestrand kurz vor der Abreise zur Ausbildung in Deutschland und Österreich. Von links: SS-Standarten-Oberjunker Ole Selnes und SS-Obersturmführer Otto Holmen.

Marching exercise in Holmestrand.

Marschübung in Holmestrand.

The cadet walking alongside his soldiers is *SS-Standarten-Oberjunker* Ole Selnes.

SS-Standarten-Oberjunker Ole Selnes zusammen mit seinen Soldaten.

The *Schijäger Battalion* celebrates Christmas in Gdánsk before travelling on to Finland.

Vor der Abfahrt nach Finnland feiert das Schijäger-Bataillon Weihnachten in Danzig.

Another view of the *Schijäger Battalion* celebrating Christmas in Gdánsk before travelling on to Finland.

Vor der Abfahrt nach Finnland feiert das Schijäger-Bataillon Weihnachten in Danzig.

Kåre Westby entertains with songs during the Christmas party.

Kåre Westby unterhält mit Gesang bei der Weihnachtsfeier.

The *Schijäger Battalion* is loaded up and ready to depart for Finland.

Das Schijäger-Bataillon vor der Abreise nach Finnland.

The boat trip to Finland across the Baltic Sea.

Die Schifffahrt nach Finnland über die Ostsee.

To Finland by boat across the Baltic Sea.

Mit dem Schiff nach Finnland über die Ostsee.

From the left: two unknowns, Hans Jakob Bruun and Håkon Helland.

Von links: zwei Unbekannte, Hans Jakob Bruun und Håkon Helland.

SS-Schijäger-Bataillon an der Front | *SS-Schijäger-Bataillon* at the front

Upon their arrival in Finland, the soldiers were transported closer to the front by rail.

In Finnland wurden die Soldaten mit dem Zug näher an die Front geschickt.

The *Schijäger* having arrived at the front. Here, just behind Kiestinki, was a *Soldatenheim*, a meeting place and recreation facility for soldiers. Part of the battalion's HQ staff was also located here.

Die Schijäger sind an der Front angekommen, hier gleich hinter Kiestinki, wo sich ein Soldatenheim befand. Auch ein Teil des Bataillonsstabs befand sich hier.

The battalion arranged a ski competition behind the front. *SS-Untersturmführer* Ole Selnes, left, and *SS-Untersturmführer* Odd Skui lead the competition.

Skimeisterschaft des Bataillons hinter der Front. Von links: SS-Untersturmführer Ole Selnes und SS-Untersturmführer Odd Skui, der in der Meisterschaft in Führung lag.

A group of *Schijäger* from HQ company.

Eine Gruppe Schijäger der Stabskompanie.

Graveyard of the *6. SS-Division 'Nord'* at Mayweg, with a funeral ceremony attended by German, Norwegian and Finnish officers.

Soldatenfriedhof der 6. SS-Division "Nord" am Mayweg. Hier eine Beerdigung unter Anwesenheit deutscher, norwegischer und finnischer Offiziere.

Another view of the graveyard of the *6. SS-Division 'Nord'* at Mayweg, with a funeral ceremony attended by German, Norwegian and Finnish officers.

Soldatenfriedhof der 6. SS-Division "Nord" am Mayweg. Hier eine Beerdigung unter Anwesenheit deutscher, norwegischer und finnischer Offiziere.

SS-Untersturmführer Rolf Ugelstad, left, commander of HQ company.

Von links: SS-Untersturmführer Rolf Ugelstad, Kompanieführer der Stabskompanie.

A funeral ceremony.

Beerdigung.

A funeral ceremony.

Beerdigung.

Field post office in Kiestinki. All the mail for the volunteers arrived here before being forwarded to the various positions.

Feldpostamt in Kiestinki. Die Post für die Freiwilligen kam hier an, und wurde an die verschiedenen Stellungen weiterverteilt.

SS-Untersturmführer Sverre Kjelstrup, left, the battalion's German physician, and *SS-Untersturmführer* Rolf Ugelstad.

Von links: SS-Untersturmführer Sverre Kjelstrup, der deutsche Bataillonsarzt des SS-Jäg.Schi.Btls. "Norge", und SS-Untersturmführer Rolf Ugelstad.

Munin
På vakt for Norge
i Finnlands skoger
Se SS-PK Ulf Tur's beretning
fra «SS-Skijægerbataljon
Norge» i dette nummer
Auf Wache für Norwegen
in Finnlands Wäldern
Siehe unseren Bericht vom
»SS-Skijägerbataillon Norwegen«.
NR. 6 • 3. ÅRG.
2. MARSHEFTE 1944
PRIS 50 ØRE

Munin.

Norske frivillige klar til utrykning. — Norwegische Freiwillige fertig zum Einsatz

SS Untersturmführer Skjefstad var en av de første frivillige som dro ut, den gang som menig. No leder han sitt eget kompani i Finnland.

SS-Untersturmführer Skjefstad war einer der ersten Freiwilligen. Nun führt er als Kampaniechef eine bewährte Einheit in Finnland

↓ En av de yngste norske guttene på vakt i Finnlands skoger. 17 år, men kampånden er der
Ein 17jähriger Freiwilliger auf Wache in Finnlands Wäldern

På vakt for Norge i Finnlands skoger

En bildeberetning fra „SS-Skijægerbataljon Norge" av SS-PK Ulf Tur

Tusener av norske frivillige har stått og står i dag ved fronten. Fra Karelen i nord til Svartehavet i sør har de norske guttene kjempet.

Etter opprettelsen av «SS-Skijegerbataljon Norge», har de norske frivillige inntatt sin naturlige plass ved fronten på Finnlands side.

Kart og kompass er nødvendig i Karelens urskoger.

↓ Karte und Kompass spielen in den Urwäldern Kareliens eine grosse Rolle

Munin.

Bak trestammene står også nordmenn klare
Der Spähtruppführer beobachtet die Feindbewegungen

Den norske speiderpatrulje i Karelen har hatt føling med fienden og går forsiktig fram
Ein Spähtrupp hat Feindberührung und geht vorsichtig vor

Auf Wache für Norwegen in Finnlands Wäldern

Tausende norwegische Freiwillige kämpfen an den Fronten gegen den Bolschewismus — der grösste Teil von ihnen in Finnland. Dass die meisten gerade in Finnland eingesetzt sind, erklärt sich daraus, dass die dort nicht nur mit ihren finnischen Kameraden aus dem Brudervolk Seite an Seite kämpfen, sondern darüber hinaus auch die Grenzen ihres eigenen Vaterlandes sichern. Norwegens Freundschaft mit Finnland — ausgedrückt im Kampf Schulter an Schulter für die Erhaltung der Freiheit wird für die Zukunft von grösster Bedeutung sein.

»Munin« bringt heute einige Bilder von ᛋᛋ-Kriegsberichter Ulf Tur, die den Einsatz der norwegischen Freiwilligen in Finnland zeigen. Gleichzeitig überbringen wir von den im Einsatz befindlichen Kameraden an alle die noch daheim sitzen, folgende Grüsse: »Wir sind zwar schon viele hier draussen auf Wache für Norwegen, aber auch für euch ist noch Platz.«

↓ Norske frivillige i Karelen gir fyr. Han har trening med maskingeværet no.
Garbe auf Garbe jagen die Freiwilligen den Bolschewisten entgegen

Munin.

Norsk offiser i Finnland — en ekte germaner. Elverum kan være stolt av ham.

Das Gesicht des norwegischen Freiwilligen Offiziers. Zuversicht und Entschlossenheit spiegeln sich in seinen Zügen

←

«Vi greier det nok», sier de norske frivillige da de tar avskjed til en 100 kilometers speidertur innover Sovjets ødemarker i nord

»Wir werden es schon schaffen«, meinen sie beim Aufbruch zu einem Spähtrupp-Unternehmen das in die Ödmarken Nordfinnlands führt

→

Bunkeridyll
En norsk frivillig på Finskefronten tar seg en velfortjent røyk etter dagens strabaser

Nach den Strapazen eines harten Kampftages schmeckt die Pfeife dem Kriegsberichter besonders gut

Munin.

A group prepares for a scouting expedition and receives final orders before setting out on their mission.

Eine Gruppe bereitet sich auf einen Spähtrupp vor und erhält die letzten Befehle vor dem Auftrag.

Radio contact with the command post during a scouting expedition.

Funkverbindung mit der Leitung des Spähtrupps.

Ottar Hansen, left (KIA), and Knut Gårder.

Von links: Ottar Hansen (gefallen) und Knut Gårder.

Shooting practice with an MG-34. The older model was preferred by scout squads, since it required less ammunition to be taken along.

Schießübung mit einem MG 34. Das ältere Modell wurde von Spähtrupps bevorzugt, da es weniger Munition verbrauchte.

Shooting practice with an MG-42. Its was favoured as a weapon in the defence of positions.

Schießübung mit einem MG 42, das für die Abwehr bevorzugt wurde.

The *Schijäger* often had little food, since supply routes were long and in poor condition. Here, some skilled hunters have shot a wood grouse that will provide food for the soldiers. From the left: Knut Gårder, Paul Kristiansen, Anton Moss, Einar Vassbø and Rolf Jacobsen.

Die Schijäger hatten oft wenig zu essen, da die Versorgungswege lang und in schlechtem Zustand waren. Hier haben tüchtige Jäger einen Auerhahn geschossen und können den Soldaten somit eine zusätzliche Kost bieten. Von links: Knut Gårder, Paul Kristiansen, Anton Moss, Einar Vassbø und Rolf Jacobsen.

Preparing the wood grouse are Knut Gårder, left, and Anton Moss.

Beim Zubereiten des Auerhahns. Von links: Knut Gårder und Anton Moss.

The German company commander, *SS-Hauptsturmführer* Fritz Grondt, gives orders before a scout squad starts to move towards enemy lines.

Der deutsche Kompanieführer SS-Hauptsturmführer Fritz Grondt gibt einen Befehl bevor sich der Spähtrupp in Bewegung setzt.

Knut Gårder on patrol.

Knut Gårder bei einem Spähtrupp.

Einar Vassbø on patrol.

Einar Vassbø bei einem Spähtrupp.

A wounded soldier is transported back to his position. Because of the terrain and the long distances, sleds were frequently used to transport equipment and wounded soldiers.

Ein verwundeter Kamerad wird zurück zur eigenen Stellung gebracht. Auf Grund des Geländes und der großen Abstände wurden oft Schlitten für den Transport von Ausrüstung und Verwundeten benutzt.

SS-Oberscharführer Rolf Jacobsen with American canned food, found on dead Russian soldiers. The cans were labelled in Russian.

SS-Oberscharführer Rolf Jacobsen mit auf Russisch beschrifteten Konserven aus den USA, die bei toten Russen gefunden wurden.

On patrol in the Karelian forests. Patrols could last for many hours and often several days, with the constant fear of a Russian ambush.

Auf Spähtrupp in den karelischen Wäldern. Spähtrupps konnten mehrere Stunden und auch Tagen dauern, mit ständiger Angst vor russischen Lauerstellungen.

On patrol in the Karelian forests. Patrols could last for many hours and often several days, with the constant fear of a Russian ambush.

Auf Spähtrupp in den karelischen Wäldern. Spähtrupps konnten mehrere Stunden und auch Tagen dauern, mit ständiger Angst vor russischen Lauerstellungen.

Finally back in Kiestinki, with food and a roof over their head after a long scouting expedition.

Endlich zurück in Kiestinki nach einem langen Spähtrupp, mit Essen und einem Dach über dem Kopf.

German company commander *SS-Hauptsturmführer* Fritz Grondt, left, and platoon leader *SS-Untersturmführer* Torgeir Lofthus. The latter was awarded the Iron Cross 2nd Class on the same day.

Von links: der deutsche Kompanieführer SS-Hauptsturmführer Fritz Grondt und sein Zugführer SS-Untersturmführer Torgeir Lofthus, dem noch am gleichen Tag das Eiserne Kreuz 2. Klasse verliehen wurde.

Supplies were transported by horse and mule when trucks were unable to navigate the landscape.

Verpflegung wurde mit Pferd und Maultier geschickt, wenn der LKW nicht weiter vorwärts kam.

A group from HQ chopping wood.

Mitglieder des Stabs beim Holzhacken.

One of the battalion's three trucks.

Einer der drei LKWs des Schijäger-Bataillons.

A sled is loaded with supplies for the various strongpoints.

Hier wird der Schlitten mit Verpflegung für die Stützpunkte geladen.

Field kitchen at Hill 200, where the ski battalion was positioned for a while.

Die Feldküche an der Höhe 200, wo das Schijäger-Bataillon eine Weile lag.

From the left: Ottar Hansen (KIA), Åge Fagerli and Magnar Tømte.

Von links: Ottar Hansen (gefallen), Åge Fagerli und Magnar Tømte.

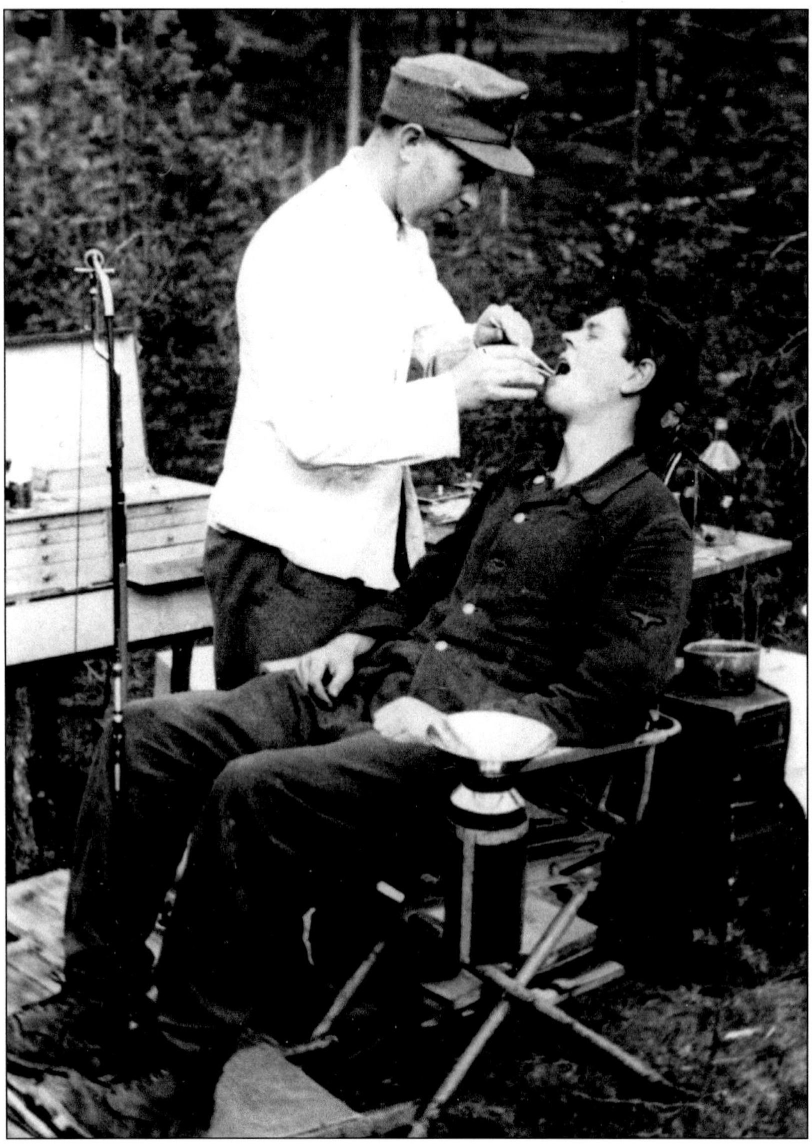

On the left is Anton Bieltvedt, the dentist of the *Schijäger Battalion*, treating a soldier suffering from a toothache.

Von links: Anton Bieltvedt, der Zahnarzt des Schijäger-Bataillons. Hier behandelt er einen Schijäger, der Zahnschmerzen hat.

A medic treats lice bites on a soldier's leg. Lice were a frequent problem at the front.

Ein Sanitäter behandelt Läusebisse am Bein eines Soldaten. Läuse waren en häufiges Problem an der Front.

A break while building a sauna behind the front.

Ruhepause während des Baus einer Sauna hinter der Front.

Distributing the field mail. In the centre is first sergeant *SS-Oberscharführer* Per Henrik Bae.

Verteilung der Feldpost. In der Mitte der Spieß, SS-Oberscharführer Per Henrik Bae.

Handing out packages from the front-fighter office and field mail at Hill 200.

Verteilung von Päckchen und Feldpostbriefen vom Frontkämpferbüro an der Höhe 200.

Squad leader *SS-Standarten-Junker* Arild Jadar gives final orders before a scouting expedition. All have rolled up their sleeves in order to be able to recognise each other, since the Russians also wore white camouflage uniforms.

Gruppenführer und SS-Standarten-Junker Arild Jadar gibt dem Spähtrupp einen letzten Befehl. Alle hatten die Ärmel hochgekrempelt um einander erkennen zu können, da auch die Russen weiße Tarnbekleidung benutzten.

Out on patrol against Russian positions.

Spähtrupp gegen russische Stellungen.

An ambush in a forest clearing. This tactic was used by both sides.

Lauerstellung im Wald. Diese Taktik wurde von beiden Seiten benutzt.

An ambush in a forest clearing. This tactic was used by both sides.

Lauerstellung im Wald. Diese Taktik wurde von beiden Seiten benutzt.

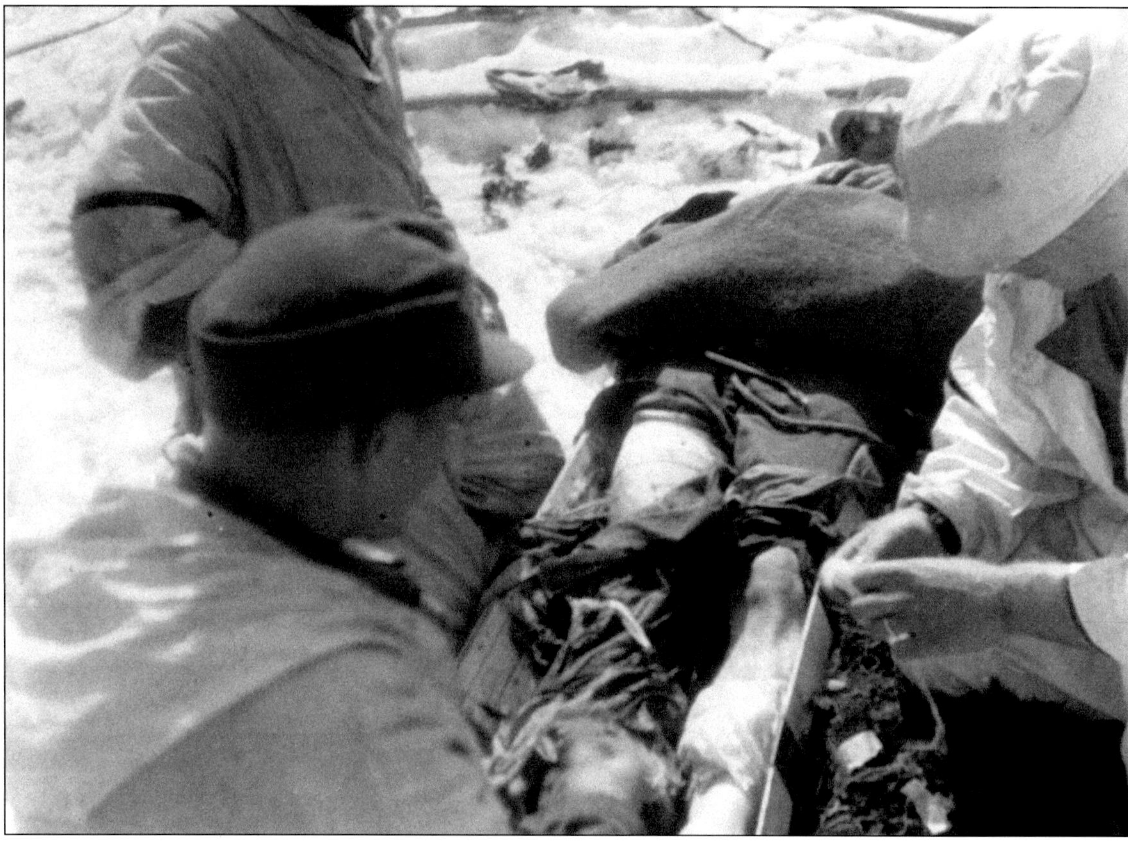

A wounded *Schijäger* is bandaged before being sent back from the front on a ski sled.

Ein verwundeter SS-Jäger bekommt Erste Hilfe bevor er mit dem Schlitten zurücktransportiert wird.

Some were not so lucky and died before making it back to their own lines for medical attention.

Einige der Soldaten hatten weniger Glück und fielen, bevor sie die eigenen Linien erreichten.

Det smaker godt med en matbit. — Her har de norske skijegerne tendt en liten nying inne i urskogen og lar maten vederfares all rettferdighet.

Eine Portion warmes Essen schmeckt immer gut. Hier haben sich norwegische Schijäger ein kleines Feuer mitten im Urwald angemachen

KJEMPERNE fra KARELEN

Guttene i «Skijegerbataljon» Norge» har i lang tid gjort en enestående innsats i Karelens uendelige urskoger. Dag og natt stod de på vakt ved nordens østgrense beredt til forsvar for land og folk. Disse norske kjemperne fra Karelen vil aldri bli glemt. Deres innsats vil alltid bli stående som en bauta i vår historie.

*

Die jungen Soldaten des »Schijägerbataillons Norwegen« haben schon längere Zeit einen einzigartigen Einsatz in Kareliens unendlichen Urwäldern geleistet.

For første gang i «seng» på lang tid. Guttene hviler ut etter turen. De ligger fullt påkledd, for kulden er slem. No leser de ukegamle aviser fra heimlandet og koser seg så godt de kan

Zum ersten Male seit langer Zeit wieder im »Bett«. Sie ruhen sich nach langer Zeit wieder einmal richtig aus nach all den Strapazen. Sie liegen vollständig angezogen da, denn die Kälte ist schlimm. Nun lesen sie wochenalte Zeitungen aus der Heimat und machen es sich so gut wie möglich bequem.

Munin.

En speidertropp gjør seg klar til utmarsj inn på fiendtlig område. Provianten fordeles. Det er ikke stort de kan ta med seg. Oppakningen må være så liten som mulig på de lange anstrengende turene.

Ein Spähtrupp macht sich abmarschbereit für seine Aufgabe, das feindliche Gebiet zu erkunden. Der Proviant wird verteilt. Es ist aber nicht viel, was er mitnehmen kann. Die mitgeführten Lasten müssen auf diesen langen, anstrengenden Touren so gering wie nur möglich sein

Her står en SS-frivillig klar til avmarsj. Over ryggen bærer han et maskingevær, forsynt med truger

Hier steht ein finnischer SS-Freiwilliger fertig zum Abmarsch. Über dem Rücken trägt er ein Maschinengewehr, das mit einem »Schneeschuh« versehen ist

Rapporten fra siste speidertakt nedskrives

Der Bericht über das letzte Spätruppunternehmen wird niedergeschrieben

Føling med fienden? Skulder ved skulder med våpnene skuddklare speider to unge nordmenn inn mellom trærne. Ikke noe unngår oppmerksomheten.

Fühlung mit dem Feinde? Schulter an Schulter, die Waffen schussklar, spähen zwei junge Norweger zwischen den Bäumen umher. Nichts entgeht ihrer Aufmerksamkeit.

Munin.

En gledelig overraskelse: Brev og pakker fra Norge

Eine freudige Überraschung: Briefe und Pakete von Norwegen

«Heime» igjen. Skijegerens smilende fjes røper Ola Nordmann på lang avstand. Etter en uvanlig slitsom oppklaringstur glir maten fort ned. Ekte norsk «Viking Melk» er ikke å forakte.

Wieder »zu Hause«. Das lächelnde Antlitz des Schijägers tritt wieder nach langer Zeit in Erscheinung. Nach einer aussergewöhnlichen, anstrengenden Aufklärungspatrouille rutscht das Essen schnell herunter. Echte norwegische »Viking-Milch« ist aber auch nicht zu verachten!

Troppen på marsj. Mil etter mil går ferden gjennom skogene inne på fiendtlig område

Trupp auf dem Marsch. Kilometer um Kilometer geht die Fahrt durch die Wälder innerhalb der feindlichen Gebiete

Karelen er intet sted for kresne mammagutter. Her gjelder det å innrette seg så godt som forholdene tillater det. De norske guttene klarer det og tar alle strabaser med godt humør

Karelien ist keine Stätte für wählerische Muttersöhnchen. Hier gilt es, sich so gut wie möglich, je nachdem es die Verhältnisse zulassen, einzurichten

Under til høyre: Støvlene smøres. Det kan være utrolig kalt i Karelens urskoger og guttene må være påpasselig med utstyret for å unngå forfrysninger

Unten rechts: Die Stiefel werden eingeschmiert. Es kann unglaublich kalt in Kareliens Urwäldern werden und die Soldaten müssen sich mit ihrer Ausrüstung den Verhältnissen anpassen, um Erfrierungen zu entgehen

Munin.

Celebrating Norway's National Day on 17 May at Kaprolat. Some of the men receive homemade awards. From the left: unknown, *SS-Unterscharführer* Peder Habbestad, unknown, *SS-Untersturmführer* Axel Steen, unknown and Bjarne Sørum.

Norwegens Nationalfeiertag am 17. Mai bei Kaprolat. Einige der Männer erhalten handgefertigte Auszeichnungen. Von links: ein Unbekannter, SS-Unterscharführer Peder Habbestad, ein Unbekannter, SS-Untersturmführer Axel Steen, ein Unbekannter und Bjarne Sørum.

SS-Oberscharführer Yngvar Kofoed, left, and *SS-Unterscharführer* Einar Skjærbekk before setting out on a patrol from Kaprolat.

Von links: SS-Oberscharführer Yngvar Kofoed und SS-Unterscharführer Einar Skjaerbekk bevor sie von Kaprolat aus auf Patrouille gehen.

SS-Oberscharführer Yngvar Kofoed, right, and *SS-Untersturmführer* Axel Steen at Kaprolat.

Von rechts: SS-Oberscharführer Yngvar Kofoed und SS-Untersturmführer Axel Steen auf der Kaprolat-Höhe.

First row: all unknown. Second row from the left: Ola Sælie, Syver Stormoen and Tov Kyllosdal.

Erste Reihe: alle unbekannt. Zweite Reihe von links: Ola Saelie, Syver Stormoen und Kyllosdal.

A fully equipped team is ready to move to new positions.

Eine voll ausgestattete Gruppe macht sich klar zum Stellungswechsel.

SS General and commander of the *6. Division 'Nord'*, Walter Krüger, visits the *Skijäger-Bataillon*. From the left: battalion adjutant *SS-Untersturmführer* Hans Petter Hoff, Krüger, Hans-Heinz Küchle and chief of HQ company *SS-Untersturmführer* Rolf Ugelstad.

SS-General und Kommandeur der 6. SS-Geb.Div. "Nord", Walter Krüger, besucht die Stellung des SS-Schijäger-Bataillons "Norge". Von links: Bataillonsadjutant SS-Untersturmführer Hans Petter Hoff, Hans-Heinz Küchle, und der Chef der Stabskompanie, SS-Untersturmführer Rolf Ugelstad.

General Walter Krüger visits the kitchen bunker.

General Walter Krüger zu Besuch im Küchenbunker.

Fetching water from the frozen lake below the position at Kaprolat.

Wasserholen aus dem eisigen See unterhalb der Kaprolat-Stellung.

Supplies are carried up the long steep road from the lake to the Kaprolat position.

Verpflegung wird vom See hoch zur Kaprolat-Stellung transportiert.

From the left: three unknowns and *SS-Unterscharführer* Magne Rødvik.

Von links: drei Unbekannte und SS-Unterscharführer Magne Rødvik.

Meal break and relaxation in the spring sun.

Essenspause und Entspannung in der Sonne.

Keeping weapons in good shape was important to ensure that the equipment was always ready for use.

Die Gewehre müssen gereinigt werden, um immer einsatzbereit zu sein.

Excitement all around while a package from Norway is opened.

Ein Päckchen aus Norwegen wird erwartungsvoll ausgepackt.

Uniform inspection before the veterans of the Ski Company are demobilised and sent home to Norway after completion of their contract.

Musterung der Veteranen der Schikompanie vor der Entlassung nach Norwegen.

The veterans of the *Schikompanie* march back to Kiestinki for the last time.

Die Veteranen der Schikompanie marschieren ein letztes Mal zurück nach Kiestinki.

The veterans of the *Schikompanie* are transported to Oulu by truck before continuing on to Norway.

Die Veteranen der Schikompanie werden mit dem LKW nach Oulo transportiert, bevor es weiter nach Norwegen geht.

A lookout point at Kaprolat.

Ein Beobachtungsposten an der Kaprolat-Höhe.

Peaceful spring days at Kaprolat before the Russians take the position a few days later, killing nearly all the men.

Ruhige Frühjahrstage auf der Kaprolat-Höhe, bevor die Stellung einige Tage später von den Russen niedergekämpft wird und nahezu alle Männer fallen.

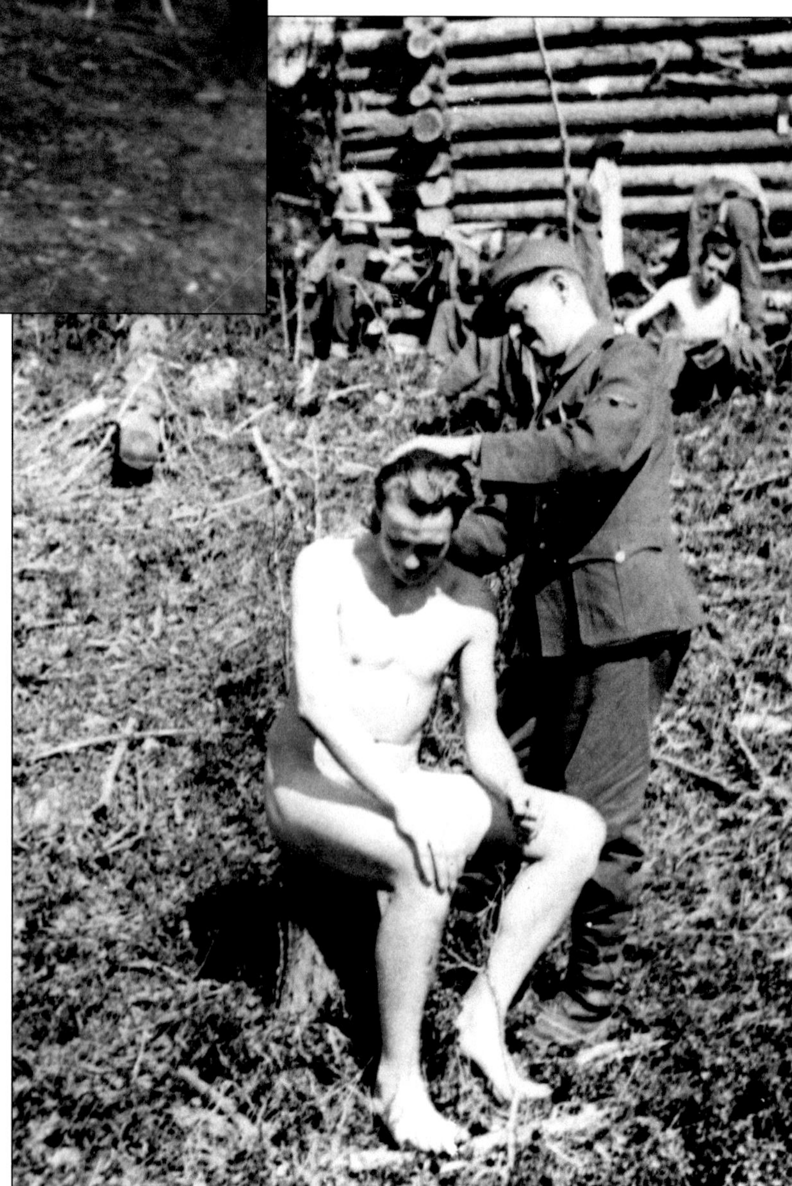

Peaceful spring days at Kaprolat before the Russians take the position a few days later, killing nearly all the men.

Ruhige Frühjahrstage auf der Kaprolat-Höhe, bevor die Stellung einige Tage später von den Russen niedergekämpft wird und nahezu alle Männer fallen.

Guard duty in a bunker at Kaprolat, machine gun and hand-grenades ready.

Eine Wache im Bunker auf der Kaprolat-Höhe. Maschinenpistole und Handgranaten liegen bereit.

On 25 June 1944, *SS-Unterscharführer* Kjell Eger was captured by the Russians at Kaprolat and died in Russian captivity one year later.

SS-Unterscharführer Kjell Eger wurde von den Russen am 25.06.1944 auf der Kaprolat-Höhe gefangengenommen, und starb ein Jahr später in russischer Gefangenschaft.

SS-Oberscharführer Yngvar Kofoed succeeded in making his way from Kaprolat to Hasselmann Hill, where he was killed some time later. He was a veteran of *Division 'Wiking'*.

SS-Oberscharführer Yngvar Kofoed schaffte es, von Kaprolat zur Hasselmann-Höhe zu entkommen, wo er später fiel. Er war ein Veteran der Division "Wiking".

John Hellblad managed to escape from Hasselmann Hill and swim to safety across Lake Kapanez.

John Hellblad flüchtete von der Hasselmann-Höhe, und schwamm über den Kapanez-See.

After the Battle of Kaprolat and Hasselmann, the *Schijäger Battalion* was once again positioned at Pundom. Here is the first line-up of those who survived, together with the new recruits.

Nach den Kämpfen um Kaprolat und Hasselmann richtete das SS-Schijäger-Bataillon "Norge" bei Pundom eine neue Stellung ein. Hier die erste Aufstellung der Überlebenden zusammen mit den neuen Rekruten.

From the left: unknown, Leif Rønningen, Magne Herseth and Torodd Lunde. The rest are unknown.

Von links: ein Unbekannter, Leif Rønningen, Magne Herseth and Torodd Lunde. Die anderen sind unbekannt.

Four unknown soldiers.

Vier Unbekannte.

From the left: Harald Åsland, Jens Petersen, Palmer Nymoen, unknown, Harald Andersen, Harald Bjørnstad, Reidar Hansen and Odd Schrøder.

Von links: Harald Åsland, Jens Petersen, Palmer Nymoen, ein Unbekannter, Harald Andersen, Harald Bjørnstad, Reidar Hansen und Odd Schrøder.

SS-Untersturmführer Ole Selnes, left, and two unknown men at the Pundom position.

Von links: SS-Untersturmführer Ole Selnes und zwei Unbekannte an der Pundom-Stellung.

Company commander *SS-Obersturmführer* Martin Skjefstad in the back of the boat at the Pundom position.

Hinten im Boot Kompanieführer SS-Obersturmführer Martin Skjefstad an der Pundom-Stellung.

Company commanders *SS-Obersturmführer* Martin Skjefstad, left, and *SS-Untersturmführer* Rolf Ugelstad at the Pundom position.

Von links: die Kompanieführer SS-Obersturmführer Martin Skjefstad und SS-Untersturmführer Rolf Ugelstad and der Pundom-Stellung.

Company commander *SS-Obersturmführer* Martin Skjefstad, left, and platoon leader Tor Arntzen at the Pundom Position.

Von links: Kompanieführer SS-Obersturmführer Martin Skjefstad und Zugführer Tor Arntzen an der Pundom-Stellung.

From the left: company commander *SS-Obersturmführer* Martin Skjefstad and platoon leaders *SS-Untersturmführer* Ole Selnes and *SS-Untersturmführer* Kristoffer Dahl.

Von links: Kompanieführer SS-Obersturmführer Martin Skjefstad und die Zugführer SS-Untersturmführer Ole Selnes und Kristoffer Dahl.

Company commander *SS-Obersturmführer* Martin Skjefstad, left, and Johan Cappelen during an award ceremony.

Von links: Kompanieführer SS-Obersturmführer Martin Skjefstad und SS-Standarten-Junker Johan Cappelen bei der Verleihung von Auszeichnungen.

Munin
Føreren for Skijegerbataljonen «Norge», Halle, lykkønsker norske frivillige som har utmerket seg
Foto: ᛋᛋ-PK Fink
Bei den Freiwilligen des Schijägerbataillons »Norwegen«. Die Tapfersten erhalten das Eiserne Kreuz
NR. 19-20 • 3. ÅRG.
OKTOBERHEFTE 1944
PRIS 1 KRONE

Munin.

Sigmund Vigerust, right, and *SS-Obersturmführer* Martin Skjefstad.

Von rechts: Sigmund Vigerust und SS-Obersturmführer Martin Skjefstad.

Sitting in the centre is *SS-Obersturmführer* Martin Skjefstad.

In der Mitte sitzend: SS-Obersturmführer Martin Skjefstad.

SS-Schijäger-Bataillon "Norge" – der Marsch nach Norwegen | *SS-Schijäger-Bataillon 'Norge'* – the march to Norway

Sommer i KARELEN

Vi bringer her en billedreportasje fra Karelen hvor de norske frivillige i over 2 år gjorde sin tjeneste.
Disse bilder som er tatt på sensommeren 1944, er hentet fra Skijægerbataljonen «Norges» stillinger, som kort tid seinere måtte rømmes på grunn av det finske regimes simple forræderi

Sommer in Karelien

Wir bringen hier einen Bilderbericht aus Karelien, wo die norwegischen Freiwilligen mehr als zwei Jahre lang ihren Einsatz geleistet haben. Diese Bilder wurden während des Spätsommers 1944 in den Stellungen des Skijägerbataillons »Norge« aufgekommen, die aber wegen des gemeinen Verrats der finnischen Regierung kurz danach geräumt werden mussten

Foto: Frode Halle

Fung. bataljonskommandør, ᛋᛋ-Obersturmführer Skjefstad mottar en melding

Der vertretende Bataillonskommandeur, ᛋᛋ-Obersturmführer Skjefstad, erhält eine Meldung

Her gjelder det å være våken. En norsk observasjonspost har inntatt en oversiktig stilling →

Hier heisst es die Augen gebrauchen. Von dieser Stellung hat der norwegische Beobachtungsposten einen guten Überblick

En hurtigående kampbåt i aktivitet

Ein Schnellkampfboot in Tätigkeit

«Toppsjøfergene» står klar til avgang

Die Gummiboote sind abfahrtsbereit

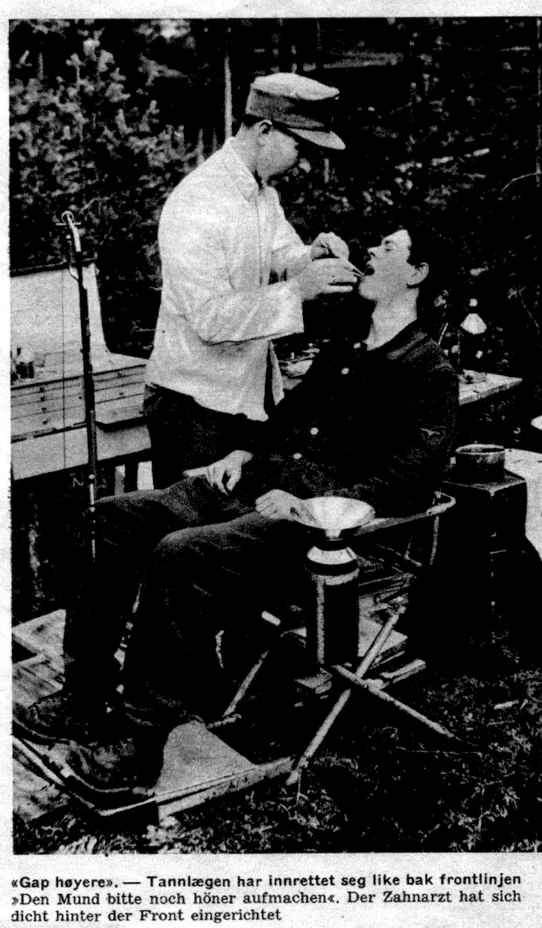

«Gap høyere». — Tannlægen har innrettet seg like bak frontlinjen

»Den Mund bitte noch höher aufmachen«. Der Zahnarzt hat sich dicht hinter der Front eingerichtet

Munin.

Sommeridyll i Karelen

Sommeridyll in Karelien

→

Personalet ved «gulasch-kanonen» tar seg en pause. Bemerk det norske flagget

Die Bedienung einer Gulasch-Kanone macht eine Pause. Bemerkt die norwegische Flagge

Utdannelsen av underførere foregår like bak fronten

Die Ausbildung von Unterführern erfolgt dicht hinter der Front

Munin.

Det 3. Politikompani har slått seg ned for dagen.
Die dritte Polizeikompanie hat an diesen Tag genug marschiert

T. v.: På veg mot Norge
Links: Nach Norwegen

Med NORGE som mål!

Finnlands kapitulasjon bragte den norske Skijægerbataljon i en vanskelig stilling. Frontlinjen lå bortimot 1000 km vekk fra Norges grenser, og noen mulighet for transport med bane var utelukket, og bilene som stod til disposisjon strakk knapt nok til for trennet. Det forelå således ingen annen mulighet enn å tilbakelegge strekningen til fots.

Den 7. november ble Skijægerbataljon «NORGE» satt i marsj med Rovaniemi som et foreløbig mål. Marsjen gikk først videre den 16. oktober.
Etter 20 dagers strabasser passertes den norske grense ved Helleskogen. Guttene var atter på norsk jord, og alle sorger og savn var blåst bort.

Foto: Frode Halle

Munin.

Finnlands Kapitulation hat das norwegische Schijägerbataillon in eine schwierige Lage versetzt. Die Front lag fast 1000 km von der norwegischen Grenze entfernt. Es gab keine Transportmöglichkeit mit der Eisenbahn, und die zur Verfügung stehenden Kraftwagen reichten kaum für den Tross aus. Es gab also keine andere Möglichkeit als die Strecke zu Fuss zurückzulegen.

Am 7. September 1944 setzte sich das Schijägerbataillon «Norge» in Bewegung mit Rovaniemi als vorläufiges Ziel, und erst am 16. Oktober d. J. wurde der Marsch fortgesetzt.

Nach 20 Tagen Strapazen wurde die norwegische Grenze bei Helleskogen überschritten. Die Männer waren wieder auf norwegischem Boden, und alle Sorgen und Entbehrungen waren vergessen.

Marsjpause underveis. Det smakte godt med en hvil

Marschpause unterwegs. Das Ausruhen tat gut

Under: — og «trennet» fulgte etter

Unten: — und der Tross kam nach

Munin.

The officers prepare for the long march home to Norway.

Die Offiziere bereiten sich auf den langen Marsch in die Heimat vor.

The soldiers set out on their long march, walking at night and resting during the day.

Die Soldaten treten den langen Marsch in die Heimat an. In der Nacht wird marschiert, tagsüber ruht man sich aus.

From the left: deputy commander of the *3. Police Company*, *SS-Obersturmführer* Oscar Rustand, the commander of the *Schijäger Battalion*, *SS-Hauptsturmführer* Frode Halle, and platoon leader *SS-Untersturmführer* Torgeir Lofthus during their return march.

Von links: der stellvertretende Kompanieführer der 3. SS-und Polizeikompanie SS-Obersturmführer Oscar Rustand, der Kommandeur des SS-Schijäger-Bataillons "Norge" SS-Hauptsturmführer Frode Halle, und der Zugführer SS-Untersturmführer Torgeir Lofthus während des Rückmarsches.

From the right: *SS-Untersturmführer* Tor Arntzen, *SS-Untersturmführer* Kristoffer Dahl and *SS-Hauptscharführer* Per Henrik Bae.

Von rechts: die SS-Untersturmführer Tor Arntzen und Kristoffer Dahl, sowie SS-Hauptscharführer Per Henrik Bae.

Marching home with a full pack.

Rückmarsch mit vollem Tornister.

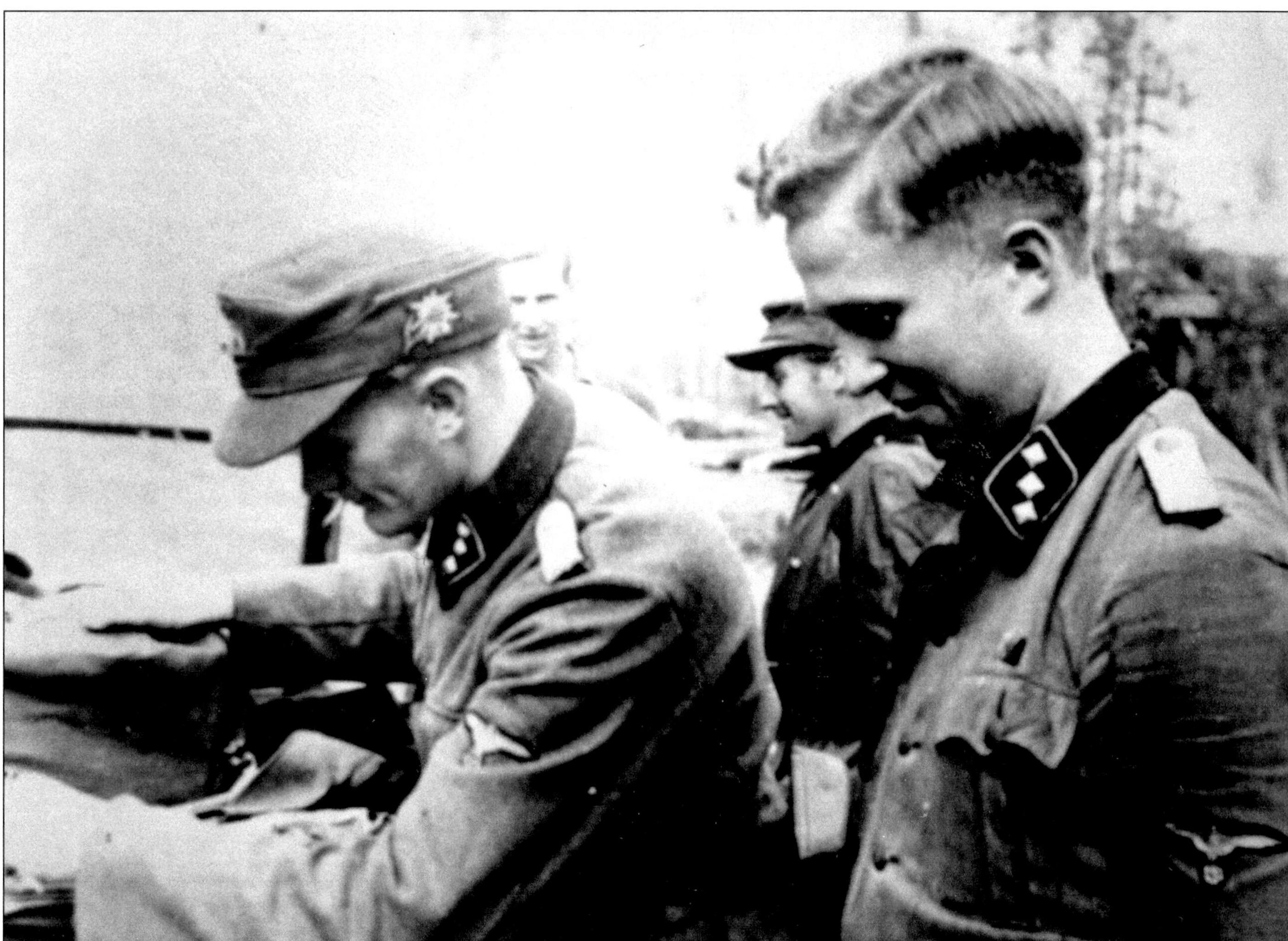

Front row from the left: *SS-Untersturmführer* Rolf Ugelstad and *SS-Untersturmführer* Torgeir Lofthus.

Vorne von links: die SS-Untersturmführer Rolf Ugelstad und Torgeir Lofthus.

The chief of HQ company, *SS-Untersturmführer* Rolf Ugelstad, and *SS-Untersturmführer* Torgeir Lofthus in front of Ugelstad's car.

Der Chef der Stabskompanie, SS-Untersturmführer Rolf Ugelstad, und SS-Untersturmführer Torgeir Lofthus an Ugelstads Wagen.

The car of the *Schijäger Battalion*'s commander, Frode Halle.

Das Auto des Kommandeurs des SS-Schijäger-Bataillons "Norge", Frode Halle.

Leaving in the evening. The trucks were loaded with all the equipment the men were unable to carry.

Aufbruch am Abend. Die LKWs beförderten Ausrüstung und Geräte, die von der Mannschaft nicht getragen werden konnten.

A platoon is ready to leave.

Ein Zug bereitet sich auf den Abmarsch vor.

Some were lucky and got a ride by truck. Among the soldiers this was known as an 'HH-trip' (*Heil Hitler Fahrt*).

Einige hatten Glück und wurden vom LKW mitgenommen. In der Landsersprache war dies als "HH-Fahrt" (Heil Hitler Fahrt) bekannt.

The march followed the road to a fixed meeting point every morning.

Der Marsch ging jeden Morgen die Straße entlang zu einem festen Treffpunkt.

From the left: *SS-Obersturmführer* Otto Holmen, an unknown person with his back to the camera and the commander of the *Schijäger Bataillon*, *SS-Hauptsturmführer* Frode Halle.

Von links: SS-Obersturmführer Otto Holmen, ein Unbekannter mit dem Rücken zur Kamera, und der Kommandeur des Schijäger-Bataillons, SS-Hauptsturmführer Frode Halle.

Time for a break in Rovaniemi. In the centre is company commander *SS-Untersturmführer* Arnfinn Vik.

Eine Ruhepause in Rovaniemi. In der Mitte Kompanieführer SS-Untersturmführer Arnfinn Vik.

Unknown *Schijäger* in Rovaniemi.

Unbekannte SS-Jäger in Rovaniemi.

The men approach Norway.

Die SS-Jäger nähern sich der norwegischen Grenze.

SS-Schijäger-Bataillon "Norge" – Heimkehr | *SS-Schijäger-Bataillon 'Norge'* – back in Norway

The men of the *Schijäger Bataillon* were celebrated upon their arrival in Narvik. Second from the right is Martin Skjefstad.

Es wurde gefeiert, als die SS-Jäger in Narvik einrückten. Nr. 2 von rechts: Martin Skjefstad.

The celebration in Narvik, attended by both German and Norwegian guests.

Bei dem Fest in Narvik waren deutsche und norwegische Gäste anwesend.

Two *Schijäger* after their return home.

Zwei heimgekehrte SS-Jäger.

Survivors of the Battle of Kaprolat and Hasselmann. From the left: Sverre Torgersen, Ragnar Nystrøm, Otto Carlson and Henrik Nordbach, all from *3. Company*.

Überlebende der Kämpfe um Kaprolat und Hasselmann. Von links: Sverre Torgersen, Ragnar Nystrøm, Otto Carlson und Henrik Nordbach, alle bei der 3. Kompanie.

The banquet dinner in Oslo following the return of the *Schijäger Bataillon*. From the left: platoon leader *SS-Untersturmführer* Tor Arntzen, company commander *SS-Obersturmführer* Martin Skjefstad and platoon leader *SS-Untersturmführer* Helge Staff.

Festessen in Oslo nach der Heimkehr des SS-Schijäger-Bataillons "Norge". Von links: Zugführer SS-Untersturmführer Tor Arntzen, Kompanieführer SS-Obersturmführer Martin Skjefstad und Zugführer SS-Untersturmführer Helge Staff.

6

3. SS-und Poliziekompanie

Die 3. SS-und Polizeikompanie, mit einer Mannschaftsstärke von 150 Mann, wurde im März 1944 unter der Führung von SS-Hauptsturmführer Aage Henry Berg und seinem Stellvertreter SS-Obersturmführer Oscar Rustand aufgestellt. Die Kompanie bestand aus drei Zügen, kommandiert von SS-Obersturmführer Oscar Rustand und den SS-Untersturmführern Sigurd Fodnes und Sverre Lyngstad. Die Freiwilligen hatten sich zu einem sechsmonatigen Fronteinsatz gemeldet, und sollten die 2. SS-und Polizeikompanie an der Front ablösen. Ein Drittel der Freiwilligen hatte schon früher an der Ostfront gedient. Einige der Bewerber kamen aus den Reihen der Polizei und des Arbeitsdiensts, während andere weder zuvor an der Front gedient hatten, noch Mitglieder einer landesweiten Organisation waren. Ein Beispiel für die Letztgenannten ist die Anwerbung von Abiturienten aus den staatlichen Gymnasien der NS.

Vor dem Fronteinsatz mussten die Norweger eine harte militärische Grundausbildung absolvieren. Diese fand Ende April bis Ende Juli 1944 im Ausbildungslager Sennheim statt, bevor es weiter mit dem Zug nach Danzig ging, und von dort mit dem Schiff nach Oulu in Finnland. Von Oulo ging der Transport durch die karelischen Wälder an die Front in eine etwa 100 Kilometer östlich von Kuusamo gelegene Gegend. Ursprünglich war die Kompanie für den Winterkrieg aufgestellt und ausgestattet worden, aber da es schon Sommer war als die Kompanie an der Front eintraf, wurden alle Streifen zu Fuß gemacht. Die Kompanie wurde der 6. SS-Geb.Div. "Nord" unterstellt, und hatte die Aufgabe, Aufklärungsaufträge im Niemandsland zu unternehmen. Da die Kompanie nie direkt an Kämpfen mit russischen Streitkräften beteiligt war, gab es weder Verwundete noch Gefallene während der Zeit in Finnland.

Die Waffenruhe zwischen Finnland und der Sowjetunion trat am 4. September 1944 in Kraft. Eine der Bedingungen der russischen Seite war der deutsche Rückzug aus finnischen Gebieten. Die 3. SS-und Polizeikompanie bildete die Nachhut während der deutschen Evakuierung aus Rovaniemi. Während des Rückzugs wurde die Kompanie von SS-Obersturmführer Oscar Rustand geführt und überquerte am 4. November 1944 die norwegische Grenze zu Fuss, um weiter nach Skibotn zu marschieren. Von hier ging es nach Bardufoss, bevor die Kompanie am 14. November 1944 in Øyjord nördlich von Narvik ankam. Da die Vertragszeit für den sechsmonatigen Fronteinsatz noch nicht abgelaufen war, wurde die Kompanie dem deutschen XIX. Gebirgs-Armeekorps (19) Armee-Abteilung Narvik unterstellt, und die drei Züge der Kompanie auf neun Stützpunkte von Tysfjord im Süden bis Porsangerfjorden im Norden verteilt. Die wichtigsten Aufgaben der Stützpunkte waren die Sicherung des deutschen Rückzugs von der Nord-Front, die Überwachung der SIS (Secret Intelligence Service) Radiosender, die über den deutschen Schiffsverkehr berichteten, und die Beobachtung von Aktivitäten der norwegischen Sepals-Basen, die vom amerikanischen Sicherheitsdienst OSS unterstützt wurden und auf der schwedischen Seite der Grenze operierten. Jeder Stützpunkt bestand aus 10 bis 25 Mann. Die nördlichen Stützpunkte wurden von Norwegern und österreichischen Gebirgsjägern bemannt, und konnten aus bis zu 50 Mann bestehen. Die Stützpunke im Süden waren nur mit Norwegern besetzt.

Im Zeitraum Ende März bis 17. April 1945 wurde die gesamte Kompanie in Narvik gesammelt, um mit Schiff und Zug in südlicher Richtung nach Oslo transportiert zu werden, wo sie am 21. April 1945 ankam. Hier wurden die Mannschaften und Offiziere am 23. April 1945 beurlaubt und bekamen den Befehl, sich am 14. Mai 1945 zum Dienst zurückzumelden.

6

3. SS-und Poliziekompanie

The *3. SS-und Polizeikompanie*, with a total of about 150 men, was activated in March 1944 under the leadership of commander *SS-Hauptsturmführer* Aage Henry Berg and his deputy commander *SS-Obersturmführer* Oscar Rustand. The company consisted of three troops, led by platoon leaders *SS-Obersturmführer* Oscar Rustand, *SS-Untersturmführer* Sigurd Fodnes and *SS-Untersturmführer* Sverre Lyngstad. All of the volunteers had signed up for six months of war service, and were to replace the *2. SS-und Polizeikompanie* currently located at the front. About a third of those who signed up as volunteers had previously served at the front. Some had a background in the police force, others came from the labour service, but there were also volunteers without former war experience or affiliation with national organisations. Examples of the latter were a number of students from secondary schools run by the NS.

Before serving at the front, the Norwegian soldiers had to undergo the Germans' gruelling training regime for new recruits, that took place at the German training camp Sennheim from late April 1944 until late July 1944. After completed training in Sennheim, the company was shipped by train from Sennheim to Gdánsk in late July 1944, and from there by boat to Oulu in Finland. From here the journey continued through the Karelian forests and all the way to the front, some 100 kilometres (60 miles) east of Kuusamo. Initially, the company had been activated and equipped for winter warfare, but since summer had arrived once they reached Finland, all patrols were conducted on foot. The company was placed under the direct command of the *6. SS-Gebirgs-Division 'Nord'* as a reconnaissance unit, and mostly carried out patrols in No Man's Land. Since there were no direct encounters with Soviet forces, the company experienced no casualties or losses during its time in Finland.

The ceasefire agreement between Finland and the Soviet Union was signed on 4 September 1944. One of the Soviet conditions was the withdrawal of all German troops from Finnish territory. The *3. SS-und Polizeikompanie*, led by *SS-Obersturmführer* Rustand, formed the rearguard during the German evacuation from Rovaniemi. On 4 November 1944, the company crossed the Norwegian border and marched to Skibotn on foot. From Skibotn the journey continued to Bardufoss, before the company arrived at Øyjord just north of Narvik on 14 November. As the stipulated six months of front duty had not yet expired, the company was placed under the command of the German *XIX. Gebirgs-Armeekorps (19) Armee-Abteilung Narvik*, and the company's three platoons were distributed among a total of nine strongpoints, from Tysfjord in the south to Porsangerfjord in the north. These strongpoints were primarily assigned the task of securing the German withdrawal from the northern front and monitoring SIS (Secret Intelligence Service) radio transmissions that reported on ship traffic and German vessels, as well as any activity at the allied Sepals bases, a Norwegian intelligence operation based in Sweden and supported by the American OSS. Each strongpoint comprised between 10 and 25 men. The northern strongpoints were frequently manned by both Norwegian soldiers and Austrian *Bergjäger* (mountain hunters), and could consist of as many as 50 men. The southern strongpoints were more or less exclusively Norwegian.

From the end of March 1945 until 17 April 1945, the entire company was gathered in Narvik and was subsequently transported southward by ship and train. Upon their arrival in Oslo on 21 April, the company was granted leave on 23 April, with orders to report back for duty on 14 May.

3. SS-und Polizeikompanie – Abreise aus Norwegen | *3. SS-und Polizeikompanie* – departure from Norway

Company commander *SS-Obersturmführer* Aage Henry Berg is handed the company's banner by Jonas Lie's adjutant, Hans Haug, in Oslo.

Jonas Lies Adjutant Hans Haug überreicht dem Kompanieführer SS-Obersturmführer Aage Henry Berg die Standarte der Kompanie in Oslo.

Company commander *SS-Obersturmführer* Aage Henry Berg in front of his company during the banner ceremony.

Kompanieführer SS-Obersturmführer Aage Henry Berg vor seiner Kompanie während der Standartenüberreichung.

A different view of company commander *SS-Obersturmführer* Aage Henry Berg in front of his company during the banner ceremony.

Kompanieführer SS-Obersturmführer Aage Henry Berg vor seiner Kompanie während der Standartenüberreichung.

The company marches through the streets of Oslo. At the front in the centre is Bjarne Dramstad.

Die Kompanie marschiert durch die Straßen Oslos. Vorne in der Mitte: Bjarne Dramstad.

Banquet dinner for the company before their departure for training in Germany. From the left: two unknown Germans, *SS-Obersturmführer* Aage Henry Berg and Hans Haug.

Festessen für die Kompanie vor dem Abmarsch zur Ausbildung in Deutschland. Von links: zwei Unbekannte, SS-Obersturmführer Aage Henry Berg und Hans Haug.

3. SS-und Polizeikompanie – Ausbildung in Sennheim | *3. SS-und Polizeikompanie* – training in Sennheim

The company filing out in Sennheim. First row from the left: an unknown German, *SS-Hauptsturmführer* Aage Henry Berg and *SS-Hauptsturmführer* Jouko Itälä from Finland. Second row from the left: an unknown German, *SS-Untersturmführer* Oscar Rustand, *SS-Oberscharführer* Rolf Huseby, unknown and *SS-Oberscharführer* Dagfinn Gjertsen.

Die Kompanie beim Ausmarsch in Sennheim. Erste Reihe von links: ein unbekannter Deutscher, SS-Hauptsturmführer Aage Henry Berg und SS-Hauptsturmführer Jouko Itälä aus Finnland. Zweite Reihe von links: ein unbekannter Deutscher, SS-Untersturmführer Oscar Rustand, SS-Oberscharführer Rolf Huseby, ein Unbekannter und SS-Oberscharführer Dagfinn Gjertsen.

Company commander *SS-Hauptsturmführer* Aage Henry Berg gives orders during a line-up in Sennheim, handing out specific tasks and military ranks to all the men.

Kompanieführer und SS-Hauptsturmführer Aage Henry Berg gibt während der Aufstellung in Sennheim Befehle, und erteilt jedem Mann eine besondere Aufgabe und einen militärischen Rang.

Company commander *SS-Hauptsturmführer* Aage Henry Berg greeting an unknown *SS-Unterscharführer.*

Kompanieführer SS-Hauptsturmführer Aage Henry Berg begrüßt einen unbekannten SS-Unterscharführer.

Company commander *SS-Hauptsturmführer* Aage Henry Berg and deputy commander *SS-Untersturmführer* Oscar Rustand.

Kompanieführer SS-Hauptsturmführer Aage Henry Berg und sein Stellvertreter, SS-Untersturmführer Oscar Rustand.

A break during the line-up.

Eine Ruhepause während der Aufstellung.

Training with an MG-42 in Sennheim, using live ammunition.

Übung mit einem MG 42 in Sennheim. Es wurde mit scharfer Munition geschossen.

Czech machine guns were also used during training in Sennheim, but mostly as backup weapons.

Auch tschechische Maschinengewehre wurden bei der Ausbildung in Sennheim benutzt, aber vorwiegend als Reservewaffe.

There was a lot of hard training in Sennheim to prepare the soldiers for the rigours of life on the front.

In Sennheim wurde hart trainiert, um die Soldaten auf das anstrengende Leben an der Front vorzubereiten.

The food tasted particularly good after a training session. At the back in the centre is company commander Aage Henry Berg.

Nach den Übungen schmeckte das Essen besonders gut. Hinten in der Mitte Kompanieführer Aage Henry Berg.

Preparing for the departure to Finland by train and boat.

Klarmachen zur Abreise nach Finnland mit Zug und Schiff.

Preparing for the departure to Finland by train and boat.

Klarmachen zur Abreise nach Finnland mit Zug und Schiff.

3. SS-und Polizeikompanie an der Front | *3. SS-und Polizeikompanie* at the front

The company is lodged in plywood tents, having arrived in Finland.

Die Kompanie ist in Finnland angekommen und wird in finnischen Sperrholz-Zelten untergebracht.

Establishing a telephone connection with HQ and the various troops.

Die Fernsprechverbindung mit dem Stab und den verschiedenen Zügen wird hergestellt.

Company commander *SS-Hauptsturmführer* Aage Henry Berg, left, in front of one of the camouflaged plywood tents.

Von links: Kompanieführer SS-Hauptsturmführer Aage Henry Berg vor einem der getarnten finnischen Zelte.

Occasionally the soldiers also built small timber huts to live in.

Holzhütten wurden auch gezimmert.

The men's teeth were checked by dentists during their time in Finland. One of the members of *3. Police Company* was a dentist.

Die Zähne wurden von den Zahnärzten in Finnland untersucht. Ein Freiwilliger der 3. Kompanie war Zahnarzt.

The hairdresser was busy as well during quiet times behind the front.

Auch der Friseur hatte viel zu tun, wenn es ruhig hinter der Front war.

The armament artificer of *3. Police Company, SS-Unterscharführer* August Amundsen, fills out the soldiers' pay books. He was a veteran of the *Norwegian Legion* and had previously spent several years with the French Foreign Legion in Africa.

Der Waffenwart der Kompanie, SS-Unterscharführer August Amundsen, füllt die Soldbücher aus. Er war ein Veteran der SS-Frw.-Legion Norwegen, und hatte 1931–36 in der französischen Fremdenlegion in Afrika gedient.

SS-Unterscharführer August Amundsen, left, inside his tent.

Links: SS-Unterscharführer August Amundsen in seinem Zelt.

A party in a tent behind the front.

Eine Feier in einem Zelt hinter der Front.

It was crowded inside the tents, with little space to sleep.

Es war eng in den Zelten und wenig Platz zum Schlafen.

Platoon leader *SS-Untersturmführer* Sverre Lyngstad came from the police force and had been trained as a Norwegian officer. He was strict, but popular among his men.

Zugführer SS-Untersturmführer Sverre Lyngstad war ausgebildeter norwegischer Offizier, und kam aus den Reihen der Polizei. Obwohl er sehr streng war, war er beliebt bei seiner Mannschaft.

First sergeant *SS-Oberscharführer* Dagfinn Gjertsen was a veteran of the *Norwegian Legion*. He was disliked by the soldiers, since he snitched about everything to the company commander.

Feldwebel und SS-Oberscharführer Dagfinn Gjertsen war ein Veteran der SS-Frw.-Legion Norwegen. Er war nicht beliebt bei seinen Soldaten, da er sie beim Kompanieführer ständig verpetzte.

From the left: *SS-Unterscharführer* Finn Forsberg, *SS-Unterscharführer* Gunnar Preus Olsen (a veteran of *1. Police Company*) and *SS-Unterscharführer* Olav Bleka. All three had been police officers by profession before joining the company.

Von links: die SS-Unterscharführer Finn Forsberg und Gunnar Preus Olsen, letzterer ein Veteran der 1. SS-und Polizeikompanie, gefolgt von Olav Bleka. Vor dem Fronteinsatz waren alle drei als Polizeibeamten tätig gewesen.

3. SS-und Polizeikompanie – der Marsch in die Heimat | *3. SS-und Polizeikompanie* – the march to Norway

The company prepares for the march home to Norway, following Finland's ceasefire agreement with the Soviet Union.

Nach dem Waffenstillstandsabkommen mit der Sowjetunion macht sich die Kompanie für den Rückzug nach Norwegen bereit.

Normann Quist, left, during the return march.

Von links: Normann Quist während des Rückmarsches.

MG-gunners had a demanding job, since they had to haul along the heavy machine gun.

Die MG-Schützen hatten schwer zu tun, da es ihre Aufgabe war, das Maschinengewehr zu befördern.

From the left: *SS-Untersturmführer* Sverre Lyngstad, three unknowns, *SS-Hauptsturmführer* Frode Halle and *SS-Untersturmführer* Willy Amundsen during the return march.

Von links: SS-Untersturmführer Sverre Lyngstad, drei Unbekannte, SS-Hauptsturmführer Frode Halle und SS-Untersturmführer Willy Amundsen bei dem Rückzug.

A meal break during the return march to Norway.

Essenspause beim Rückmarsch nach Norwegen.

Company commander *SS-Hauptsturmführer* Aage Henry Berg on a motorcycle during the return march.

Kompanieführer SS-Hauptsturmführer Aage Henry Berg auf einem Krad während des Rückmarsches.

The field kitchen was always appreciated during the tiring march back home.

Die Feldküche war während des harten Rückmarsches immer gefragt.

In the front row are *SS-Oberscharführer* Dagfinn Gjertsen, left, and Nils Wathne.

Erste Reihe von links: SS-Oberscharführer Dagfinn Gjertsen und Nils Wathne.

3. Police Company preparing for the night's march.

Die 3. Kompanie macht sich für den nächtlichen Marsch bereit.

Sometimes the soldiers found a house to sleep in, and didn't have to put up tents.

Manchmal fanden die Soldaten ein Haus zum Schlafen, und brauchten nicht ihre Zelte aufzustellen.

From the left: two/three unknowns, followed by platoon leader Olav Fodnes.

Von links: zwei/drei Unbekannte, dann Zugführer Olav Fodnes.

Company commander *SS-Hauptsturmführer* Aage Henry Berg in conversation with a front-line nurse after the company arrived in Norway.

Die Kompanie ist in Norwegen angekommen. Kompanieführer SS-Hauptsturmführer Aage Henry Berg im Gespräch mit einer DRK-Schwester.

3. SS-und Polizeikompanie im Dienst in Nord-Norwegen | *3. SS-und Polizeikompanie* on duty in Northern Norway

Company line-up in Narvik after the return to Norway.

Aufstellung der Kompanie in Narvik nach der Ankunft in Norwegen.

Company commander *SS-Hauptsturmführer* Aage Henry Berg addresses the soldiers, informing them that they will be assigned to various strongpoints.

Kompanieführer SS-Hauptsturmführer Aage Henry Berg hält eine Ansprache an die Soldaten und teilt ihnen mit, dass sie an verschiedene Stützpunkte versetzt werden.

The company lines up before being assigned to various strongpoints.

Die Kompanie wird gemustert und an die verschiedenen Stützpunkte verteilt.

The funeral of the company's only fallen soldier, Otto Moen. Reportedly, his death was illness-related.

Die Beerdigung Otto Moens, des einzigen Gefallenen der Kompanie. Vermutlich starb er an einer Krankheit.

Company commander *SS-Hauptsturmführer* Aage Henry Berg delivers a speech at the funeral.

Kompanieführer SS-Hauptsturmführer Aage Henry Berg hält eine Ansprache bei der Beerdigung.

From the left: Arne Kroken, *SS-Untersturmführer* Sverre Lyngstad and *SS-Oberscharführer* Dagfinn Gjertsen in Narvik.

Von links: Arne Kroken, SS-Untersturmführer Sverre Lyngstad und SS-Oberscharführer Dagfinn Gjertsen in Narvik.

SS-Untersturmführer Sverre Lyngstad, left, and *SS-Oberscharführer* Dagfinn Gjertsen in Narvik.

Von links: SS-Untersturmführer Sverre Lyngstad und SS-Oberscharführer Dagfinn Gjertsen in Narvik.

A group from *3. Police Company* on patrol together with German soldiers. Here they are taking a lunch break during a ski patrol.

Eine Gruppe der 3. SS-und Polizeikompanie auf Aufklärungsfahrt zusammen mit deutschen Soldaten. Hier bei einer Essenspause.

Soldiers from *3. Police Company* and members of the German Navy. The photo was taken in Sør-Skjomen near Narvik, where the German Navy's *14. U-Boot-Flottille* was based from December 1944 to May 1945.

Soldaten der 3. SS-und Polizeikompanie und Angehörige der deutschen Kriegsmarine. Aufnahme aus Sør-Skjomen in der Nähe von Narvik, wo die 14. U-Boot-Flottille von Dezember 1944 bis Mai 1945 stationiert war.

A break during patrol duty. To the right is *SS-Unterscharführer* Finn Forsberg.

Eine Ruhepause während der Aufklärungsfahrt. Rechts: SS-Unterscharführer Finn Forsberg.

An unknown police soldier.

Ein unbekannter Soldat.

Patrol duty in the spring of 1945 outside Narvik.

Aufklärungsfahrt im Frühjahr 1945 außerhalb von Narvik.

Company commander *SS-Hauptsturmführer* Aage Henry Berg visiting the various strongpoints in the southern sector by boat.

Kompanieführer SS-Hauptsturmführer Aage Henry Berg besichtigt die verschiedenen Stützpunkte im südlichen Abschnitt per Boot.

SS-Oberscharführer Dagfinn Gjertsen at his office in Narvik.

SS-Oberscharführer Dagfinn Gjertsen in seinem Büro in Narvik.

Lining up for the award ceremony for *3. Police Company* in Narvik.

Aufstellung und Verleihung von Auzeichnungen an Angehörige der 3. SS-und Polizeikompanie.

Front row from the left: *SS-Untersturmführer* Sverre Lyngstad and Sverre Knarud.

Erste Reihe von links: SS-Untersturmführer Sverre Lyngstad und Sverre Knarud.

The General of the *Gebirgskorps Norwegen* (Mountain Corps Norway), Ferdinand Alfred Friedrich Jodl, conferred the awards.

Der General des Gebirgskorps Norwegen, Ferdinand Alfred Friedrich Jodl, verlieh die Auszeichnungen.

Company commander *SS-Hauptsturmführer* Aage Henry Berg receives the War Merit Cross 1st Class with Swords. He was the only Norwegian to be awarded this distinction.

Kompanieführer SS-Hauptsturmführer Aage Henry Berg erhält das Kriegsverdienstkreuz (KVK) 1. Klasse mit Schwertern. Er war der einzige Norweger, dem diese Auszeichnung verliehen wurde.

SS-Untersturmführer Sverre Lyngstad receives the War Merit Cross 2nd Class with Swords.

SS-Untersturmführer Sverre Lyngstad erhält das Kriegsverdienstkreuz 2. Klasse mit Schwertern.

An unknown *SS-Unterscharführer* receives the War Merit Cross 2nd class with Swords.

Ein unbekannter SS-Unterscharführer erhält das Kriegsverdienstkreuz 2. Klasse mit Schwertern.

Ferdinand Alfred Friedrich Jodl and company commander *SS-Hauptsturmführer* Aage Henry Berg after the ceremony.

Ferdinand Alfred Friedrich Jodl und Kompanieführer SS-Hauptsturmführer Aage Henry Berg nach der Verleihung.

Following the award ceremony, the company marches to the banquet dinner.

Nach der Verleihungsfeier marschiert die Kompanie zum Festessen.

From the left: Henrik Preus Olsen, Gunnar Preus Olsen, Anders Lysne, Arne Wallas and Finn Forsberg, all of whom were an *SS-Unterscharführer.*

Von links: die SS-Unterscharführer Henrik Preus Olsen, Gunnar Preus Olsen, Anders Lysne, Arne Wallas und Finn Forsberg.

Company commander *SS-Hauptsturmführer* Aage Henry Berg and *SS-Untersturmführer* Sverre Lyngstad.

Kompanieführer SS-Hauptsturmführer Aage Henry Berg und SS-Untersturmführer Sverre Lyngstad.

Company commander *SS-Hauptsturmführer* Aage Henry Berg awarding the Iron Cross 2nd Class to Odd Stigen for his efforts in Finnmark.

Kompanieführer SS-Hauptsturmführer Aage Henry Berg verleiht Odd Stigen das Eiserne Kreuz 2. Klasse für seinen Einsatz in Finnmark.

The *3. Police Company* prepares for departure from Narvik after completing its mission in the North.

Die 3. SS-und Polizeikompanie macht sich nach beendetem Auftrag im Norden zum Abmarsch aus Narvik bereit.

3. SS-und Polizeikompanie – Heimkehr nach Oslo | *3. SS-und Polizeikompanie* – the return to Oslo

The soldiers load equipment into the train before departing for Oslo.

Bevor es in Richtung Oslo geht, wird die Ausrüstung in den Zug geladen.

A police soldier with a full pack getting ready for the trip to Oslo.

Ein Soldat mit vollem Gepäck macht sich für die Fahrt nach Oslo bereit.

Cattle wagons were used to transport the men all the way to Oslo.

Mit dem Kuhwagen ging es ganz nach Oslo.

Some soldiers spent part of the trip in open wagons. The picture shows two soldiers watching the field kitchen.

Einige Soldaten verbrachten Teile der Fahrt in offenen Waggons. Hier zwei Soldaten, die sich um die Feldküche kümmern.

Odd Stigen on his way to Oslo with his Karelian walking cane.

Odd Stigen auf dem Weg nach Oslo mit seinem karelischen Wanderstock.

At last, the *3. Police Company* arrive home in Oslo and meet their loved ones. It was the end of April 1945, and everyone was granted two weeks of leave until 14 May. The war was over before they ever had a chance to return.

Endlich war die 3. SS-und Polizeikompanie zurück in Oslo angekommen. Es war Ende April 1945, und die Angehörigen der Kompanie bekamen zwei Wochen Urlaub bis zum 14.05. Bevor sie zurückkehren konnten, war der Krieg zu Ende.

The train journey to Oslo.

Die Zugfahrt nach Oslo.

7

23. SS-Panzergrenadier-Regiment "Norge"

Mitte Februar 1943 besuchte Reichsführer-SS Heinrich Himmler die SS-Freiwilligen-Legion Norwegen, die von der Front zurückgezogen und dem Ersatzbataillon in Mitau (Jelgava), Lettland, zugeführt worden war. In seiner Rede an die Mannschaften und Offiziere der Legion forderte er sie auf, sich beim neuen Regiment "Norge" weiterhin zu verpflichten. Als Lockmittel wurde den Soldaten ein Heimaturlaub in Norwegen angeboten, während die Offiziere mit einer Beförderung rechnen konnten.

Im März 1943 begann die Anwerbung mit einem Aufruf des Ministerpräsidenten Vidkun Quisling in der Presse. Gleichzeitig hatte der Stabsleiter der Germanischen SS Norwegen (GSSN), SS-Obersturmführer Olaf Lindvig, die Mitglieder der GSSN aufgefordert, eine gesammelte Kompanie für das neue Regiment aufzustellen.

Im Mai 1943 versammelte sich die SS-Frw.-Legion Norwegen am Truppenübungsplatz Grafenwöhr in Bayern, und wurde am 10. Mai 1943 zur Entlassung nach Norwegen geschickt. Das neue Regiment unterlag deutscher Leitung: das I./SS-Pz.Gren.Rgt. 23 "Norge" bestand aus Norwegischen Angehörigen der aufgelösten SS-Frw.-Legion Norwegen samt einer Reihe von Reichsdeutschen unter der Leitung von SS-Sturmbannführer Finn Finson; das II./SS-Pz.Gren.Rgt 23 "Norge" wurde mit Offizieren und Angehörigen des II./SS-Inf.Rgts. "Nordland" unter der Leitung von SS-Sturmbannführer Albrecht Krügel besetzt; und das III./SS-Pz.Gren.Rgt. 23 "Norge" ging aus dem ehemaligen I./SS-Inf.Rgt. "Nordland" unter der Leitung von SS-Sturmbannführer Hans-Heinrich Lohmann hervor. Am 1. Juni 1943 wurde das Regiment offiziell aufgestellt. Im Juli 1943 stellte es sich heraus, dass der Nachschub an freiwilligen Norwegern zu gering war, um das neue Regiment auf die Beine zu stellen. Daher wurde eine große Anzahl von Freiwilligen aus Rumänien und Ungarn – Siebenbürger Sachsen und Banater Schwaben – zugeteilt, die im Regiment die Mehrzahl ausmachten. Die Norweger wurden über sämtliche Kompanien verteilt, während die "norwegischen" Kompanien des I. Bataillons aufgelöst wurden. Die einzige Ausnahme war die 1. Kompanie, in der die Norweger der Germanischen SS Norwegen die Mehrheit behielten.

Ende August 1943 wurde das Regiment nach Kroatien verlegt, wobei das I. und III. Bataillon in Kostanica stationiert wurde, und das II. Bataillon nach Bosn Nowi kam. Während die Ausbildung fortgesetzt wurde, gab es eine Reihe von Sicherungsaufträgen, und es kam auch zu Kämpfen mit Partisanen. Einige der Norweger wollten unter diesen Umständen nicht am Krieg teilnehmen, und hatten überdies Schwerigkeiten mit der deutschen Kommandosprache. Daher stellten sie den Antrag, als Freiwillige zum SS-Jäg.Schi.Btl. "Norge" versetzt zu werden. Es kam zu Streitigkeiten um die Mannschaft, und alle, die sich freiwillig zum Dienst in Finnland gemeldet hatten, wurden von ihren Kameraden unter Druck gesetzt. Mitte November 1943 verließen die betroffenen Norweger das Regiment "Norge", und bekamen einige Zeit später den Befehl, sich beim Abschnitt Oranienbaum zu melden.

Das Regiment wurde mit dem Zug nach Oranienbaum transportiert und kam dort Anfang Dezember 1943 an. In der Nacht zum 12. Dezember 1943 wurde das II. und III./Norge, sowie der Regimentsstab samt Stabskompanie and die Frontlinie verlegt, während das I./Norge als Korpsreserve nach Golubowitzy geschickt wurde. Am Morgen des 14. Januar 1944 unternahm die 2. russische Stoßarmee eine Offensive um aus dem Oranienbaumer Kessel auszubrechen. Der Hauptangriff richtete sich direkt gegen die 10. Luftwaffen-Feld-Division, und am Nachmittag erhielt das I./Norge den Befehl einzugreifen und die Frontlinie zu stabiliseren. Das Bataillon wurde frühmorgens am 15. Januar zwischen Sajostrowja und Korpowitzy (?) in Kämpfe verwickelt, und musste sich bis zum 24. Januar in eine Verteidigungsstellung bei Kosherizy zurückziehen. In der Nacht zum 27. Januar hatte das gesamte III. (Germ.) SS-Pz.Korps den Rückzug nach Jamburg angetreten, und um den 30. Januar nahm das Regiment "Norge" eine Stellung südlich von Jamburg ein, wo bis zum nächsten Tag gekämpft wurde. Daraufhin wurde eine neue Verteidigungsstellung bei Dubrowka eingenommen, die am 2. Februar 1944 nach schweren Kämpfen verlassen wurde. Mitte Februar 1944 wurde das I./Norge in Narwa aufgelöst und die Mannschaften an das II. und III./Norge verteilt. Das Regiment "Norge" wurde in seine Verteidigungsstellungen südlich der Stadt geschickt, und im Februar/ März 1944 kämpfte ein Einsatzkommando unter Leitung von SS-Sturmbannführer Krügel mit drei Kompanien (7., 11. und 16./Norge) um das Dorf Siivertsi .

Im Juni 1944 wurden die Mannschaften des aufgelösten I./Norge nach Hammerstein in Pommern befördert [transportiert], wo die Neuaufstellung der Einheit begonnen hatte. Dieses Bataillon kehrte nie wieder zu seinem Stammregiment zurück, wurde aber im November 1944 an die Front in Modlin, Polen, verlegt und dem IV SS-Pz.

7

23. SS-Panzergrenadier-Regiment 'Norge'

In mid-February 1943, *Reichsführer-SS* Heinrich Himmler visited the *SS-Freiwilligen-Legion Norwegen*, which had been withdrawn from the front and relocated to the replacement battalion in Mitau (Jelgava), Latvia. In his speech to the soldiers and officers of the Legion, Himmler encouraged the men to continue serving in the newly activated *Regiment 'Norge'*. To provide an incentive, anyone willing to enlist for further service would immediately be granted leave in Norway and many of the officers were given a promotion.

Enlistment began in early March 1943 in Norway, following an appeal by Minister-President Vidkun Quisling in the media. At the same time, the chief of staff of the *Germanic SS Norway* (GSSN), *SS-Obersturmführer* Olaf Lindvig, had urged members of the GSSN to assemble a company-sized unit to place at the disposal of the new regiment.

In May of 1943, the *Norwegian Legion* was assembled at the military training area Grafenwöhr in Bavaria to be sent back to Norway for discharge around 10 May 1943. The new regiment, *I./SS-Pz.Gren.Rgt. 23 'Norge'*, was activated under German leadership with Norwegians from the dissolved Legion as well as ethnic German volunteers, and placed under the command of *SS-Sturmbannführer* Finn Finson. The *II./SS-Pz.Gren.Rgt. 23 'Norge'* was activated with soldiers and officers from the *II./SS-Inf.Rgt. 'Nordland'* under the leadership of *SS-Sturmbannführer* Albrecht Krügel, while the *III./SS-Pz.Gren.Rgt. 23 'Norge'* consisted of former members of the *I./SS-Inf.Rgt. 'Nordland'*, commanded by *SS-Sturmbannführer* Hans-Heinrich Lohmann. On 1 June 1943, the *SS-Pz.Gren.Rgt. 'Norge'* was formally activated. In early July of 1943 it became clear that there was an insufficient supply of Norwegian volunteers to complete the new regiment, and a large number of Transylvanian Saxons from Romania and Banat Swabians from Hungary were enlisted. These were to make up the bulk of volunteers in the regiment.

The Norwegians were spread throughout all the companies. With the exception of *1. Company*, which retained most of the Norwegians from the GSSN, the 'Norwegian' companies of *I. Battalion* were split up and redistributed.

Towards the end of August 1943, the regiment was transferred to Croatia, where *I.* and *III./Norge* were sent to Kostanica, and *II./Norge* was sent to Bosn Nowi. While their training continued, they carried out security tasks and also had a number of encounters with partisans. The realities of serving in Croatia, as well as the fact that the command language was German, led a large part of the Norwegian volunteers to apply for transfer to the newly activated *SS-Jäg.Schi.Btl. 'Norge'*, which was bound for Finland. A quarrel ensued about the issue, and those who expressed a wish to be transferred to Finland were pressured by their fellow soldiers and officers to remain in the regiment. In mid-November 1943, those Norwegians wishing to be transferred to Finland left *Regiment 'Norge'*. Some time later, the regiment received orders for transfer to Oranienbaum.

The regiment was transported to Oranienbaum by train and arrived in early December 1943. On the night of 12 December 1943, *II.* and *III./Norge*, together with the regimental staff and HQ company, were ordered to the battlefront, while *I./Norge* was sent to Golubowitzy as a corps reserve. On the morning of 14 January 1944, two Russian shock armies launched their main attack from Oranienbaum. The attack was directed at the field division of the *10. Luftwaffe*, and that afternoon *I./Norge* received orders to be inserted in order to stabilise the front line. On the morning of 15 January, the battalion became engaged in fighting between Sajostrowja and Korpowitzy (?)[AQ28: is this name confirmed or not?It is], and subsequently pulled back to Kosherizy, where it took up a defensive position that was held until 24 January. On the night of 26/27 January, the entire *III. (Germ.) SS-Pz.Korps* retreated towards Jamburg, and on or around 30 January, *Regiment 'Norge'* went into position south of the city. Here the fighting continued until 31 January, when a new defensive position was established near Dubrowka., but the position was abandoned following encounters with the enemy on 2 February. In mid-February, *I./Norge* was dissolved in Narva, and the men distributed across the remaining two battalions. Consequently, *Regiment 'Norge'* was transferred to a defensive position south of the city, and a task force led by *Sturmbannführer* Krügel fought together with three companies (*Nos. 7, 11* and *16/23*) to conquer the village of Siivertsi in February/March.

In early June 1944, the members of the disbanded *I./Norge* were transported to Hammerstein in Pomerania, where the formation of the new *I./Norge* was under way. The battalion never returned to its core regiment, but was relocated to Modlin, Poland, in late November 1944 and attached to the *IV SS Panzer Corps*. In late December, the battalion was transferred to Hungary to join in the relief of Budapest, which had been encircled by Soviet forces since

Korps unterstellt. Ende Dezember 1944 wurde das Bataillon nach Ungarn beordert, um an den Kämpfen um die Stadt Budapest, die seit Dezember 1944 von russischen Truppen eingekesselt war, teilzunehmen. Das Bataillon beteiligte sich an den Unternehmen "Konrad I" und "Konrad III", kämpfte sich aber im März aus Ungarn heraus und löste sich im Mai 1945 in Österreich auf.

Am 25. Juli 1944 begann der Rückzug in die Tannenberg-Stellung, deren Verteidigung bei den Kämpfen um die Höhen Kinderheim, Grenadier und Höhe 69,9 zu großen Verlusten auf beiden Seiten führte. Die Front bewegte sich hin und zurück, stabilisierte sich aber am 30. Juli bis zum Rückzug am 18. September.

Daraufhin kam das Regiment vom 23.–27. September zum Einsatz bei Baldone südöstlich von Riga, und kehrte ins Kurland zurück. Hier nahm das Regiment am 16. und 17. Oktober an drei schweren Kämpfen teil, wobei die Frontlinie immer näher an Preekuln heranrückte.

Nach den Kämpfen im Januar 1945 wurde das Regiment per Schiff nach Pommern verlegt, wo es durch neue Mannschaften und Soldaten des Volkssturms ergänzt wurde. Am 15. Februar hatten die Kämpfe bei Schlagenthin und Arnswalde wieder begonnen, und das Regiment zog sich im März nach Stettin-Altdamm zurück. Danach wurde es an die Westseite der Oder verlegt, und beteiligte sich ab 17. April an den Verteidigungskämpfen um Berlin, bis zum Endkampf und der Kapitulation am 2. Mai 1945.

December 1944. The battalion participated in Operation 'Konrad' I and III, but fought its way out of Hungary in March 1945 and disintegrated two months later in Austria.

The retreat towards the Tannenberg position began on 25 July 1944, its defence leading to great losses on both sides in the battles for the hills of Kinderheim, Grenadier and Höhe 66.9. The front wavered back and forth, but stabilised on 30 July until the withdrawal on 18 September.

At Baldone, south-east of Riga, the regiment encountered enemy forces between 23 and 27 September and retreated further back into Courland. Here they participated in three major battles on 16 and 27 October while the front line drew closer to Prekuln (Priekule).

After further battles in early January 1945, the regiment was shipped to Pomerania by boat and supplied with new troops from the German national militia *Volkssturm* ('people's assault'). Fighting resumed on 15 February at Schlagenthin and Arnswalde, where the regiment retreated to Stettin-Altdamm in March 1945. Subsequently, the regiment was sent to the western side of the river Oder, participating in defensive battles and retreating all the way to Berlin until the capitulation on 2 May 1945.

23. SS-Panzergrenadier-Regiment "Norge" – Abreise aus Norwegen | *23. SS-Panzergrenadier-Regiment 'Norge' – departure from Norway*

Recruitment brochure for *Regiment 'Norge'*.

Anwerbungsblatt des Regiments "Norge".

GSSN Company, led by *SS-Obersturmführer* Olaf Lindvig, marching down Karl Johans gate in Oslo, in the spring of 1943.

Die Kompanie der GSSN, geführt von SS-Obersturmführer Olaf Lindvig beim Marsch durch Oslos Karl Johans gate, Frühjahr 1943.

New recruits to the *Norwegian Legion* at Holmestrand before their departure for training in Germany. Since the Legion was disbanded, none of them ever joined. Instead, all of them signed up with *Regiment 'Norge'*.

Neue Rekruten der SS-Frw.-Legion Norwegen in Holmestrand vor der Abreise zur Ausbildung in Deutschland. Keiner von ihnen trat jemals der Legion bei, da die Einheit aufgelöst wurde. Stattdessen kamen sie zum Regiment "Norge".

23. SS-Panzergrenadier-Regiment "Norge" in Sennheim | *23. SS-Panzergrenadier-Regiment 'Norge' in Sennheim*

Standing, first row from the right, is Johan Peter Balstad, an instructor at Sennheim between 1941 and 1943 due to his excellent knowledge of German. The picture shows the training staff at Sennheim.

Stehend, erste Reihe von rechts: Johan Peter Balstad, der Dank seiner guten Deutschkenntnisse 1941–43 Hilfsausbilder in Sennheim war. Die Gruppenaufnahme zeigt das Ausbildungspersonal in Sennheim.

Shooting practice in Sennheim.

Schießausbildung in Sennheim.

Rifle practice with a K-98 in Sennheim.

Gewehrdrill mit einem K 98 in Sennheim.

Johan Peter Balstad in Sennheim, aiming his gun at the photographer.

Johan Peter Balstad in Sennheim, mit dem Gewehrlauf zum Fotografen.

SS-Sturmmann Johan Peter Balstad at Sennheim, wearing a forage cap.

SS-Sturmmann Johan Peter Balstad mit Schiffchen in Sennheim.

23. SS-Panzergrenadier-Regiment "Norge" in Grafenwöhr/Auerbach | *23. SS-Panzergrenadier-Regiment 'Norge'* in Grafenwöhr/Auerbach

The *7. Company 'Norge'* in Auerbach, in the summer of 1943. In the first row are company NCOs; with an accordion is Gunnar Verpe. From the left: *SS-Unterscharführer* Winkels, sergeant and *SS-Hauptscharführer* Hans Engels and troop leader *SS-Hauptscharführer* Karl Peter Theilacker.

7. Kompanie "Norge" in Auerbach, Sommer 1943. Erste Reihe: Unteroffiziere der Kompanie. Mit Akkordeon: Gunnar Verpe. Von links: 1. SS-Unterscharführer Winkels, 2. Spieß und SS-Hauptscharführer Hans Engels und 3. Zugführer SS-Hauptscharführer Karl Peter Theilacker.

Auerbach, in the summer of 1943. Bjørn Noreger, head of the front-fighter office, is giving a speech during a visit. The room is filled with Norwegians. First row from the left: battalion adjutant of *III./Norge, 1. SS-Untersturmführer* Per Halse; battalion commander of *III./Norge, SS-Sturmbannführer* Hans Heinrich Lohmann; regimental adjutant *SS-Hauptsturmführer* Frode Halle; company commander of *1./Norge, SS-Hauptsturmführer* Olaf Lindvig; head of the GSSN, Leif Schjøren; company commander of *2./Norge, SS-Obersturmführer* Tor Marstrander; company commander of *7./Norge, SS-Obersturmführer* Hans Georg Holter; and platoon leader with *1./Norge, SS-Untersturmführer* Wolfgang Rendemann. The latter became company commander of *2./Norge* when Marstrander returned to Norway.

Auerbach, Sommer 1943. Besuch vom Leiter des Frontkämpferbüros, Bjørn Noreger, der eine Rede hält. Der Saal ist gefüllt mit Norwegern. Erste Reihe von links: Bataillonsadjutant III./Norge, 1. SS-Untersturmführer Per Halse; Bataillonskommandeur III./Norge, SS-Sturmbannführer Hans Heinrich Lohmann; Regimentsadjutant, SS-Hauptsturmführer Frode Halle; Kompanieführer 1./Norge, SS-Hauptsturmführer Olaf Lindvig; Leiter der GSSN, Leif Schjøren; Kompanieführer 2./Norge, SS-Obersturmführer Tor Marstrander; Kompanieführer 7./Norge, SS-Obersturmführer Hans Georg Holter; und Zugführer in der 1./Norge, SS-Untersturmführer Wolfgang Rendemann. Er übernahm die 2./Norge, als Marstrander entlassen wurde und nach Norwegen zurückkehrte.

Auerbach, in the early summer of 1943. Standing from the left: sixth, *Hauptsturmführer* Olaf Lindvig; seventh, *SS-Obersturmführer* Tor Marstrander; 10th, *SS-Untersturmführer* Willy Amundsen; 11th, *SS-Untersturmführer* Sverre Hagtun.

Auerbach, Frühsommer 1943. Stehend von links: Nr. 6 SS-Hauptsturmführer Olaf Lindvig, Nr. 7 SS-Obersturmführer Tor Marstrander, Nr. 10 SS-Untersturmführer Willy Amundsen, Nr. 11. SS-Untersturmführer Sverre Hagtun. (?)

The *10. Company 'Norge'* during an MG exercise in Auerbach, in the summer of 1943. Standing second from the leftis Knut Baardseth.

Die 10. Kompanie "Norge" bei einer MG-Übung in Auerbach, Sommer 1943. Stehend Nr. 2 von links: Knut Baardseth.

Auerbach, in the summer of 1943. Henrik Møllmann-Osmoen from *10. Company 'Norge'* behind an MG-42.

Auerbach, Sommer 1943. Henrik Møllmann-Osmoen von der 10. Kompanie hinter einem MG 42.

Visitors at *Regiment 'Norge'* in Auerbach, in the late July of 1943. At the front is Minister Axel Stang together with General Felix Steiner.

Besuch beim Regiment "Norge" in Auerbach, Ende Juli 1943. Vorne Minister Axel Stang zusammen mit General Felix Steiner.

Auerbach training camp, in the summer of 1943.

Auerbach Truppenübungsplatz, Sommer 1943.

During a weekend outing in Auerbach, some of the Norwegian volunteers of *Regiment 'Norge'* met Hermann Göring, whose hunting lodge lay nearby. From the left: Oddvar Halbostad, Göring, unknown and Finn Røsshammer.

Norwegische Freiwillige des Regiments "Norge" in Auerbach während eines Ausflugs mit Hermann Göring, der ein Jagdschloss in der Nähe besaß. Von links: Oddvar Halbostad, Göring, ein Unbekannter und Finn Røsshammer.

Food queue in Auerbach.

Warteschlange zum Essenfassen in Auerbach.

The *16. Company* in Auerbach. Seated from the left: Audbjørn Fiskum and Nils Bu. The rest are unknown. Standing from the left: third, Wilhelm Forberg; fifth, Ola Thorshaug.

Die 16. Kompanie in Auerbach. Sitzend von links: Audbjørn Fiskum und Nils Bu, die anderen sind unbekannt. Stehend von links: Nr. 3. Wilhelm Forsberg, Nr. 5. Ola Thorshaug.

Standing from the left: Dahl, Einar Sundve, Lars Furulund, Sverre Ryen, Odd Seljelid, Ole Welde and two unknowns. Seated in front from the left: unknown, Julius Salthammer, Kjell Kaastad and Bjarne Mork.

Stehend von links: Dahl, Einar Sundve, Lars Furulund, Sverre Ryen, Odd Seljelid, Ole Welde und zwei Unbekannte. Vorne sitzend von links: ein Unbekannter, Julius Salthammer, Kjell Kaastad und Bjarne Mork.

Veterans of the *Norwegian Legion*. Third from the left is *SS-Unterscharführer* Bjørn Breive; the rest are unknown.

Veteranen der SS-Frw.-Legion Norwegen. Von links: zwei Unbekannte, SS-Unterscharführer Bjørn Breive. Die anderen sind unbekannt.

A group of Norwegian volunteers from *10.* and *11. Company* taking a break during training. Seated in front on the left is John Lyngstad.

Eine Gruppe norwegischer Freiwilliger der 10. und 11. Kompanie bei einer Ruhepause während der Übung. Vorne links sitzend: John Lyngstad.

From the left: Ole Welde, Julius Salthammer and unknown.

Von links: Ole Welde, Julius Salthammer und ein Unbekannter.

From the left: Gunnar Amundsen, Einar Sundve and Johansen.

Von links: Gunnar Amundsen, Einar Sundve und Johansen.

Punitive drill in Auerbach. Unlucky soldiers had to run around the barracks with their mattresses.

Strafexerzieren in Auerbach. Als Bestrafung musste man mit der Matratze um die Baracken laufen.

A group of recruits in front of their barracks before leaving for Croatia.

Eine Gruppe Rekruten vor ihrer Baracke vor der Abreise nach Kroatien.

An unknown Norwegian.

Ein unbekannter Norweger.

Line-up before leaving for Croatia.

Aufstellung vor der Abreise nach Kroatien.

23. SS-Panzergrenadier Regiment "Norge" – Pionierausbildung in Dresden | *23. SS-Panzergrenadier-Regiment 'Norge'* – pioneer training in Dresden

The *16. Pioneer Company* of *Regiment 'Norge'* in Prague. Seated second from the left is *SS-Obersturmführer* Harald Normann Sødahl; third, *SS-Hauptsturmführer* Egil Reidar Hoel; sixth, *SS-Oberscharführer* Harald Løvaas. Standing in the next row third from the left is *SS-Unterscharführer* Albert Endresen; fifth, with a ski hat, *SS-Sturmmann* Bjørn Richard Folvik.

16. Pionierkompanie des Regiments "Norge" in Prag. Sitzend Nr. 2 von links: SS-Obersturmführer Harald Normann Sødahl, Nr. 3 SS-Hauptsturmführer Egil Reidar Hoel, Nr. 6 SS-Oberscharführer Harald Løvaas. Stehend in der nächsten Reihe von links: Nr. 3 SS-Unterscharführer Albert Endresen, Nr. 5 mit Skimütze SS-Sturmmann Bjørn Richard Folvik.

Swearing-in of the *16. Pioneer Company 'Norge'* in Czechoslovakia. At the lectern is the commander of the *SS Pioneer Battalion 11 'Nordland'*, *SS-Sturmbannführer* Fritz Bunze. Front centre is *SS-Hauptsturmführer* Egil Reidar Hoel.

Vereidigung der 16. Pionier-Kompanie "Norge" in der Tschechoslowakei. Am Rednerpult Kommandeur des SS-Pionier-Bataillons 11 "Nordland", SS-Sturmbannführer Fritz Bunze. Vorne in der Mitte: SS-Hauptsturmführer Egil Reidar Hoel.

Swearing-in of the *16. Pioneer Company 'Norge'*. Standing in front of the lectern is *SS-Hauptsturmführer* Egil Reidar Hoel.

Vereidigung der 16. Pionier-Kompanie "Norge". Vor dem Rednerpult stehend: SS-Hauptsturmführer Egil Reidar Hoel.

Swearing-in of *SS Pioneer Battalion 11 'Nordland'*, *16. Pioneer Company 'Danmark'* and *16. Pioneer Company 'Norge'*.

Vereidigung des SS-Pionier-Bataillons 11 "Nordland", 16. Pionier-Kompanie "Danmark" und 16. Pionier-Kompanie "Norge".

23. SS-Panzergrenadier-Regiment "Norge" in Kroatien | *23. SS-Panzergrenadier-Regiment 'Norge'* in Croatia

10. Company 'Norge' on its way to Croatia, August 1943. In the middle of the wagon is Gabriel Wartano from Russia, serving as a *HiWi* (volunteer assistant).

Die 10. Kompanie "Norge" auf dem Weg nach Kroatien, August 1943. In der Mitte des Wagens der Russe Gabriel Wartano als HiWi.

1. Company 'Norge' en route to Croatia, August 1943. *SS-Unterscharführer* Andreas Nilsson, left, and *SS-Unterscharführer* Tor Svenneby sitting in the doorway.

1. Kompanie "Norge" auf dem Weg nach Kroatien, August 1943. Von links: 1. SS-Unterscharführer Andreas Nilsson, 2. SS-Unterscharführer Tor Svenneby in der Türöffnung sitzend.

10. Company 'Norge' en route to Croatia, August 1943. Sitting in the middle with black hair without a hat is *HiWi* Gabriel Wartano from Baku, followed by *SS-Hauptscharführer* Robert Stock from Tyrol with a forage cap.

10. Kompanie "Norge" auf dem Weg nach Kroatien. In der Mitte sitzend mit schwarzem Haar ohne Mütze ist der HiWi Gabriel Wartano aus Baku, dann SS-Hauptsturmführer Robert Stock aus Tirol mit Schiffchen.

In the front row on the left is *SS-Unterscharführer* Willy Schakesby.

Vorne links: SS-Unterscharführer Willy Schakesby.

A break during the train journey to Croatia.

Eine Pause während der Zugfahrt nach Kroatien.

Visiting *4. Company 'Norge'* in Kostanica, 1943. First from the left is *SS-Unterscharführer* Bjørn Heisholdt, with Jarl Wathne third from the left, both from *1./23*.

Besuch bei der 4. Kompanie in Kostanica, 1943. Von links: Nr. 1 SS-Unterscharführer Bjørn Heisholdt, Nr. 3 Jarl Wathne, beide von der 1. Kompanie "Norge".

Unknown Norwegian from *10. Company 'Norge'*.
Photo taken in Croatia, autumn 1943.

Ein unbekannter Norweger der 10. Kompanie.
Aufnahme aus Kroatien, Herbst 1943.

Driving practice on the German Autobahn for those who were to serve as drivers.

Fahrunterricht auf der Autobahn in Deutschland.

A group of grenadiers from *3. Company 'Norge'* in Dvor, autumn 1943.

Eine Gruppe Grenadiere der 3. Kompanie "Norge" in Dvor, Herbst 1943.

The Croatian village of Kostanica, where *I.* and *III. Battalion 'Norge'* were deployed on both sides of the nearby river Una.

Das Dorf Kostanica in Kroatien, wo das I. und III. Bataillon "Norge" an beiden Seiten des Flusses Una im Einsatz waren.

The companies of *II./Norge* are lined up to be sworn in at Bosn Nowi , autumn 1943.

Herbst 1943. Die Kompanien des II./Norge sind in Bosn Nowi zur Vereidigung aufgestellt.

SS-Untersturmführer Kristoffer Dahl of *12. Company 'Norge'* borrowed a fez for the occasion.

SS-Untersturmführer Kristoffer Dahl von der 12./Norge trägt zum Anlass einen Fez.

Samobor, autumn 1943. To the left are *SS-Untersturmführer* Per Kjølner of *3. Company SS-Pz.Abt. 11 'Hermann von Salza'* and *SS-Untersturmführer* Thomas Hvistendahl of *4. Company SS-Pz.Abt. 11 'Hermann von Salza'*.

Samobor, Herbst 1943. Links: SS-Untersturmführer Per Kjølner von der 3./SS-Pz.Abt. 11 “Hermann von Salza” und SS-Untersturmführer Thomas Hvistendahl von der 4. Kompanie.

The men of *SS-Pz.Abt. 11 'HvS'* in Samobor, Croatia, 1943.

Die Mannschaft der SS-Pz.Abt. 11 "HvS" in Samobor, Kroatien, Herbst 1943.

23. SS-Panzergrenadier-Regiment "Norge" an der Front | *23. SS-Panzergrenadier-Regiment 'Norge' at the front*

Soldiers from *11. Company 'Norge'* at Oranienbaum, January 1944. In the middle with binoculars is company commander *SS-Obersturmführer* Karl-Heinz Reinecke. He was killed on 2 February 1944 at Dubrovka.

Soldaten der 11. Kompanie "Norge" bei Oranienbaum, Januar 1944. In der Mitte mit Fernglas der Kompanieführer SS-Obersturmführer Karl-Heinz Reinecke. Er fiel am 2.2.44 bei Dubrowka.

Narva, 1944. On the left is *SS-Unterscharführer* Albert Maacke *of 9. Company 'Norge'*, with *SS-Unterscharführer* Fritz Meisse of *10. Company 'Norge'* on the right. Both survived the war.

Narwa, 1944. Links: SS-Unterscharführer Albert Maacke von der 9. Kompanie "Norge", rechts SS-Unterscharführer Fritz Meisse von der 10. Kompanie "Norge". Beide überlebten den Krieg.

SS-Unterscharführer Fritz Meisse of *10. Company 'Norge'* at Narva in the spring of 1944.

SS-Unterscharführer Fritz Meisse von der 10. Kompanie "Norge" bei Narwa, Frühjahr 1944.

Unknown soldiers of *III. Battalion 'Norge'* at Narva, 1944.

Unbekannte Soldaten des III. Bataillons "Norge" bei Narwa, 1944.

SS-Hauptscharführer Heinz Twesmann, a platoon leader in *3. Company 'Norge'*. He was severely wounded on 17 January 1944 and never returned to his unit. In 1945, he attended the last training course for the disabled at Bad Tölz and fought against the Americans with the *38. SS-Pz.Gren.Div. 'Nibelungen'*. He survived the war.

SS-Hauptscharführer Heinz Twesmann, Zugführer in der 3. Kompanie "Norge", wurde am 17.1.44 schwer verwundet und kehrte nicht zurück zu seiner Einheit. 1945 war er Junker beim letzten Invalidenlehrgang an der SS-Junkerschule Tölz, und kämpfte in der 38. SS-Pz.Gren.Div. "Nibelungen" gegen die Amerikaner. Er überlebte den Krieg.

Two Norwegian members of the regimental staff. Both worked as drivers and mechanics.

Zwei Norweger vom Stab des Regiments. Beide dienten als Fahrer und Mechaniker.

SS-Obergruppenführer and General of the *Waffen-SS* Felix Martin Julius Steiner (1896–1966) was commanding general of the *III. SS Panzer Corps (Germanic)*. From 1940 until 1943 he was Division Commander of the *5. SS-Pz.Div. 'Wiking'*. After the Second World War, he wrote several books about volunteers during the war and settled in Munich. He never married.

SS-Obergruppenführer und General der Waffen-SS, Felix Martin Julius Steiner (1896–1966), war Kommandeur des III. (germ.) SS-Panzer-Korps. Von 1940 bis 1943 war er Divisionskommandeur der 5. SS-Pz.Div "Wiking". Nach dem Krieg schrieb er mehrere Bücher über Freiwillige im Krieg und lebte in München. Er hat nie geheiratet.

SS-Brigadeführer and General of the *Waffen-SS* Fritz von Scholz. From 1940 until 1943 he commanded the *SS Infantry Regiment 'Nordland'*, attached to the *5. SS-Pz.Div. 'Wiking'*. In January 1943, he became leader of the *2. SS Infantry Brigade (mot.)*, to which the *Norwegian Legion* was attached. In the spring of 1943, he was appointed commander of the *11. SS-Pz.Gren.Div. 'Nordland'*, which he led until his death on 28 July 1944.

SS-Brigadeführer und General der Waffen-SS, Fritz von Scholz. Von 1940 bis 1943 war er Regimentskommandeur des SS-Infanterie-Regiments "Nordland" bei der 5. SS-Pz.Div. "Wiking". Im Januar 1943 wurde er Kommandeur der 2. SS-Infanterie-Brigade (mot.), der die SS-Frw.-Legion Norwegen unterstellt war. Im Frühjahr 1943 wurde er zum Kommandeur der 11. SS-Pz.Gren.Div. "Nordland" befördert, die er bis zu seinem Tod am 28.7.44 führte.

Der verlorene Haufen

In der Nacht zum 27. Januar 1944 hatte sich das Regiment "Norge" mit dem II. und III. Bataillon aus den Stellungen bei Oranienbaum zurückgezogen. Das II./Norge sollte zwischen den Dörfern Martynowo im Norden und Ssawoltschina im Süden eine Sperrstellung halten. Die 7. Kompanie wurde an die linke Flanke bei Martynowo kommandiert, während die 6. Kompanie die rechte Flanke bei Ssawoltschina sichern sollte. Als die 6. Kompanie von den Russen angegriffen wurde, entstanden harte Kämpfe. Der Btl.Kdr. SS-Sturmbannführer Albrecht Krügel musste die 5. und später die 8. Kompanie einsetzen, um der 6. Kompanie beizustehen. Gleichzeitig hielt die 7. Kompanie ihre Stellung bei Martynowo im Norden. Die Kommandantur der Züge war folgendermaßen verteilt:

Kp.fhr 5./23 SS-Hauptsturmführer Erich Dahm, Zugfhr. SS-Untersturmführer Clemens Dederichs.
Kp.fhr 6./23 SS-Obersturmführer Erhard Göttlich, Zugfhr. SS-Obersturmführer Harald Sødahl.
Kp.fhr 7./23 SS-Obersturmführer Kristian Prytz, Zugfhr. SS-Untersturmführer Arne Hanssen.
Kp.fhr 8./23 SS-Obersturmführer Walter Körner.

Zu dieser Zeit, als das Bataillon im Süden an harten Kämpfen beteiligt war, hatte SS-Obersturmführer Prytz vermutlich keinen Kontakt mit dem Bataillon, und entschloss sich, das Bataillon auf Ski zu erreichen um weitere Befehle zu bekommen. Als er sich auf den Weg machte, übernahm SS-Untersturmführer Arne Hanssen die Führung der Kompanie. Im Rückblick behauptete SS-Unterscharführer Artur Ewerth, dass die Kompanie während der Abwesenheit des Kompanieführers per Funkmeldung den Befehl zum Rückzug erhalten hatte, was auch geschah. Als SS-Obersturmführer Kristian Prytz zurückkehrte, war die Kompanie verschwunden. Daher lief er auf Skiern nach Lamocha, wo er SS-Untersturmführer Richard Børesen vom II./SS-Art.Rgt. 11 traf und ihm mitteilte, er hätte seine Kompanie "verloren". Vermutlich begleitete Prytz das II./SS-Art.Rgt. 11 nach Jamburg, wo er zum Stab des Regiments "Norge" kam.

Die Kompanie begann nun ihren abenteuerlichen Marsch gegen Westen. Ein Norweger hat berichtet, dass die Kompanie nach und nach alle MG 42 und andere schwere Ausrüstung vergraben wurde. Nach fünf Tagen, am 01.02.44, geriet die Kompanie in ein Feuergefecht mit russischen Truppen, und der "Haufen" wurde in zwei Gruppen geteilt. Die erste Gruppe unter der Leitung von SS-Unterscharführer Haase wurde niedergekämpft, und viele der Männer fielen oder wurden in Gefangenschaft genommen. Der anderen Gruppe unter der Führung von SS-Untersturmführer Hanssen gelang es, den Russen zu entkommen und in Richtung Westen zu ziehen, wo ihr Weg sie nördlich bis an die Ostsee führte.

Am 1.2.44 wurde Haases Gruppe bis zum nächsten Tag in einen Nahkampf mit den Russen verwickelt, und alle Überlebenden endeten in Gefangenschaft. Laut russischer Unterlagen war der 2.2.44 der Tag der Gefangennahme. Alle Verwundeten, die nicht zu Fuß gehen konnten, wurden erschossen.

Ein kurzgefasster Bericht des 106. Grenzregiments des NKVD (Innenministerium der UdSSR), das die 7. Kompanie niedergekämpft hatte, gibt den Zeitpunkt der Kämpfe an, und die Zahl der Soldaten die in Gefangenschaft geraten waren.

Als der "verlorene Haufen" in der Nacht zum 10.2.44 eine deutsche Stellung in der Nähe von Hungerburg passierte, wurden SS-Untersturmführer Hanssen und SS-Unterscharführer Weermeister auf dem Eis erschossen. Zwei Fotos, die vor dem Offizierskasino in Hungerburg aufgenommen wurden, zeigen 21 Mann, darunter auch SS-Rottenführer Kåre Bergersen. Die Überlebenden erhielten später das Eiserne Kreuz 2. Klasse.

Der verlorene Haufen (The forlorn hope)

During the night of 26/27 January 1944, the *II.* and *III. Battalion* of *Regiment 'Norge'* left their position at Oranienbaum. The *II. Battalion* was charged with setting up a blocking position between the villages of Martynowo in the north and Ssawoltschina in the south. The *7. Company* was assigned to the left flank and the area around Martynowo, while the *6. Company* maintained the right flank near Ssawoltschina. When the Russians launched a main attack against the latter, the company found itself enmeshed in fierce fighting at Ssawoltschina, and the commander of the battalion, *Sturmbannführer* Albrecht Krügel, decided to deploy *5. Company* and some time later *8. Company* to come to the aid of *6. Company*, while *7. Company* continued to maintain the blockade at Martynowo in the north. The companies were disposed as follows:

5./23 – company commander *SS-Hauptsturmführer* Erich Dahm, platoon leader *SS-Untersturmführer* Clemens Dederichs.
6./23 – company commander *SS-Obersturmführer* Erhard Göttlich, platoon leader *SS-Obersturmführer* Harald Sødahl.
7./23 – company commander *SS-Obersturmführer* Kristian Prytz, platoon leader *SS-Untersturmführer* Arne Hanssen.
8./23 – company commander *SS-Obersturmführer* Walter Körner.

It was probably at this time, while the rest of the battalion was engaged in fierce fighting further south, that *SS-Obersturmführer* Prytz lost contact with the leadership of the battalion and decided to set out on skis to obtain new advance directives. At least we know that he took along his skis and left the company under the command of *SS-Untersturmführer* Arne Hanssen. *SS-Unterscharführer* Artur Ewerth later claimed that a wireless message ordering the company to retreat was received during Prytz's absence. The order was carried out, and when Prytz returned to Martynowo, he was unable to locate the company. He decided to return to Lamocha, where he met *SS-Untersturmführer* Richard Børesen of the *II./SS-Artillerie-Regiment 11*, telling him that he has 'lost his company'. In all likelihood, Prytz accompanied the *II./SS-A.R. 11* to Jamburg, where he joined the regimental staff.

Now began the company's adventurous trek to the west. According to a Norwegian source, the men eventually buried their MG-42s and disposed of all heavy equipment. After five days, on 1 February 1944, things went wrong when the company was attacked by Russian forces and the 'Haufen' decided to split into two groups. The first group, commanded by *SS-Unterscharführer* Haase, was defeated and killed, while others were taken prisoner. The group bringing up the rear, under the leadership of *SS-Untersturmführer* Hanssen, succeeded in escaping the Russians and moved westward. At one point, they advanced as far north as the Baltic Sea.

On 1 February, Haase's group became involved in battles with Russian forces until the next day, when the survivors were taken captive. Russian sources indicate that the soldiers were captured on 2 February. Those who were wounded and unable to walk were shot.

The *106. Border Regiment* of the Russian NKVD (People's Commissariat for Internal Affairs) that had defeated Haase's company issued a brief report specifying when the fighting began, and the number of prisoners taken captive.

When the '*verlorene Haufen*' passed Hungerburg during the night of 10 February 1944, the commanding officer, *SS-Untersturmführer* Hanssen, and a German *Unterscharführer* were shot on the frozen Narva River. Later, two group pictures were taken of the 'Haufen', depicting 21 men in front of the officers' mess in Hungerburg, among them *SS-Rottenführer* Kåre Bergersen. Later, the survivors received the Iron Cross 2nd Class.

10 February 1944. The survivors of *7. Company 'Norge'*, *'Der verlorene Haufen'*, standing on the stairs in front of the officers' mess in Hungerburg near Narva after having penetrated the main front line (*Hauptkampflinie*, or HKL). The company was reported missing on 27 January 1944 at Martynowo, and had to return to Narva under the leadership of *SS-Untersturmführer* Arne Hanssen from Sandefjord. The only food they had for the 16-day long march was a sack of flour.

10. Februar 1944. Auf der Treppe des Offizierskasinos in Hungerburg bei Narwa stehen die Überlebenden der 7. Kompanie – der "verlorene Haufen" – nach dem Durchbrechen der Hauptkampflinie. Die Kompanie wurde am 27.1.44 bei Martynowo als vermisst gemeldet, und musste unter Führung von SS-Untersturmführer Arne Hanssen aus Sandefjord zu Fuß nach Narwa zurückkehren. Der einzige Proviant für den 16 Tage langen Marsch war ein Sack Mehl.

7. Company 'Norge' at Hungerburg, 10 February 1944. Four survivors of the *'verlorene Haufen'* are, from the left: Andreas Manchen, *SS-Unterscharführer* Max Gryska (who was killed on 27 October 1944), *SS-Oberscharführer* Franz Schacherl and *SS-Unterscharführer* Heinz Kienast (who was killed in 1945).

7. Kompanie "Norge" bei Hungerburg am 10.2.44. Vier Überlebende des "verlorenen Haufens". Von links: Andreas Manchen, SS-Unterscharführer Max Gryska (gefallen am 27.10.44), SS-Oberscharführer Franz Schacherl und SS-Unterscharführer Heinz Kienast (gefallen 1945).

7. Company 'Norge'. Three survivors of the '*verlorene Haufen*' during the departure for Narva on 2 October 1944 are, from the left: Werner Köpke, *SS-Unterscharführer* Henz Kienast and *SS-Unterscharführer* Artur Ewerth. Ewerth survived the war.

7. Kompanie "Norge". Drei Überlebende des "verlorenen Haufens" während des Abmarsches nach Narwa am 10.2.44. Von links: Werner Köpke, SS-Unterscharführer Heinz Kienast und SS-Unterscharführer Artur Ewerth. Ewerth überlebte den Krieg.

SS-Standarten-Oberjunker Arne Einar Olav Hanssen from Sandefjord. He attended the 9th Kriegsjunker-Lehrgang (cadet training course) at Bad Tölz, and in the summer of 1943 was assigned to the newly activated *11. SS-Panzergrenadier-Division 'Nordland'*, where he became a platoon leader in *7. Company 'Norge'*. When the company commander disappeared on 27 January 1944, Hanssen led the company through the forest towards Narva. On 10 February 1944, he was killed on the frozen river Narva at Hungerburg while trying to reach his own lines, shot by a soldier from the German *Wehrmacht*. The Danish *SS-Brigadeführer* Christian Kryssing led the ceremony at his burial some time later. Today, Hanssen's remains rest at the German cemetery in Toila, Estonia.

SS-Standarten-Oberjunker Arne Einar Olav Hanssen aus Sandefjord. Er hatte den 9. Kriegsjunker-Lehrgang an der SS-Junkerschule Tölz durchgeführt, und wurde im Sommer 1943 an die neuaufgestellte 11. SS-Pz.Gren.Div. "Nordland" kommandiert, wo er als Zugführer in der 7. Kompanie eingesetzt wurde. Als der Kompanieführer am 27.1.44 bei einer Skifahrt verschwand, führte er die Kompanie durch den Wald nach Narwa. Er fiel auf dem Eis des Flusses Narwa, erschossen von einem Soldat der Wehrmacht. Bei seinem Begräbnis leitete der dänische SS-Brigadeführer Christian Kryssing die Zeremonie. Heute ruht er auf dem deutschen Soldatenfriedhof in Toila, Estland.

SS-Sturmmann Knut Skjolden from Mysen, a member of *11. Company 'Norge'*, was killed at Siiversti on 14 February 1944. He had previously served in *Division 'Wiking'* and *Regiment 'Westland'*. His epaulettes show a 'W' for '*Westland*'.

SS-Sturmmann Knut Skjolden aus Mysen, ein Angehöriger der 11. Division "Norge", fiel am 14.02.44 bei Siiversti . Früher hatte er in der SS-Division "Wiking" und im Regiment "Westland" gedient. Auf den Schulterstücken ist der Buchstabe "W" für "Westland" zu erkennen.

The battles for Narva, 1944.

Die Kämpfe um Narwa, 1944.

The battles for Narva, 1944.

Die Kämpfe um Narwa, 1944.

Hermann Castle (*Hermannsfeste*) on the Estonian side of the Narva River under Russian bombardment in the spring of 1944.

Die Festung Hermannsfeste auf der estnischen Seite der Narwa unter russischem Feuer, Frühjahr 1944.

Overview of Narva, spring of 1944. The Russian fortress Ivangorod is on the right bank of the river, with a bridge leading across the Narwa to Hermann Castle on the Estonian side. The castle is shrouded in smoke from Russian artillery fire.

Überblick über Narwa, Frühjahr 1944. An der rechten Seite des Flusses liegt die russische Festung Iwangorod, und eine Brücke führt über den Fluss zur Festung Hermannsfeste auf der estnischen Seite. Die Festung ist durch russisches Artilleriefeuer in Rauch gehüllt.

The cemetery of *Division 'Nederland'* in Narva.

Soldatenfriedhof der Division "Nederland" bei Narwa.

Spring of 1944. On the left is *SS-Sturmbannführer* Albrecht Krügel, battalion commander of the *II. Battalion 'Norge'*. In the middle is *SS-Brigadeführer* Fritz von Scholz, and on the right the newly appointed commander of *Regiment 'Norge'*, *SS-Obersturmbannführer* Fritz Knöchlein. Knöchlein came from the *3. SS-Panzer-Division 'Totenkopf'* and had participated in the French Campaign of 1940. Here he was guilty of committing war crimes at Le Paradis, where he ordered the murder of British POWs. He was hanged as a war criminal on 28 January 1949.

Frühjahr 1944. Von links: SS-Sturmbannführer Albrecht Krügel, Bataillonskommandeur des II./Norge. In der Mitte SS-Brigadeführer Fritz von Scholz, rechts der neue Kommandeur des Regiments "Norge", SS-Obersturmbannführer Fritz Knöchlein. Er kam von der 3. SS-Pz.Div. "Totenkopf", und hatte 1940 am Feldzug im Westen Frankreichs teilgenommen. Hier hatte er sich an Kriegsverbrechen gegen englische Kriegsgefangene schuldig gemacht, als er den Befehl für deren Ermordung gab. Er wurde 1949 von den Engländern in Hameln hingerichtet.

Narva, spring of 1944. Outside the headquarters of division commander Fritz von Scholz, standing with his arm in a sling. An unknown general from the German *Wehrmacht* greets *SS-Brigadeführer* Franz Augsberger, commander of the *20. SS-Waffen-Grenadier-Division (estnische No. 1).*

Narwa, Frühjahr 1944. Vor dem Gefechtsstand des Divisionskommandeurs Fritz von Scholz, mit Arm in der Schlinge. Ein unbekannter General der Wehrmacht begrüßt SS-Brigadeführer Franz Augsberger, Kommandeur der 20. SS-Waffen-Grenadier-Division (estnische Nr. 1).

SS-Pz.Abt. 11 'Hermann von Salza' with *Panzer IV* Panther tanks in Narva, spring of 1944.

SS-Pz.Abt. 11 "Hermann von Salza" mit Panzer IV Panther Kampfwagen in Narwa, Frühjahr 1944.

Unknown unit, photographed by a Norwegian with *10. Company 'Norge'*, Narva 1944.

Unbekannte Einheit, fotografiert von einem Norweger der 10. Kompanie, Narwa 1944.

SS-Pz.Abt. 11 'HvS', Panther tank labeled *315, 3. Company, 1. platoon, 5. tank*. Narva, spring of 1944.

SS-Pz.Abt. 11 "HvS", Panther Kampfwagen mit Kennzeichen *315, 3. Kompanie, 1. Zug, 5. Panzer*. Narwa, Frühjahr 1944.

Unknown infantryman from *10. Company 'Norge'*, photographed by a Norwegian in the spring of 1944.

Unbekannter Grenadier der 10. Kompanie, fotografiert von einem Norweger, Frühjahr 1944.

Unknown infantryman in position at Narva Bridgehead, spring of 1944.

Unbekannter Grenadier in Stellung am Brückenkopf von Narwa, Frühjahr 1944.

In position south of Narva. *SS-Untersturmführer* Kåre Brynestad of *10. Company 'Norge'*, left, and an unknown *Oberscharführer*, spring of 1944.

In Stellung südlich von Narwa. Von links: SS-Untersturmführer der 10. Kompanie, Kåre Brynestad, und ein unbekannter SS-Oberscharführer, Frühjahr 1944.

SS-Unterscharführer Fritz Ihlen, a radio correspondent with the *SS-Standarte 'Kurt Eggers'*, near Narva, spring of 1944. Ihlen made a large number of tape recordings at the front, which were broadcast by the Norwegian Broadcasting Corporation between 1942 and 1944. In 1942, Ihlen joined the *5. SS-Division 'Wiking'* on the southern front and produced audio recordings of the battles around Rostov and the Caucasus. He had studied journalism in England, where he had also gained practical experience. Before the war, Ihlen had been a member of the National Socialist Workers' Party of Norway, and was a friend of Per Imerslund. Ihlen died in 1991 in Oslo.

SS-Unterscharführer Fritz Ihlen, SS-Rundfunkberichter bei der SS-Standarte "Kurt Eggers", in der Nähe von Narwa, Frühjahr 1944. Ihlen hatte etliche SS-PK-Reportagen an der Front gemacht, die vom norwegischen Rundfunk (NRK) zwischen 1942 und 1944 gesendet wurden. 1942 war er bei der 5. SS-Pz.Div. "Wiking" an der Südfront zwischen Rostow und dem Kaukasus. Ihlen war in England als Journalist ausgebildet. Vor dem Krieg war er Mitglied der Norwegischen Nationalsozialistischen Arbeiterpartei, und war mit Per Imerslund befreundet. Ihlen starb 1991 in Oslo.

At the Narva River, spring of 1944. Infantrymen cross the bridge from east to west.

Am Narwa-Fluss, Frühjahr 1944. Grenadiere überqueren die Brücke in westlicher Richtung.

A Panther IV tank from *SS-Pz.Abt. 11 'HvS'* outside Narva, 1944.

Ein Panther IV Kampfwagen der SS-Pz.Abt. 11 "HvS" außerhalb von Narwa, 1944.

A German war cemetery in Kreenholm, a suburb of Narva, 1944. For a while, the headquarters and graveyard of *Division 'Nordland'* were located here.

Deutscher Soldatenfriedhof in Kreenholm, einem Vorort von Narwa, 1944. Der Gefechtsstand und die Gräber der Division "Nordland" lagen eine Zeit lang hier.

A German war cemetery in Kreenholm, a suburb of Narva, 1944. For a while, the headquarters and graveyard of *Division 'Nordland'* were located here.

Deutscher Soldatenfriedhof in Kreenholm, einem Vorort von Narwa, 1944. Der Gefechtsstand und die Gräber der Division "Nordland" lagen eine Zeit lang hier.

Soldiers from the staff of *III. Battalion 'Norge'* bury one of their fallen soldiers in the spring of 1944. Standing with a spade is Edgar Schweitzer.

Soldaten des Bataillonstabs des III./Norge beerdigen einen gefallenen Kameraden im Frühjahr 1944. Stehend mit Spaten, Edgar Schweitzer.

Norwegian *SS-Unterscharführer* Helge Nilsen was a member of *1.* and later *10. Company 'Norge'.* On 25 February 1944, he was severely wounded during the battles for the 'Westsack', and lost his glass eye; Nilsen had originally lost his eye when he was with the *1. Company* of the *Norwegian Legion*. Westsack is an area near Sirgala, 20 km (12 miles) west of Narva and south of Kinderheimhöhe (Orphanage Hill). Here, *Regiment 'Norge'* was engaged in heavy fighting between 25 January and 3 March 1944. As the Russians had managed to advance to the main road between Narva and Tallinn, it was imperative to defeat them in order to secure the supply lines to Narva.

SS-Unterscharführer der 1 und 10. Kompanie, Helge Nilsen, wurde am 25.02.44 bei den Kämpfen um den Westsack schwer verwundet, und verlor sein Glasauge. (Er hatte sein Auge einige Zeit früher bei der 1. Kompanie der SS-Freiwilligen Legion Norwegen verloren.) Westsack ist der Name des Gebietes um Sirgala, 20 km westlich von Narwa und südlich der Kinderheimhöhe. Hier war das Regiment "Norge" vom 25.02.44 bis zum 03.03.44 an schweren Kämpfen beteiligt. Da die Russen schon bis zur Hauptstraße zwischen Narwa und Tallinn vorgerückt waren, war es von entscheidender Bedeutung sie zu besiegen, um die Versorgungsleitung nach Narwa zu sichern.

Zuggefechtsstand (troop headquarters) of *1. platoon, 7. Company 'Norge'* at Kulgubach, May 1944. From the left: two unknowns, *SS-Unterscharführer* Werner Köpke, *SS-Unterscharführer* Ernst Richters, two unknowns, *SS-Unterscharführer* Arthur Ewerth, *SS-Standarten-Oberjunker* Johan Peter Balstad, *SS-Hauptscharführer* Karl-Peter Theilacker (KIA 16 February 1945), *SS-Unterscharführer* Niels Bonnichsen (from Denmark) and *SS-Standarten-Oberjunker* Olai Rønningen (KIA 4 August 1944).

Zuggefechtsstand des 1. Zugs der 7. Kompanie bei Kulgubach, Mai 1944. Von links: zwei Unbekannte, SS-Unterscharführer Werner Köpke, SS-Unterscharführer Ernst Richters, zwei Unbekannte, SS-Unterscharführer Artur Ewerth, SS-Standarten-Oberjunker Johan Peter Balstad, SS-Hauptscharführer Karl-Peter Theilacker (gefallen am 16.02.45), SS-Unterscharführer Niels Bonnichsen (ein Däne) und SS-Standarten-Oberjunker Olai Rønningen (gefallen am 04.08.44).

From the left: *SS-Oberscharführer* Deckstahl, *SS-Hauptscharführer* Dürr, *SS-Unterscharführer* Müller and *SS-Standarten-Oberjunker* Asbjørn Jäger Wiik with *13. Company 'Norge'*, Narva, spring of 1944.

Von links: SS-Oberscharführer Deckstahl, SS-Hauptscharführer Dürr, SS-Unterscharführer Müller und SS-Standarten-Oberjunker Asbjørn Jäger Wiik bei der 13. Kompanie, Narwa, Frühjahr 1944.

13. Company Norge near Narva, spring of 1944. From the left: *SS-Standarten-Oberjunker* Asbjørn Jäger Wiik (KIA April 1945 in Berlin), *SS-Hauptscharführer* Dürr, *SS-Oberscharführer* Deckstahl, *SS-Unterscharführer* Müller and Danish company commander *SS-Untersturmführer* Christian Dall.

13. Kompanie bei Narwa, Frühjahr 1944. Von links: SS-Standarten-Oberjunker Asbjørn Jäger Wiik (gefallen im April 1945 in Berlin), SS-Hauptscharführer Dürr, SS-Oberscharführer Deckstahl, SS-Unterscharführer Müller und der dänische Kompanieführer SS-Untersturmführer Christian Dall.

13. Company 'Norge' near Narva, 1944. Second from the left is SS-Untersturmführer Christian Dall, and on the right is *SS-Standarten-Oberjunker* Asbjørn Jäger Wiik. The rest are unknown.

Die 13. Kompanie bei Narwa, 1944. Von links: ein Unbekannter, SS-Untersturmführer Christian Dall, ein Unbekannter und rechts SS-Standarten-Oberjunker Asbjørn Jäger Wiik.

1. Platoon of *9. Company 'Norge'*, spring of 1944. In the middle with a cane is *SS-Standarten-Oberjunker* Kjell Marthinsen, who later lost a leg during a grenade-launcher exercise in Voka on 20 August 1944. He died on October 16 1944 when his plane crashed at Skorve Mountain near Seljord, Telemark.

1. Zug der 9. Kompanie, Frühjahr 1944. In der Mitte mit Stock SS-Standarten-Oberjunker Kjell Marthinsen, der später bei Woka am 20.08.44 ein Bein bei einem Granatwerferunfall verlor. Er starb am 16.10.44, als sein Flugzeug am Skorve-Berg in der Nähe von Seljord, Telemark, abstürzte.

SS-Unterscharführer W. Schutze from *8. Company 'Norge'* in the swamps south of Narva.

SS-Unterscharführer W. Schultze von der 8. Kompanie in den Sümpfen südlich von Narwa.

A bunker of *8. Company, Regiment 'Norge'*, in the swamps south of Narva.

Ein Bunker der 8. Kompanie, Regiment ‚Norge', in den Sümpfen südlich von Narwa.

Another shot of *SS-Unterscharführer* W. Schutze of *8. Company 'Norge'* in the swamps south of Narva.

SS-Unterscharführer W. Schultz von der 8. Kompanie in den Sümpfen südlich von Narwa.

SS-Unterscharführer W Schutze from *8. Company 'Norge'*, spring of 1944, from the positions at Uferwald, south of Narva.

SS-Unterscharführer W. Schultze von der 8. Kompanie, Frühjahr 1944 bei Narwa. Hier in den Stellungen am Uferwald südlich von Narwa.

A Panther IV tank from *SS-Pz.Abt. 11 'Hermann von Salza'*, Narva, summer of 1944.

Ein Panther IV der SS-Pz.Abt. 11 "Hermann von Salza", Narwa, Sommer 1944.

SS-Untersturmführer Frank Goyvaerts, January/February 1944. He was a Flemish orderly officer with the regimental staff and took part in the fighting between Jamburg and Narva. Goyvaerts was a good friend of Henrik Pedersen and Borger Dahl Larssen, both of them Norwegian *SS-Untersturmführer* who were killed in action.

SS-Untersturmführer Frank Goyvaerts, ein flämischer Ordonanzoffizier im Regimentsstab, Januar/Februar 1944. Goyvaerts nahm an den Kämpfen von Jamburg bis Narwa teil, und war ein guter Freund der gefallenen norwegischen SS-Untersturmführer Henrik Pedersen und Borger Dahl Larssen.

SS-Sturmmann Tormod Kjekshus of *9. Company 'Norge'*. He was a member of the company from 1943 until the autumn of 1944.

SS-Sturmmann Tormod Kjekshus von der 9. Kompanie. Er gehörte der Kompanie seit der Aufstellung 1943 bis zum Herbst 1944 an.

Hunting for lice at *10. Company 'Norge'* at one of its positions south of Narva. From the left: Ørnulf Breines, Mikael Ukkestad and Harris Lund. The rest are unknown.

Läusejagd in einer Stellung der 10. Kompanie südlich von Narwa. Von links: Ørnulf Breines, Mikael Ukkestad und Harris Lund. Die anderen sind unbekannt.

Soldiers from *10. Company 'Norge'* near Narva, winter of 1944, at their position south of the city. Front row from the left: unknown, Harris Lund, Ørnulf Breines and Reidar Andresen. Back row from the left: Einar Sundve, two unknown Germans and Mikael Ukkestad.

Soldaten der 10. Kompanie bei Narwa, Winter 1944, in ihrer Stellung südlich der Stadt. Vorne von links: ein Unbekannter, Harris Lund, Ørnulf Breines und Reidar Andresen. Hinten von links: Einar Sundve, zwei Deutsche und Mikael Ukkestad.

SS-Untersturmführer Thomas Hvistendahl from his time with the *4./SS-Pz.Abt. 11 'Hermann von Salza'* in the summer of 1944. Standing in front of the sign labelled *'Gef.Stand 3./SS-Pz.Abt. 11 "HvS"'* is *SS-Hauptsturmführer* Ernst Richard Stübben.

SS-Untersturmführer Thomas Hvistendahl aus seiner Zeit bei der 4./SS-Pz.Abt. 11 "Hermann von Salza". Vor dem Schild mit dem Text "Gefechtsstand 3./SS-Pz.Abt. 11 ‚HvS'", SS-Hauptsturmführer Ernst Richard Stübben, Sommer 1944.

Repairing the tank of *SS-Sturmbannführer* Paul Albert Kausch, a Panther IV S28. Kausch was commander of the *SS-Pz.Abt. 11 'Hermann von Salza'.*

Reparatur des Panzers von SS-Sturmbannführer Paul Albert Kausch, ein Panther IV S28. Kausch war Kommandeur der SS-Pz. Abt. 11 "Hermann von Salza".

A crew of *SS-Pz.Abt. 11 'Hermann von Salza'* near Narva, 1944.

Eine Mannschaft der SS-Pz.Abt. 11 "Hermann von Salza" bei Narwa, 1944.

SS-Untersturmführer Per Kjølner. He was a platoon leader in *3. Company, SS-Pz.Abt. 11 'Hermann von Salza'.*

SS-Untersturmführer Per Kjølner. Er war Zugführer in der 3./ SS-Pz.Abt. 11 "Hermann von Salza".

SS-Untersturmführer Johan Petter Balstad, the only Norwegian to wipe out three enemy tanks.

SS-Untersturmführer Johan Petter Balstad, der einzige Norweger der drei feindliche Panzer zerstörte.

SS-Sturmmann Martin Klein with his platoon, led by *SS-Untersturmführer* Balstad of *7. Company 'Norge'.* He was killed at Kinderheimhöhe (Orphanage Hill) during a counter-attack led by Balstad while sitting atop a Panther IV, on 29 July 1944. Klein was left on the battlefield, and his body was not found until 2010. After his family had been contacted, the remains were identified and transferred to the German War Cemetery at Toila.

SS-Sturmmann Martin Klein im Zug der 7. Kompanie des SS-Untersturmführers Balstad. Klein fiel am 29.07.44 während eines von Balstad geleiteten Gegenstoßes, als er bei der Kinderheimhöhe auf einem Panther IV saß. Klein hinterließ man im Niemandsland, und seine sterblichen Überreste wurden erst 2010 gefunden. Nachdem die Angehörigen ermittelt worden waren, konnte sein Leichnam identifiziert werden. Heute ruht er auf dem Deutschen Soldatenfriedhof in Toila.

SS-Oberscharführer Walter Diedrichs was company HQ personnel leader with *3. Company 'Norge'* between 1943 and February 1944. In January 1944, he took part in heavy fighting and was transferred to *10. Company 'Norge'* in Narva. Here he remained until he was seriously wounded as a platoon leader in a counter-attack at Pferdekopfhöhe in Courland on 30 October 1944. He survived the war.

SS-Oberscharführer Walter Diedrichs war Kompanietruppführer der 3. Kompanie von 1943 bis Februar 1944. Im Januar hatte er an schweren Kämpfen teilgenommen, und wurde in Narwa zur 10. Kompanie versetzt. Bei einem Gegenstoß wurde er am 30.10.44 als Zugführer an der Pferdekopfhöhe in Kurland schwer verwundet. Er überlebte den Krieg.

SS-Sturmmann Per Ramberg from Trondheim. He belonged to the *GSSN Company* of *SS-Hauptsturmführer Lindvig*, which became *1. Company 'Norge'*. Ramberg took part in the fighting in Croatia and later at Oranienbaum in January 1944. In February of the same year, he was transferred to *10. Company 'Norge'* and participated in the westward campaigns until he was granted leave in Norway in January 1945. For his efforts in the unit of *SS-Oberscharführer* Diedrichson on 30 October 1944, Ramberg was awarded the Iron Cross 1st Class. He was transferred to the *Schijäger Battalion* in 1945.

SS-Sturmmann Per Ramberg aus Trondheim. Er gehörte zur GSSN-Kompanie des SS-Hauptsturmführers Lindvig. Ramberg hatte an den Kämpfen in Kroatien teilgenommen, und später, im Januar 1944, bei Oranienbaum. Im Februar 1944 wurde er zur 10. Kompanie versetzt, und nahm an den Kämpfen in westlicher Richtung teil, bis er im Januar 1945 Urlaub in Norwegen bekam. Für seinen Einsatz am 30.10.44 im Zug des SS-Oberscharführers Walter Diedrichs wurde er mit dem Eisernen Kreuz 1. Klasse ausgezeichnet. 1945 wurde er zum SS-Schijäger-Bataillon "Norge" versetzt.

In 1943, *SS-Unterscharführer* Olav Thunestveit was a member of *1. Company 'Norge'*, and was actively involved on the battlefield until the company's disbandment in February 1944. Subsequently, he came to *10. Company 'Norge'* and volunteered for all scouting patrols that were undertaken. In January 1945, he attended a course for NCOs in Hammerstein and joined the *Kampfgruppe Scheibe*; he was killed on 10 February 1945 in Pomerania. He was awarded the Iron Cross 1st Class.

1943 war SS-Unterscharführer Olav Thunestveit bei der 1. Kompanie "Norge", und nahm bis Februar 1944 an den Kämpfen der Kompanie teil. Daraufhin wurde er zur 10. Kompanie versetzt und bot sich als Freiwilliger bei allen Spähtrupps an. Im Januar 1945 absolvierte er einen Lehrgang für Unteroffiziere in Hammerstein, und wurde bei der Kampfgruppe Scheibe eingesetzt, wo er am 10.02.45 in Pommern fiel. Er wurde mit dem Eisernen Kreuz 1. Klasse ausgezeichnet.

SS-Untersturmführer Njaal Bjørkelid from Marnardal, southern Norway, died on 21 March 1945 as company commander of *5. Company 'Norge'* in a field hospital in Stettin (Szczecin). He had joined *Regiment 'Nordland'* in March 1941, and participated in the fighting on the Eastern Front from December 1941. In 1943/44, he had attended the *11. Kriegsjunker-Lehrgang* at the *SS-Junkerschule Tölz*, and joined *Regiment 'Norge'* in the spring of 1944. In August 1944, Bjørkelid became battalion adjutant of *II. Battalion 'Norge'*.

SS-Untersturmführer Njaal Bjørkelid aus Marnardal, Südnorwegen, starb am 21.03.45 in einem Lazarett in Stettin als Kompanieführer der 5./Norge. Von März bis Dezember 1941 hatte er als Freiwilliger beim Regiment "Nordland" an der Ostfront gekämpft. Er besuchte den 11. Kriegsjunker-Lehrgang an der SS-Junkerschule Tölz, und kam im Frühjahr 1944 zum Regiment "Norge". Im August 1944 wurde er Bataillonsadjutant beim II./Norge.

SS-Untersturmführer Eyvind Andreas Schrøder from Langesund, southern Norway. Three of his brothers were also front line fighters. Schrøder joined the *Norwegian Legion* and was ordered to the Leningrad Front as *Leg.-Unterscharführer* and squad leader in *4. Company*. When he enlisted once again, he was sent to attend the officer school in Bad Tölz. Subsequently, he joined the *23. SS-Panzergrenadier-Regiment 'Norge', 9. Company*, as a platoon leader, and later as company commander. In Altdamm (Dąbie) he was taken prisoner by the Russians. Schrøder survived the war and died in 1994.

SS-Untersturmführer Eyvind Andreas Schrøder aus Langesund, Südnorwegen. Drei seiner Brüder waren auch Frontkämpfer. Schrøder meldete sich zur SS-Frw.-Legion Norwegen, und kam als Leg.-Unterscharführer und Gruppenführer in der 4. Kompanie an die Leningrader Front. Er ließ sich wieder anwerben, und wurde zur SS-Junkerschule Tölz geschickt. Als Zugführer und später Kompanieführer der 9./Norge kam er nach Pommern, und wurde in Altdamm von den Russen gefangengenommen. Schrøder überlebte den Krieg und starb 1994 in Oslo.

SS-Untersturmführer Håkon Windingstad volunteered for the *SS-Schikompanie* in 1942, and was sent to join the replacement battalion of the *Norwegian Legion* in Mitau after completing his training as an NCO. In the summer of 1943, he was sent to Tölz, and joined the *6. Company 'Norge'* in Narva as a platoon leader in the spring of 1944. After being wounded on 6 April 1944, he served as an orderly officer in the regimental staff and the battalion staff of *II. Battalion 'Norge'*. In 1945, he once again became company commander of *6. Company 'Norge'*, and was wounded on 3 March 1945 at Kremzow.

Nachdem SS-Untersturmführer Håkon Windingstad sich 1942 zur SS-Schikompanie gemeldet hatte, wurde er zur Ausbildung als Unteroffizier geschickt, und daraufhin zum Ersatzbataillon der SS-Frw.-Legion Norwegen in Mitau. Im Sommer 1943 kam er an die SS-Junkerschule Tölz, und im Frühjahr 1944 als Zugführer zur 6./Norge bei Narwa. Am 06.04.44 wurde er leicht verwundet, und diente als Ordonnazoffizier beim Regimentsstab und Bataillonstab des II./Norge. 1945 wurde er erneut als Kompanieführer bei der 6. Kompanie "Norge" eingesetzt, und am 03.03.45 bei Kremzow verwundet.

SS-Pz.Gren. Erland Folke Andersen joined *3. Company 'Norge'* in 1943 and was transferred to the staff of *III. Battalion 'Norge'* as a driver in 1944. He participated in all the battles for Berlin and was taken prisoner by the Russians on 2 May 1945. Andersen was repatriated in 1947.

SS-Pz.Gren. Erland Folke Andersen war seit 1943 bei der 3. Kompanie, und wurde 1944 an den Stab des III./ Norge als Fahrer versetzt. Er hatte an allen Kämpfen um Berlin teilgenommen, und wurde am 02.05.45 von den Russen gefangengenommen. 1947 kehrte er zurück nach Norwegen.

SS-Pz.Gren. Arve Moen was a member of *14. Company 'Norge'* from the time of its activation in 1943 until the surrender in Berlin in May 1945, where he managed to escape the Russians.

SS-Pz.Gren. Arve Moen war Angehöriger der 14. (Flak-) Kompanie seit der Aufstellung 1943 bis zur Kapitulation in Berlin im Mai 1945. Es gelang ihm, den Russen in Berlin zu entfliehen.

Troops from *Regiments 'Norge'* and *'Danmark'*, interned at former concentration camp Neuengamme as Western Allied POWs in the summer of 1945.

Mannschaften der Regimenter "Norge" und "Danmark", im Sommer 1945 als Kriegsgefangene im früheren KZ Neuengamme interniert.

8

SS-Polizei-Schijäger-Bataillon 506 (mot.)

Als das SS-Schijäger-Bataillon "Norge" im Dezember 1944 nach Oslo zurückkehrte, begann ein politisches Spiel zwischen den deutschen militärischen Behörden, vertreten durch SS-Obergruppenführer Wilhelm Redieß auf der einen Seite, und Ministerpräsident Quisling auf der anderen. Die Deutschen wollten das SS-Schijäger-Bataillon "Norge" für Aktionen gegen die norwegische Widerstandsbewegung einsetzen, und Redieß hoffte, dass die kriegserfahrenen Norweger des SS-Schijäger-Bataillons "Norge" hierbei von großem Nutzen sein könnten. In einem Brief an Quisling, datiert 29.1.45, schreibt Redieß, dass es auch im Interesse Quislings läge, durch die Verstärkung der Krad-Kompanien, oder der Aufstellung neuer motorisierter Einheiten diesen Typs, eine verschärfte Kontrolle der norwegischen Gebiete und die Verhinderung und Bekämpfung von Sabotage und Terror zu erzielen. Quisling fürchtete, das SS-Schijäger-Bataillon "Norge" würde auch außerhalb der Landesgrenzen eingesetzt, und erhob Einspruch gegen Redieß' Vorschlag. Zusätzlich sträubte er sich, das Schijäger-Bataillon der deutschen Leitung zu unterstellen. In einem undatierten Brief als Antwort auf Redieß' Brief vom 29.01.45 schreibt Quisling, er wünsche sich den verstärkten Einsatz freiwilliger norwegischer Einheiten auf norwegischem Boden, da ein solches Bataillon nicht nur als mobile Alarmeinheit von großem Wert wäre, sondern auch bei der Bekämpfung von Sabotage und Terroraktionen. Weiter schreibt Quisling, dass eine Auflösung des Skibataillons, das bereits als traditionsreiche Einheit anzusehen war, sowie eine Verteilung der Führer und Mannschaften an deutsche Polizeiabteilungen sicher zu Enttäuschung und Verbitterung führen würde. Quisling empfahl, die geplante Auflösung und Verteilung aufzugeben, und statt dessen ein verstärktes norwegisches Bataillon aufzustellen. Er wies darauf hin, dass die norwegischen Freiwilligen eine solche Aufgabe mit dem gleichen Eifer angreifen würden, wie schon früher als geschlossene norwegische Einheit unter norwegischen Offizieren. Das Ergebnis jedoch war, dass dem SS-Schijäger-Bataillon "Norge" drei Kradschützen-Kompanien der deutschen Ordnungspolizei zugeführt wurden. Redieß argumentierte in einem Brief vom 09.02.45 bezüglich der zukünftigen Zusammensetzung des SS-Schijäger-Bataillons 506, dass die zunehmende Tätigkeit von Sabotagegruppen und Terroristen, sowie deren wirksame Bekämpfung, es erforderlich mache, rasche und mobile Einheiten einzusetzen. Überdies lehnte Redieß auch Quislings Vorschlag für eine Verstärkung des SS-Schijäger-Bataillons "Norge" ab, da der Mangel an schweren Waffen, Kraftfahrzeugen und Fahrern, bedingt durch die jetzige Kriegsbeschaffenheit, dies nicht erlaube. Das derzeitige SS-Schijäger-Bataillon "Norge", bestehend aus drei norwegischen und drei deutschen Polizei-Kradschützen-Kompanien, werde zu sechs neuen SS-und Polizei-Schijäger-Kompanien verschmelzt. Die neue Einheit hatte damit eine Stärke von rundt 1100 Mann.

Die Führung der neuen Einheit, SS-Polizei-Schijäger-Bataillon 506 (mot.), sollte ursprünglich dem früheren Leiter des SS-Schijäger-Bataillons "Norge", Frode Halle, unterstellt werden. Halle wünschte dies aber nicht, und lehnte sich zusätzlich dagegen auf, dem SS-Schijäger-Bataillon "Norge" deutsche Einheiten zuführen zu lassen. Daraufhin wurde SS-Sturmbannführer Egil Hoel aus Kurland zurückkommandiert und mit der Führung des SS-Polizei-Schijäger-Bataillons 506 (mot.) beauftragt.

Das Bataillon wurde an verschiedene Orte im Südosten Norwegens verlegt, unter anderem Gjøvik, Skien, Holmestrand, Vikersund und Notodden. In Elverum wurde zudem eine Unterführerschule gegründet.

8

SS-Polizei-Schijäger-Bataillon 506 (mot.)

Once the *SS-Schijäger-Bataillon 'Norge'* returned to Oslo in December 1944, a political game was sparked off between the German military authorities represented by *SS-Obergruppenführer* Wilhelm Rediess on the one hand, and Minister-President Quisling on the other. The Germans wished to deploy the *Schijäger Battalion* to fight the Norwegian resistance movement, and Rediess envisioned the battalion to be of great use in this situation. In a letter to Quisling dated 29 January 1945, Rediess writes that he also believed to be acting in Quisling's interest by either reinforcing the existing motorcycle companies or establishing new ones, to thereby gain greater control over Norwegian territories and prevent and combat sabotage and terror. Fearing that the *Schijäger Battalion* might be put into action abroad, Quisling protested to Rediess. Neither did Quisling wish the *Schijäger Battalion* to be placed under direct German command. In an undated letter written in response to Rediess' letter of 29 January 1945, Quisling expresses his wish for a stronger presence of Norwegian volunteer units on Norwegian soil, believing that such a battalion-sized troop would not only be of great use as a mobile alarm unit, but also aid in the defence against sabotage and terrorist acts. Furthermore, Quisling writes that to dissolve the Ski Battalion – a military unit that had begun to develop its own traditions – and reassign its leaders and other members to German police units, would surely cause disappointment and resentment. Quisling recommended to abandon the planned dissolution and redistribution of the *Schijäger Battalion*, and reiterated his earlier plans for a reinforced Norwegian battalion. He also pointed out that the Norwegian volunteers would approach the task with the same eagerness as they had in the past, when they served as an exclusively Norwegian unit under Norwegian leadership.

The result, however, was that the *Schijäger Battalion* was augmented with three *Kradschützen* companies (motorised infantry, mostly on motorcycles) from the German *Ordnungspolizei* (order police). In a letter dated 9 February 1945, Rediess takes up the future organisation of the *SS-Schijäger-Bataillon 506*, arguing that the ever-increasing number of operations by sabotage and terrorist groups, and the ability to fight them, required fast and mobile units. Rediess also rejected Quisling's proposal for a reinforcement of the *Schijäger Battalion* by pointing out that this was not possible under the current war conditions due to a shortage of heavy weapons, vehicles and associated drivers. The *SS-Schijäger-Bataillon 'Norge'*, including its three Norwegian and three German police and motorcycle companies, would be merged into six new *SS-und Polizei-Schijäger Companies*. The new unit would amount to a force of about 1,100 men.

The leadership of this new unit – the *SS-Polizei-Schijäger-Bataillon 506 (mot.)* – was initially to be entrusted to the former commander of the *SS-Schijäger-Bataillon 'Norge'*, Frode Halle. Halle, however, declined, and also opposed reinforcing the *SS-Schijäger-Bataillon 'Norge'* with German troops. Therefore, *SS-Sturmbannführer* Egil Hoel was ordered back from Courland and assumed leadership of the *SS-Polizei-Schijäger-Bataillon 506 (mot.)* as battalion commander.

The battalion was stationed at various locations in south-eastern Norway, including Gjøvik, Skien, Holmestrand and Notodden, and ran a school for NCOs at Elverum.

Following the return of the *SS-Schijäger-Bataillon 'Norge'*, the men were stationed at Høytorp Fort and transferred to *Battalion 506*. A number of new recruits from the Norwegian National Socialist youth organisation NSUF had also joined their ranks.

Nach der Heimkehr des Schijäger-Bataillons "Norge" wurden die Mannschaften nach Høytorp Fort verlegt, und dem Bataillon 506 angeschlossen. Eine Reihe von neuen Rekruten aus dem nationalsozialistischen norwegischen Jugendverband NSUF waren auch mit dabei.

Seated in front is *SS-Unterscharführer* Einar Skjærbekk, a veteran of *Division 'Wiking'*. Second row from the left: *SS-Unterscharführer* Magne Ødegård, unknown and Georg Gundersen. Third row from the left: *SS-Unterscharführer* Henry Buran and *SS-Unterscharführer* Erik Olsen.

Vorne sitzend: SS-Unterscharführer Einar Skjærbekk, ein Veteran der Division "Wiking". Zweite Reihe von links: SS-Unterscharführer Magne Ødegård, ein Unbekannter und Georg Gundersen. Dritte Reihe von links: die SS-Unterscharführer Henry Buran und Erik Olsen.

Front row from the left: Asbjørn Filseth, the rest are unknown. Second row from the right: Harald Bjørnstad, the rest are unknown.

Erste Reihe von links: Asbjørn Filseth, die anderen sind unbekannt. Zweite Reihe von rechts: Harald Bjørnstad.

From the left: Arvid Solberg, Magnar Tømte, Asbjørn Filseth, Anders Andvik and Oddvar Syljeseth at Høytorp Fort. All were veterans of the *Schijäger Battalion 'Norge'.*

Von links: Arvid Solberg, Magnar Tømte, Asbjørn Filseth, Anders Andvik und Oddvar Syljeseth auf Høytorp Fort. Alle waren Veteranen des Schijäger-Bataillons "Norge".

Drill at Høytorp Fort for the newly activated *Battalion 506*.

Drill auf Høytorp Fort für das neuaufgestellte Bataillon 506.

The canteen at Høytorp Fort.

Die Kantine auf Høytorp Fort.

On the right is Per Ramberg, who was transferred from *Regiment 'Norge'* to *Battalion 506*.

Rechts: Per Ramberg, der vom Regiment "Norge" zum Bataillon 506 versetzt wurde.

Per Ramberg, left, instructing new recruits of *Battalion 506*.

Links: Per Ramberg unterrichtet neue Rekruten des Bataillons 506.

Kompanie z.b.V. (special deployment company) in Oslo. From the left: *SS-Unterscharführer* Magne Ødegård, a veteran of both the *Norwegian Legion* and the *Schijäger Battalion*; Bjørn Lindstad, a veteran of *Regiment 'Norge'*; unknown; and *SS-Unterscharführer* Reidar Bjørgan, a veteran of *Division 'Wiking'*.

Kompanie z.b.V. (zur besonderen Verwendung) in Oslo. Von links: SS-Unterscharführer Magne Ødegård, ein Veteran der SS-Frw.-Legion Norwegen und des Schijäger-Bataillons "Norge", Bjørn Lindstad, ein Veteran des Regiments "Norge", ein Unbekannter, und SS-Unterscharführer Reidar Bjørgan, ein Veteran der Division "Wiking".

From the left: *SS-Unterscharführer* Erik Olsen, a veteran of the *Norwegian Legion* and *Regiment 'Norge'*, and the three *SS-Unterscharführer*, Magne Ødegård, Reidar Buran and Reidar Bjørgan.

Von links: SS-Unterscharführer Erik Olsen, ein Veteran der SS-Frw.-Legion Norwegen und des Regiments "Norge", und die SS-Unterscharführer Magne Ødegård, Reidar Buran und Reidar Bjørgan.

A company stationed at Gjøvik. Here the men are filing out.

Eine Kompanie in Gjøvik beim Ausmarsch.

SS-Oberscharführer Inge Martin Bakken, a veteran of *Division 'Wiking'* and the Battle of Cherkassy, was transferred to *Battalion 506*, where he served as personnel-NCO in Holmestrand.

SS-Oberscharführer Inge Martin Bakken, ein Veteran der Division "Wiking" und der Kämpfe um Tscherkassy, wurde zum Bataillon 506 versetzt, wo er als sachbearbeitender IIa Unteroffizier in Holmestrand diente.

Standing second from the left is *SS-Untersturmführer* Odd Skui during the training for new recruits. He was a veteran of *Division 'Wiking'* and the *Schijäger Battalion*.

Stehend Nr. 2 von links: SS-Untersturmführer Odd Skui bei der Rekrutenausbildung. Er war ein Veteran der Division "Wiking" und des Schijäger-Bataillons "Norge".

Olso, 1945. *Battalion 506* has surrendered and is brought to the detention centre at Grini by truck. From the left, sitting and facing the camera, are *SS-Obersturmbannführer* Egil Hoel and *SS-Obersturmführer* Martin Skjefstad.

Das Bataillon 506 hat kapituliert und wird mit dem LKW ins Gefangenenlager Grini gebracht. Von links, sitzend und mit dem Gesicht zur Kamera: SS-Obersturmbannführer Egil Hoel und SS-Obersturmführer Martin Skjefstad.

A group from *Battalion 506* waiting to be arrested.

Eine Gruppe des Bataillons 506 wartet auf ihre Verhaftung.

Quellen

Die meisten Fotos in diesem Buch stammen aus unseren eigenen Archiven. Seit etwa Mitte 1980 sammeln wir unabhängig voneinander Bildmaterial. Nachdem wir mit ehemaligen Frontkämpfern Kontakt aufgenommen hatten, stellten sie uns ihre Bilder zum abfotografieren zur Verfügung. Außerdem hatten wir die Möglichkeit, sie zu interviewen. Daraufhin schickten wir die Bilder samt Kopien zur Identifizierung der abgebildeten Personen zurück. Wir schickten die Bilder auch an andere Frontkämpfer aus den entsprechenden Einheiten, die uns bei der Namenssuche halfen. Besondere Erwähnung verdienen Knut Baardseth und Bjørn Østring, die uns dank ihres großen Kontaktnetzes sehr geholfen haben. Sie brachten uns in Verbindung mit anderen Frontkämpfern, die auch mit Fotografien und Auskünften beitrugen. Zusätzlich haben wir Zeitschriften und Magazine aus dem zweiten Weltkrieg durchgesehen, um weitere Bilder zu finden. Wir hatten auch das Glück, dass viele Sammler uns Kopien ihrer Bilder im Austausch für Daten zur Verfügung stellten. Die Bilder, die nicht aus Brendens und Natedals Archiven stammen, kommen aus dem Archiv von Helge Tunge. Einige wenige Bilder wurden uns von der National Archives and Records Administration (NARA) in den USA zur Verfügung gestellt.

Sources

Most of the photographs in this book were taken from our own archives. Independent of one another, we both began to collect picture material in the mid-1980s. After contacting former front line fighters, we were able to borrow and reproduce their images and conduct interviews with them. We then returned their pictures together with replicas in order to get help in identifying the people in the photographs. We also sent the pictures to other front line fighters from the same units, hoping that they, too, would be able to provide us with names. A special mention goes to Knut Baardseth and Bjørn Østring, who helped us a great deal thanks to their large network of contacts, and put us in touch with other front line fighters who had pictures and information. We have also searched through magazines and newspapers from the Second World War to find more images. Additionally, we were fortunate that many collectors provided us with pictures in exchange for information. Images that were not taken from Brenden's or Natedal's archives come from the archive of Helge Tunge. A few images were provided by the National Archives and Records Administration (NARA) in the United States.